AF556335

LIMNOLOGY AND AQUATIC SCIENCE

ENV BOOKS SERIES

LIMNOLOGY AND AQUATIC SCIENCE

Editors

Dr. Shailendra Sharma

Principal

Adarsh Institute of Management & Science

(Devi Ahilya Vishwa Vidyalaya Indore), Dhamnod (M.P.), India

Dr. Pawan Kumar 'Bharti'

Vice President (Executive)

Society for Environment, Health, Awareness of nutrition & Toxicology (SEHAT)

1775, Sohan Ganj, Near Clock Tower, Delhi-7, India

E-mail: *gurupawanbharti@rediffmail.com*

DISCOVERY PUBLISHING HOUSE PVT. LTD.

NEW DELHI-110 002

Published by:
Tilak Wasan

DISCOVERY PUBLISHING HOUSE PVT. LTD.
4383/4B, Ansari Road, Darya Ganj
New Delhi-110 002 (India)
Phone : +91-11-23279245, 43596064-65
Fax : +91-11-23253475
E-mail : discoverypublishinghouse@gmail.com
sales@discoverypublishinggroup.com
web : www.discoverypublishinggroup.com

First Edition: **2015**

ISBN: 978-93-5056-735-7

Limnology and Aquatic Science

Printed at:
Infinity Imaging Systems
Delhi

ENV Books Series, India

Calls lengthy and error free chapters for further volumes of books on various environmental issues. (Send your manuscripts to envbooks@gmail.com)

Founding Editor (Editor-in-Chief)

Dr. Pawan Kumar 'Bharti'
Society for Environment, Health, Awareness of Nutrition & Toxicology (SEHAT-India)
1775, Sohanganj, Near Clock Tower, Delhi-7, India
E-mail: *gurupawanbharti@rediffmail.com*

Other titles by Editor-in-Chief:

1. **Advances in Agriculture and Ecology (2013)**
   Bharti, P.K.; Chauhan, A. and Ezeaku Peter Ikemefuna (eds.)
   (ISBN: 978-93-5056-362-5).

2. **Advances in Biotechnology and Ecological Sciences (2013)**
   Bharti, P.K., Chauhan, A. and Ray, J. (eds.)
   (ISBN: 978-93-5056-358-8).

3. **Agriculture and Environmental Biotechnology (2014)**
   Bharti, P.K. and Chauhan, A. (eds.)
   (ISBN: 978-93-5056-479-0).

4. **Agriculture Ecology and Environment (2014)**
   Bharti, P.K. and Olubukola O. Babalola (eds.)
   (ISBN: 978-93-5056-480-6).

5. **Agro-forestry and Climate Change (2014)**
   Bharti, Pawan K. and Singh, Narayan (eds.)
   (ISBN: 978-93-5056-514-8).

6. **Aquaculture and Fisheries Environment (2014)**
   Gupta, S.K. and Pawan K. Bharti (eds.)
   (ISBN: 978-93-5056-408-0).

7. **Aquatic Biodiversity and Pollution (2013)**
   Bharti, P.K.; Chauhan, A. and Kaoud, H.A.H. (eds.)
   (ISBN: 978-93-5056-359-5).

8. **Aquatic Ecology and Biotechnology (2014)**
Bharti, P.K. and Zaki, M.S.A. (eds.)
(ISBN: 978-93-5056-451-6).

9. **Aquatic Environment and Toxicology (2013)**
Bharti, Pawan K. (ed.)
(ISBN: 978-93-5056-236-9).

10. **Biodiversity of Aquatic Ecosystem: Significance, Threat and Conservation (2013)**
Bharti, P.K. and Kaoud, H.A.H. (eds.)
(ISBN: 978-93-5056-297-0).

11. **Clean Technologies and Environmental Protection (2015)**
Chauhan, A.; Sharma, S. and Bharti, P.K. (eds.)
(ISBN: 978-93-5056-731-9).

12. **Climate Change and Agriculture (2012)**
Bharti, P.K. and Chauhan, Avnish (eds.)
(ISBN: 978-93-5056-148-5).

13 **Conservation and Cultivation of Medicinal Plants (2015)**
Bharti, P.K. and Singh, Narayan (eds.)
(ISBN: 978-93-5056-740-1).

14. **Climate Change and Biodiversity (2013)**
Bharti, P.K. and Chauhan, Avnish (eds.)
(ISBN: 978-93-5056-360-1).

15. **Eco-toxicology and Eco-technology (2013)**
Bharti, P.K. and Zaki, M. (eds.)
(ISBN: 978-93-5056-313-7).

16. **Environmental Biotechnology and Application (2013)**
Bharti, P.K. and Chauhan, Avnish (eds.)
(ISBN: 978-93-5056-262-8).

17. **Environmental Conservation and Biotechnology (2014)**
Chauhan, A. and P.K. Bharti (eds.)
(ISBN: 978-93-5056-512-4).

18. **Environmental Health and Problems (2013)**
Bharti, P.K. and Gajananda, Kh. (eds.)
(ISBN: 978-93-5056-263-5).

19. **Environmental Pollution and Biodiversity (2012)**
Bharti, P.K.; Chauhan, Avnish and Kumar, P. (eds.)
(ISBN: 978-93-5056-149-2).

20. **Fisheries and Toxicology (2014)**
Zaki, M.S.A.; Bharti, P.K. and Chauhan, A. (eds.)
(ISBN: 978-93-5056-452-3).

21. **Freshwater Ecosystem and Xenobiotics (2013)**
Bharti, P.K.; Zaki, M. and Chauhan, A. (eds.)
(ISBN: 978-93-5056-299-4).

22. **Medicinal Plants: Distribution, Utilization and Significance (2015)**
Sharma, P.; Bharti, P.K. and Singh N (eds.)
(ISBN: 978-93-5056-734-0).

23. **Microbial Applications and Environment (2014)**
Bharti, Pawan K. (ed.)
(ISBN: 978-93-5056-515-5).

24. **Microbial Ecology and Habitat (2014)**
Bharti, Pawan K. (ed.)
(ISBN: 978-93-5056-514-8).

25. **Prakriti me Aushadhi (*in Hindi*) (2012)**
Singh, J.R.; Bharti, P.K. and Bharti, B.
(ISBN: 978-93-5056-200-0).

26. **Seed Technology, Plant Growth and Cropping System (2015)**
Tyagi, P.K. and Bharti, P.K. (eds.)
(ISBN: 978-93-5056-738-8).

27. **Soil Contamination and Conservation (2015)**
Ezeaku, P.I. and Bharti, P.K. (eds.)
(ISBN: 978-93-5056-737-1).

28. **Soil Quality and Contamination (2013)**
Bharti, P.K. and Chauhan, Avnish (eds.)
(ISBN: 978-93-5056-361-8).

29. **Waste Disposal and Management (2015)**
Bharti, P.K.; Tabassum, B. and Bajaj, P. (eds.)
(ISBN: 978-93-5056-729-6).

30. **Water Resources and Agriculture (2014)**
Bharti, P.K. and Ezeaku Peter Ikemefuna (eds.)
(ISBN: 978-93-5056-481-3).

Preface

Limnology is the study of the structural and functional relationships and productivity of organisms of inland aquatic ecosystems as they are related to their dynamic physical, chemical, and biotic environments. In short, it can be defined as the study of continental waters; or the study of fresh and saline waters contained within continental boundaries. Limnology and its closely related science of oceanography together cover all aquatic ecosystems. The two sciences, limnology and oceanography, share the basic principles; however they differ in that limnology covers lakes, ponds, reservoirs, streams, rivers, wetlands and estuaries – succinctly, fresh and brackish waters; while oceanography covers the open sea.

Limnology applies to lotic or lentic waters, while oceanography covers only 'lentic' waters. A major goal of limnology is to understand the functional relationships and productivity of freshwater ecosystems resulting from multiple interactions between the abiotic (physical and chemical) parameters and the biotic environment.

Limnology is aquatic ecology, the study of inland waters. The course develops a comprehensive and integrated understanding of physical, chemical and biological processes occurring in lakes, streams and wetlands using the scientific method to investigate and contrast basic ecological processes operating in various systems.

Limnology is the study of inland waters. It is often regarded as a division of ecology or environmental science. It covers the biological, chemical, physical, geological, and other attributes of all inland waters (running and standing waters (fresh and saline), natural or man-made). This includes the study of lakes and ponds, rivers, springs, streams and wetlands. A more recent sub-discipline of limnology, termed landscape limnology, studies, manages, and conserves these aquatic ecosystems using a landscape perspective.

Limnology is closely related to aquatic ecology and hydrobiology, which study aquatic organisms in particular regard to their hydrological environment.

This book provides comprehensive coverage of the fundamental principles and current practices and trends in the field of conservation of freshwater ecosystems, Aquatic Ecology, Limnology and fishery science.

This book updates the subject matter, illustrations and problems to incorporate new concepts and issues related to Aquatic Ecology, Limnology and fishery science.

Thanks are due to contributors from different institutions and publisher for their interest in this book. We hope this book will provide a multi-disciplinary forum to explore emerging areas in the field of Aquatic Ecology, Limnology, freshwater ecology and fishery science.

– Editors

(envbooks@gmail.com)

Contents

Pages: 1-16

LIMNOLOGY AND AQUATIC SCIENCE

Edited by: Dr. Shailendra Sharma; Dr. Pawan Kumar 'Bharti'

ISBN: 978-93-5056-735-7

Edition: 2015

Published by: Discovery Publishing House Pvt. Ltd., New Delhi (India)

Diversity of Water Beetles (Coleoptera) in Tropical and Subtropical Region (Khalghat) of Narmada River, M.P. India

*Shailendra Sharma; **Sudha Dubey
**Rajendra Chaurasia; **Dilip Solanki, ***Vibha Dave

ABSTRACT

The diversity of aquatic beetles at Khalghat in Tropical and Sub tropical region of Narmada River were studied from December 2012 to April 2012. Khalghat is located in the Narmada River in the state of M.P. India. The benthic macro-invertebrates (Coleoptera) encountered in the river during the study period is shown in following. Phylum Arthropoda, class Insecta, Order- Coleoptera, Suborder- Adephaga, Five (5) families, Ten (10) Subfamilies, Twenty eight (28) Genus, Six (6) Sub genus and Seventeen (17) Species were recorded.

Total 17 species of water beetles belonging to families Gyrinidae, Dytiscidae, Hydroporini, Hydrophilidae and Elmidae were recorded. Gyrinidae and Dytiscidae was the dominant family with respect to species diversity (17 species) and abundance.

* Department of Biotechnology, Adarsh Institute of Management & Science Dhamnod (M.P.) India.

** Department of Zoology, Govt. Holkar Science College Indore - 452 017, India.

*** Department of Zoology, P.M.B. Gujarati Science College Indore - 452 001, India.

Key words: Coleoptera, Water beetles, Khalghat, Narmada River.

INTRODUCTION

Indicators in continental aquatic ecosystems in Water beetles are very integral part of the biotic. Aquatic beetles water beetle in the ecosystem, the present work was are a diverse group and are excellent indicators of habitat conducted to determine the diversity, abundance and quality, age and 'naturalness (Bilton 2009). They are indicator of species composition of these beetles in the ecological diversity and habitat characteristics (Fernandez *et al.*, 2004). they meet most of the criteria generally accepted in the selection of indicator taxa (Pearson 1994). Temporary and permanent standing waters represent the most important habitats for this group of insects. Today, these fragile ecosystems are under threat due to intensive anthropogenic influences (draining, waste waters, etc.) (Celik *et al.*, 2005).

Water beetles are very integral parts of the biotic component of any water bodies or wetlands. They are indicator of ecological diversity and habitat characteristics (Foster, 1987; Eyre and Foster, 1989; Foster *et al.*, 1990; Ribera and Foster, 1993; Fernandez *et al.*, 2004) as they meet most of the criteria generally accepted in the selection of indicator texa (Pearson, 1994). The beetles are especially useful in certain habitats as peat bogs, coastal and saline lagoons, wood and wetland ponds, etc. (Ribera and Foster, 1993).

In view of the important role played by water beetle in the ecosystem, the present work was conducted to determine the diversity, abundance and species composition of these beetles in the Tropical and Sub tropical region of Khalghat M.P. India.

MATERIAL AND METHODS

Description of Narmada River

The Narmada River, hemmed between Vindhya and Satpuda range, extends over an area of 98,796 km^2. And lies between east longitudes 72 °32" to 81° 45′ and north latitudes 21° 20" to 23°45" lying on the northern extremity of the Deccan Plateau. The basin covers areas of Madhya Pradesh (86%), Gujarate (14%) and a comparatively smaller area (2%) in Maharastra. There are 41 tributaries, out of which 22 are from the Satpura rang and the rest on the right bank are from the Vindhya Range.

The Study Area

Description of Sampling Station

Before finally fixing the sampling station a general survey of river was made, samples were collected and estimated from various regions in which Narmada River flow. Accordingly and study areas were fixed. The water samples would be collected from the selected sampling station in the Narmada river which are as under.

Narmada River

Sampling site (KHALGHAT): The study will be conducted from December 2012 to April 2012 at 5 different sampling sites in Khalghat region in the Narmada River, in the state of, Madhya Pradesh. The Narmada River is located as a central offshoot of. Vindhyachal scarps lies the narrow valley of the Narmada in the state of Madhya Pradesh in Central India. The Khalghat is Tropical and Subtropical, in nature. Road Distance or driving distance from Indore to Khalghat is 85 kms (53.00 miles). Khalghat region will be selected as sampling sites for the collection of water beetles. The geographical coordinates will be noted using a GPS recorder as follows:

Latitude 22.166667/22° 10' 0.0012" Longitude 75.45/75° 27' 0.0"

Sampling Site

PHYSICO-CHEMICAL ANALYSIS

Physico-chemical analysis was carried out as per methods given A.P.H.A. (2005), Welch (1998), Golterman (1991) The sampling site will be sampled twice every month from. December 2012 to March 2012. regular collection of water were made in the first and last week of every month between 7:00 to 9:00 A.M. from station the river water was collection in a sterilized pyrex flask and brought to the laboratory for chemical analysis. The temperature, pH and transparency were noted in the field. While Dissolved Oxygen Biochemical oxygen demand, Total Hardness, Alkanity, Chloride, Nitrate, Phosphate were determined in the laboratory. All the chemicals used were of AR grade.

RESULTS AND DISSCUTION

Physico-chemical Parameters

Temperature

Temperature is one of the most important parameters that influence almost all the physical, chemical and biological properties of water and thus the water chemistry. Water temperature depends upon the water depth beside solar radiation, climate and topography. The surface water temperature of Narmada River ranged between 25°C to 35°C. (Fig. 1.1). The minimum temperature was recorded in the month of December and maximum was recorded in the month of April. Sharma *et al.,* (2001), Yogesh *et al.,* (2001) also reported the same type of fluctuation in various freshwater bodies.

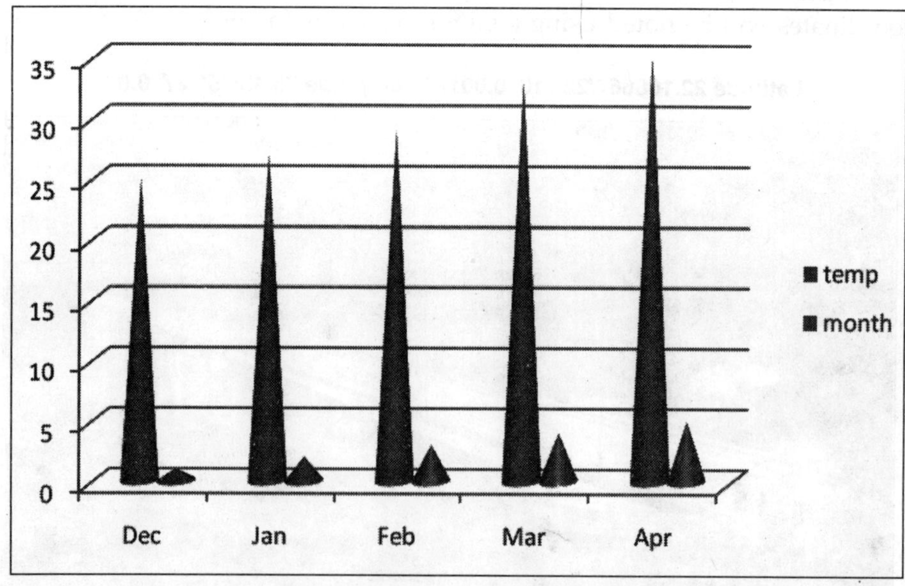

Fig. 1.1: Monthly Fluctuation of Temperature of Narmada River (Dec. 12 to Apr. 13)

pH

pH–Potential of hydrogen, is the measure of the concentration of hydrogen ions. It provides the measure of the acidity or alkalinity of a solution. pH is a most important factors that serve as an for the pollution. In the present study the observed pH values ranging from 7.4 and 8.6 show that the present water samples are slightly alkaline (Fig. 1.2). These values are within maximum permissible limited prescribed by WHO (1993). Our results tally with the findings of Sharma *et al.*, (2004).

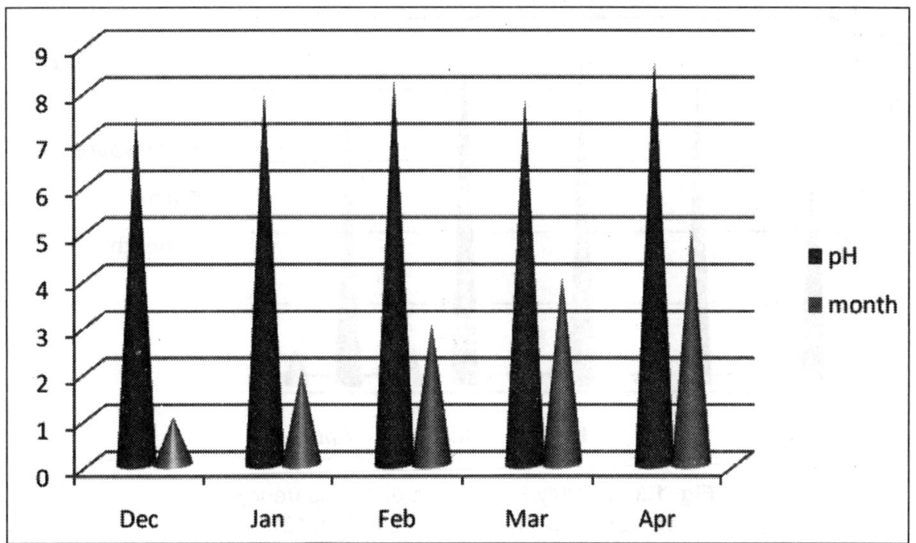

Fig. 1.2: Monthly Fluctuation of pH of Narmada River (Dec. 12 to Apr.13)

Transparency

Transparency is a characteristic of water that varies with the combined effect of colour and turbidity. It measures the depth to which light penetrates in the water body. In the present study the value of transparency varied from 35(NTU) – 52 (NTU). The highest Transparency unit was 52 (NTU) obtained in the month of March and the lowest was 35 (NTU) in December. (Fig. 1.3), Jain and Sharma (2000) also reported lowest transparency in rainy season and maximum in winter.

Dissolved Oxygen (D.O.)

Dissolved oxygen in natural and waste water depends on the physical, chemical and biological activities in the water body. Dissolved Oxygen content, plays a vital role in supporting aquatic life and is susceptible to slight environment changes. Dissolved Oxygen is important for aquatic system and also essential for the metabolism in the organisms. There are two main sources of dissolved oxygen in water i.e. by diffusion from air and photosynthetic activity. D.O. an important limnological parameter indicating level of water quality and organic pollution in the water body (Wetzel and Likens, 2006). In present study concentration of D.O. in Narmada river water samples varied from 7.1 mg/l. to 8.8 mg/l. with minimum in the month of March and maximum in the month of April (Fig. 1.4). The seasonal variation of D.O. in water depends upon the temperature of the water body which influences the oxygen solubility in water.

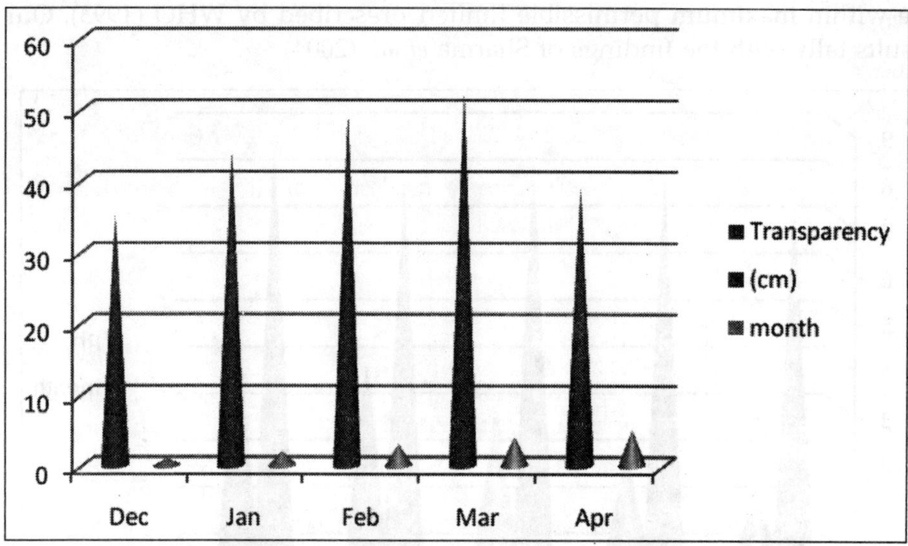

Fig. 1.3: Monthly Fluctuation of Transparency of Narmada River (Dec. 12 to Apr. 13)

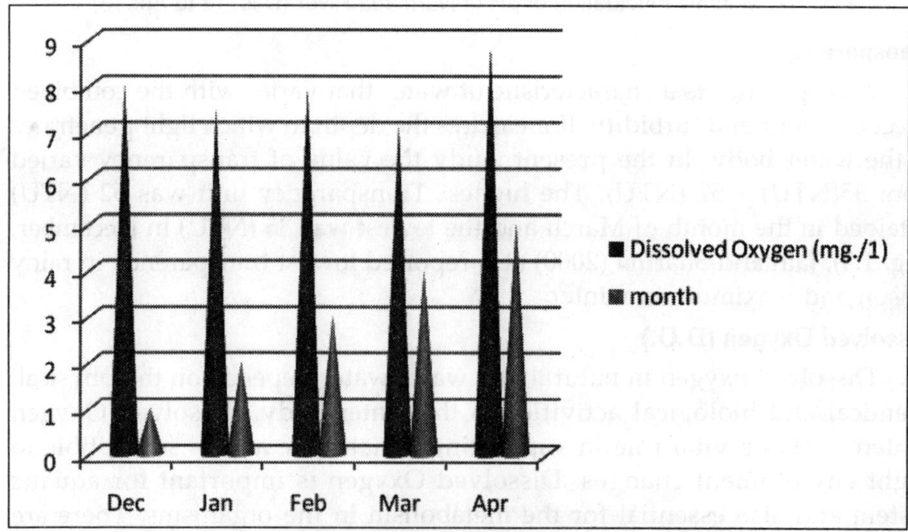

Fig. 1.4: Monthly Fluctuation of Dissolved Oxygen of Narmada River (Dec. 12 to Apr. 13)

Total Suspended solid (TSS)

The total Suspended solid varied between 146-170 mg/l. The minimum and maximum value was recorded at station (Fig. 1.5) in December and April. The minimum total Suspended solid was recorded February Month and maximum total Suspended solid was recorded in December.

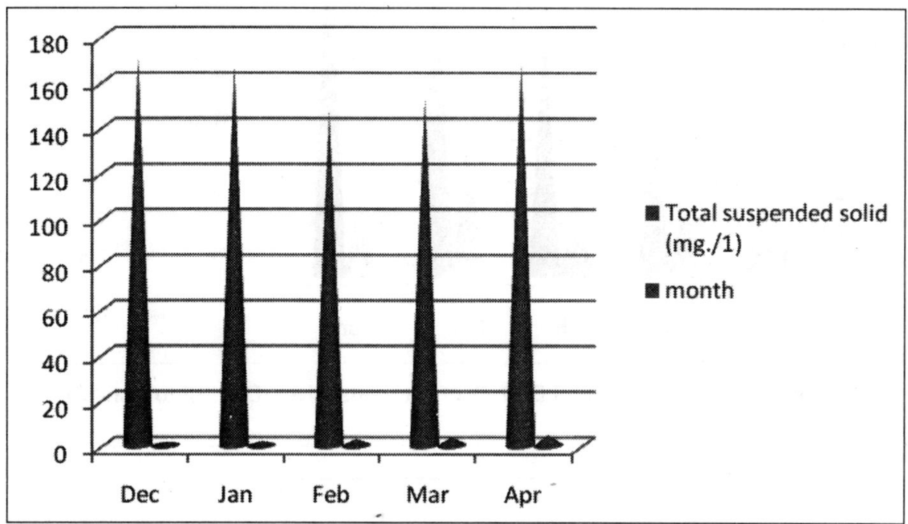

Fig. 1.5: Monthly Fluctuation of Total Suspended Solid of Narmada River (Dec. 12 to Apr. 13)

Biochemical Oxygen Demand (BOD)

The biochemical oxygen demand, abbreviated as BOD, is a test for measuring the amount of biodegradable organic material present in a sample of water. In present study the BOD was ranged between 0.5 mg/l. to 1.6 mg/l. with minimum BOD were recorded in the month of December and maximum BOD was recorded in the month of Marc h (Fig. 1.6). similar observations were confirmed by many other workers such as Pathak and Mudgal (2005), Khanna (2003). The high level of BOD might have been attributed to the discharge of pollutants into the river through washing, sewage contamination, industrial affluent and a like.

Alkalinity

Alkalinity of water is a measure of weak acid present in it and of the cations balanced against them. Alkalinity is a measure of buffering capacity of the water. The range of total alkalinity in Indian waters resources. Ranges between 40 mg/l. to 100 mg/l. Jhingran 1982.The observation of alkalinity reveals that the monthly variation ranged from a minimum of 164 mg/l. to 180mg/l. (Fig. 1.7) the minimum value were recorded in the month of April and maximum in the month of December. (Same results were also reported by Sharma *et al.,* (2004).

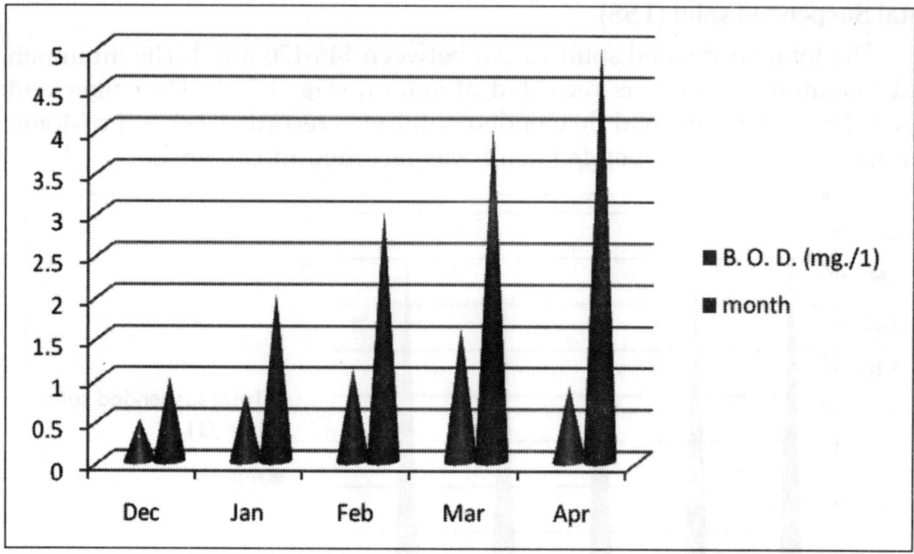

Fig. 1.6: Monthly Fluctuation of B. D. O. of Narmada River (Dec. 12 to Apr. 13)

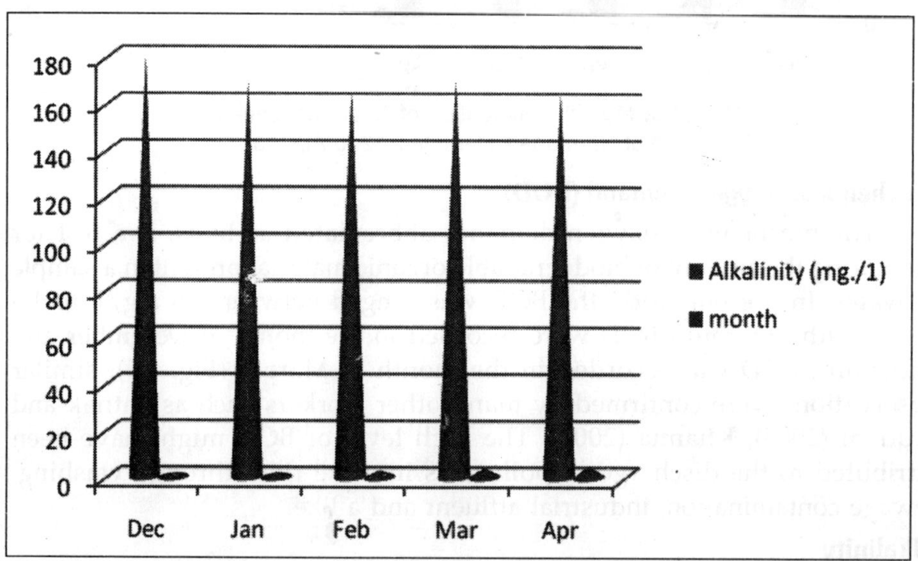

Fig. 1.7: Monthly Fluctuation of Alkalinity of Narmada River (Dec. 12 to Apr. 13)

Nitrate

Nitrate (Nitrogen) is the basic constituent of all organisms and plays a vital role in metabolism, growth, reproduction, and transmission of heritable characters. In an aquatic ecosystem, nitrogen is present in the form of organic nitrogen compounds, ammonia, nitrate, and as nitrite. Nitrates are the most oxidised forms of nitrogen and the end product of the aerobic decomposition of organic nitrogenous matter. Nitrogen is an essential building block in the synthesis of protein. The evaluation of nitrogen is therefore an important parameter in understanding the nutritional status of water bodies. The concentration of nitrate in Narmada river water was found to be in the range of 0.42mg/l. to 0.70 mg/l. Minimum nitrate concentration was recorded in the month of December and maximum was also recorded in the month of February (Fig. 1.8) Nitrate is attributed mainly due to anthropogenic activities such of run of water from agricultural lands, industrial wastes, discharge of house hold and municipal sewage from the market place and other effluents containing nitrogen. Such observations were also reported by Royer *et al.*, (2004).

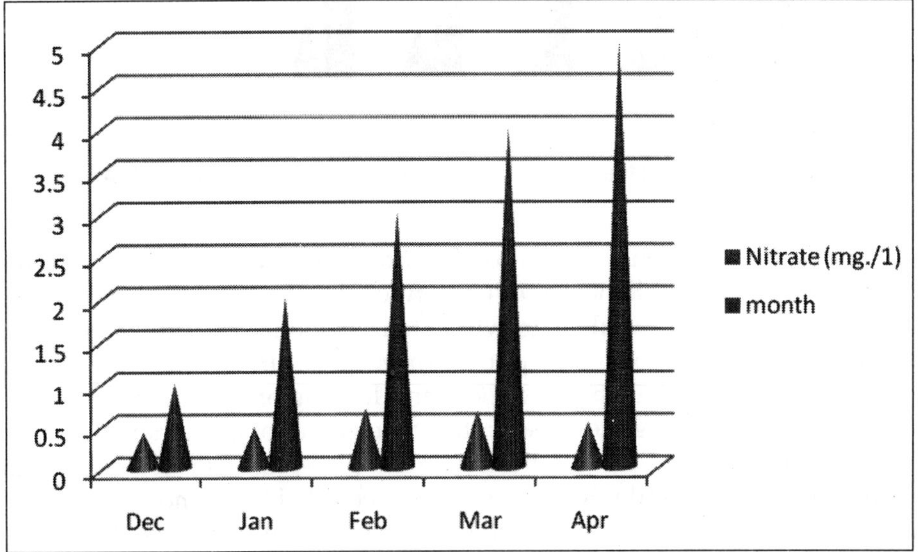

Fig. 1.8: Monthly Fluctuation of Nitrate of Narmada River (Dec. 12 to Apr. 13)

Chloride

Chloride is one of the major inorganic anion in water and waste water. Chloride in present in fresh water in the form of calcium, magnesium and sodium salts. The concentration of chloride content is also used as an indicator of pollution of fresh water (Ganpati 1960). In present study the values of chloride varied between 20.0 mg/l. to 32.0 mg/l. The minimum value was recorded in the month of December and Maximum in the month of April (Fig. 1.9). Higher chloride contents during summer due to high temperatue. There by causing reduction in water volume, as well as the increased microbial activity and decompositions of organic matter. Similar results have been observed by Ahmad (2004).

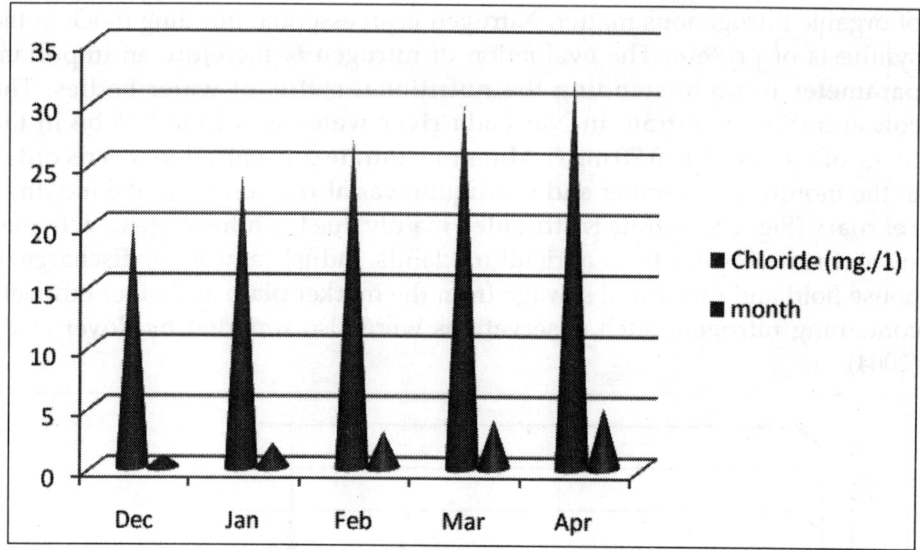

Fig. 1.9: Monthly Fluctuation of Chloride of Narmada River (Dec. 12 to Apr. 13)

Phosphate

Phosphorous is one of the most important nutrients limiting the growth of autotrophs and biological productivity of the system. High phosphorus content causes increased algal growth, often as blooms, till nitrogen becomes limiting. The main source of phosphorus in natural water comes from weathering of phosphate bearing rocks and leading of soils in the catchment (Jhingran 1982). During the present study the values of phosphate fluctuated between 0.8 mg/l. to 1.2 mg/l. the maximum phosphate was recorded in the month of December and minimum was also recorded in the month of January (Fig. 1.10). High value of phosphate in the present study may be due to high productivity of river in present investigation phosphate showed direct reduction with nitrate. The increased use of fertilizers, use of detergents and domestic sewage greatly contribute to the heavy loading of phosphorus in the water.

Calcium

Calcium is an important micronutrient in aquatic ecosystem. Calcium is found in abundance in all natural water bodies. It being an important contributor to hardness in water audit reduces. In the present study the calcium value varied between 77.0 mg/l. to 91.0 mg/l. The minimum value 77.0 mg/l. was observed during in month of December and maximum value during March month (Fig. 1.11) of in present study, higher calcium value was recorded during summer due to attributed evaporation of surface water, calcium showed positive correlation with temperature and hardness.

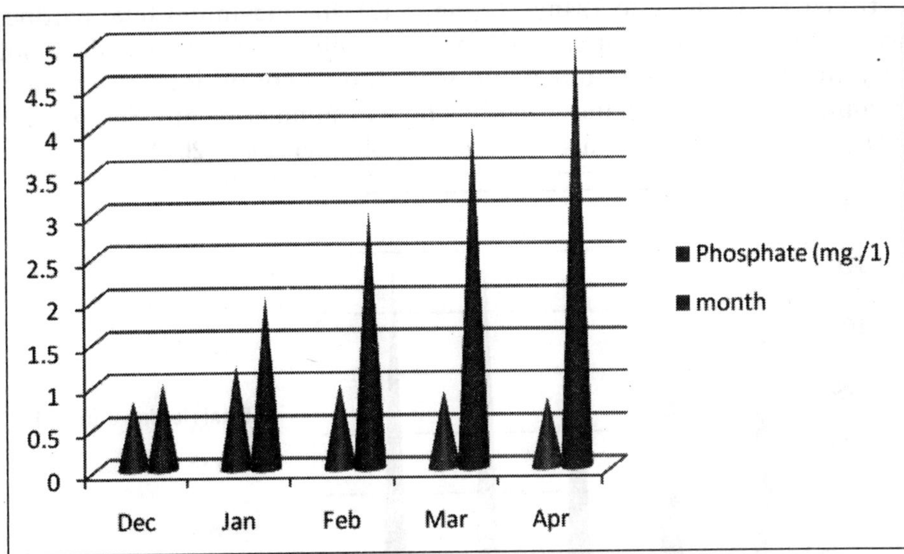

Fig. 1.10: Monthly Fluctuation of Phosphate of Narmada River (Dec. 12 to Apr. 13)

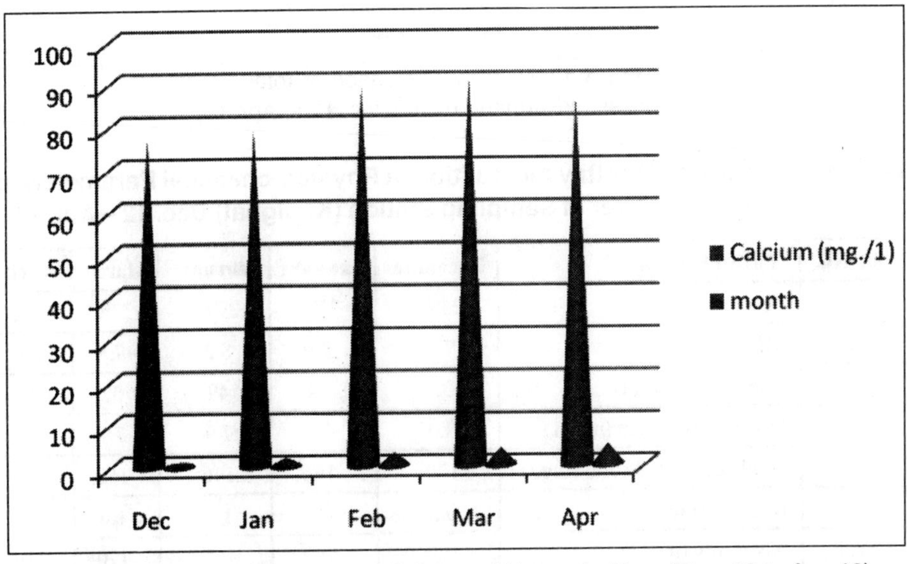

Fig. 1.11: Monthly Fluctuation of Calcium of Narmada River (Dec. 12 to Apr. 13)

Total Hardness

Total hardness is the parameter of water quality used to describe the effect of dissolved minerals (mostly Ca and Mg), determining suitability of water for domestic, industrial and drinking purposes. Its depends on a complex mixture of a cations and anions is predominantly contributed by a calcium and magnesium. The total hardness of Narmada River varied between 113.0 mg/l. to 124mg/l. (Fig. 1.12). the maximum total hardness was recorded during in month of March and minimum during in the month of January. The maximum value was due to continuous teaching an accumulation of salts in the absence of how in summer month (Sharma *et al.*, 2006). Same results were also reported by Sharma *et al.*, (2012).

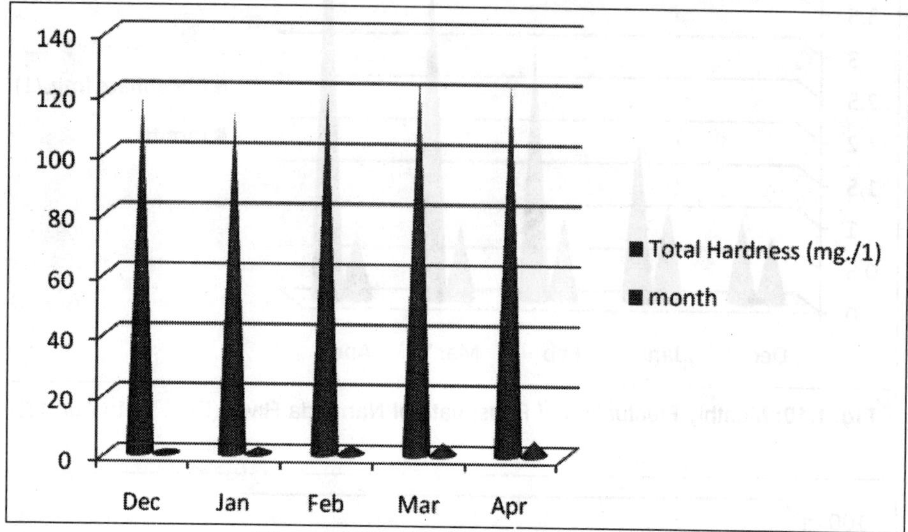

Fig. 1.12: Monthly Fluctuation of Total Hardness of Narmada River (Dec. 12 to Apr. 13)

Table 1.1: Showing Monthly Fluctuation in Physico-chemical Parameters of Narmada River at Sampling Station (Khalghat) Dec. 12 – Apr. 13

Sl. No.	Parameters	December	January	February	March	April
1.	Temperature	25ºC	27ºC	29ºC	33ºC	35ºC
2.	pH	7.4	7.9	8.2	7.8	8.6
3.	Transparency(cm)	35	44	49	52	39
4.	Dissolved Oxygen (mg./1)	8.0	7.5	7.9	7.1	8.8
5.	Total suspended solid (mg./1)	170	166	146	152	167
6.	B. O. D. (mg./1)	0.5	0.8	1.1	1.6	0.9
7.	Alkalinity (mg./1)	180	169	165	170	164
8.	Nitrate (mg./1)	0.42	0.47	0.70	0.66	0.52
9.	Chloride (mg./1)	20.0	24.0	27.0	30.0	32.0
10.	Phosphate (mg./1)	0.8	1.2	0.97	0.89	0.90
11.	Calcium (mg./1)	77.0	79.0	89.0	91.0	86.0
12.	Total Hardness (mg./1)	118.0	113.0	120.0	124.0	123.0

Systematic List Coleoptera of Narmada River

The benthic macro-invertebrates (Coleoptera) encountered in the river during the study period is shown in following. Phylum Arthropoda, class Insecta, Order- Coleoptera, Suborder- Adephaga, Five (5) families, Ten (10) Subfamilies, Twenty eight (28) Genus, Six (6) Sub genus and Seventeen (17) Species were recorded.

ORDER: COLEOPTERA
SUBORDER I: ADEPHAGA
Family I. GYRINIDAE
Subfamily 1. ENHYDRINAE
Genus 1.*Dineutus* Macleay,
Subgenus: *Protodineutus*,

1. *Dineutus (Protodineutus) indicus*
2. *Dineutus (Spinosodineutus) spinosus* (Fabricius) 1781
3. *Dineutus (Spinosodineutus) unidentatus* 1833

Subfamily 2. GYRININAE
Genus 2. *Aulonogyrus* Motschulsky, 1853

4. *Aulonogyrus sp.*(Walker) 1858

Genus 3. *Gyrinus* Geoffroy, 1762

5. *Gyrinus convexiusculus* Macleay 1871
6. *Gyrinus smaragdinus* Regimbart, 1891

Genus 4. *Metagyrinus* Brinck 1955

7. *Metagyrinus arrowi* (Regimbart)1907

Subfamily 3. ORECTOCHILINAE
Genus 5. Orectochilus Eschscholtz, 1833
Subgenus: *Patrus* , Aube, 1836

8. *Orectochilus (Patrus) andamanicus* Regimbart , 1884

Family II. DYTISCIDAE
Subfamily 1.: COLYMBETINAE
Tribe 1: Copelatini
Genus 6. Copelatus Erichson, 1832

9. *Copelatus assamensis* Vazirani 1970
10. *Copelatus freudei* Guignot, 1954
11. *Copelatus indicus* Sharp, 1882

Subfamily 3. HYDROPORINAE
Tribe1.: Hyphydrini
Genus 7. *Metheles* Sharp

12. *Metheles indicus* Regimbart

Genus 08. *Hyphydrus* Illiger, 1807

13. *Hyphydrus (Apriophorus) birmanicus* Regimbart, 1888

Tribe III. HYDROPORINI
Genus 09. *Hyphophorus* Sharp, 1882
Subfamily 4. LACCOPHILINAE.
Genus 10. Laccophilus Leach, 1817

14. *Laccophilus anticatus* Sharp, 1890

Subfamily 5. NOTERINAE
Tribe HYDROCANTHINI
Family: IV.Hydrophilidae
Subfamily 1. : Hydraeninae
Genus 11. *Hydraena* Kugelann, 1794
Subfamily 2. : Sphaeridinae
Tribe I : Sphaeridini d'Orchymont
Genus 39. *Dactylosternum* Wollaston. 1854

15. *Dactylosternum hydrophiloides* (M'Leay), 1825

Genus 40. *Sphaeridium* Fabricius,. 1775
Subfamily 7: Hydrophilinae
Tribe 1. Hydrobinii
Genus 44. *Crenetis* Bedel 1881
Genus 50. Hydrophilus Leach, 1764

16. *Hydrophilus indicus* (Bedel)1892

Family V : Elmidae
Genus 55. Stenelmis Dufour, 1835

17. *Stenelmis sp.*

Genus 10. Laccophilus Leach, 1817
14. Laccophilus anticatus Sharp, 1890

Water beetle is adapted to live in water. There are few water species that live in the intertidal zone. Some species of water beetles have aquatic larvae and terrestrial adults. Water beetles from family Gyrinidae, Haliplidae, Noteridae, Amphizoidae, Dytiscidae and Hydroscaphidae are aquatic in all life stages. The adult water beetles from family Hydroscaphidae, Hydrophilidae, Lutrochidae, Dyropidae, Elmidae, Eulichadidae, Heteroceridae, Limnichidae, Psephenidae, Ptilodactylidae and Sphaeriusidae are not aquatic.

Hebauer *et al.*, (1998) reported that water beetle fauna of the alluvial riparian swamp system Take China in West Malaysia revealed a total of 21 species representing the families Noteridae, Dytiscidae, Hydrophilidae, Hydraenidae and Hydrochidae. The Hydrophilidae Helochares Cinensis, H. Discus, H. Yangae and H. lacustris are described as new. Recent survey of the water beetle fauna of Pulau Tioman revealed 11 species of the families Noteridae, Dytiscidae, Hydrophilidae, Hydraenidae, Scirtidae and Limnichidae. All identified species (Canthydrus Flammulatus, Lacconectus krikkeni, Lacconectus Corayi, Sternolophus, Rufipes, Helochares, fuliginosus, Oocyclus, Sumatrensis, Tiomanensis and Amphiops Coomani) are widespread in the Indo-Malayan region.

Macro-invertebrates were studied as bioindicators (Coleoptera: Psephenidae) to monitor the water quality of wetlands Uniyal *et al.*, (2007) undertook a major pioneering study on the ecological study on tiger beetles as indicator for monitoring biodiversity in the protected areas of the Shivalik landscape of north western Himalaya. So far, in India, not much of the work has been done on the bioindicators role of many abundant Coleopteran families. In view of the important role played by water beetle in the ecosystem. This research work gives an opportunity to explore an uninvestigated site to determine the spatial distribution of various families, species number and endemics of the order Coleoptera to apply it as its potential role as bioindicators, which will be thus an important technique for the preliminary decision-making of conservation efforts.

REFERENCES

1. A.P.H.A. (2005), American Water Works Association and Water Pollution Control Federation Standard Methods for the Examination of Water & Waste Water 21 Edition American Public Health Association (A.P.H.A.) Washington D.C.
2. Ahmed, A.M. (2004), Ecological Studies of the River Padma at Mawa Ghat, Munshiganj Physico-chemical Properties. Pakistan Journal of Biological Sciences. 7(11):1865-1869pp.
3. Bilton, V., (2009), Report of Aquatic Coleoptera Value of Water Beetle Fauna Found that the Correlation Conservation Trust, I:\print\David Bilton.mht.
4. Celik, T., I. Zelnik, V. Babij, B. Vres, A. Pirnat, A. Seliskar and B. Drovenik, (2005): Inventari za cija kalov in lokev na Krasu ter njihov pomen za biotsko raznovrstnost. In: Voda in zivljenje v kamniti pokrajini, Kras, (Eds.) Mihevec, A., Zalozba. ZRC SAZU, Ljubljana, pp: 72-82.
5. Eyre, M.D. and G.N. Foster, (1989), A Comparison of Aquatic Heteroptera and Coleoptera Communities as a Basis for Environmental and Conservation Assessments in Statistic Water sites. J. Appl. Entomol., 108: 355-362.

6. Fernandez, S., D.P. Abellan, J. Velasco and A. Millan, (2004), Selecting Areas to Protect the Biodiversity of Aquatic Ecosystems in Semiarid Mediterranean Region Using Water Beetle. Aquatic Conservation: Marine and Freshwater Ecosystems, 14: 465-479.
7. Foster, G.N., (1987), The Use of Coleoptera Records in Assessing the Conservation Status of Wetlands. In: The Use of Invertebrates in Site Assessment for Conservation Newcastle Upon Tyne, Luff, M.L. (Ed.). University of Newcastle Upon Tyne, UK., pp. 8-17.
8. Foster, G.N., A.P. Foster, M.D. Eyre and B.T. Bilton, (1990), Classification of Water Beetle Assemblages in Arable Fenland and Ranking of sites in Relation to Conservation Value. Freshwater Biol., 22: 343-354.
9. Ganapati, S.V. (1960), Ecology of Tropical Waters. In. P. Kachroo (ed.), Proceedings in the Symposium on Ecology. Indian Council of Agricultural Research, New Delhi.
10. Golterman, H. L. (1991), Physiological Limnology: An Approach to the Physiology of Lake Ecosystem. Elsvier Scientific Publication Comp. Amsterdam. Oxford, New York, 249-277pp.
11. Hebauer, F., & Klausnitzer, B., (1998), Insecta: Coleoptera: Hydrophiloidea (exkl. Helophorus). Süâwasserfauna von Mitteleuropa 20, Part 7, 8, 9, 10-1. Gustav Fischer, Stuttgart, Jena, Lübeck, Ulm, p. 134.
12. Jain R. and Sharma D. (2000), Water Quality of Rampur Reservoir of Guna District (M.P. India) Environ. Cons. J. 1(2): 99-102pp.
13. Jhingran, V.G. (1982), Fish and Fisheries of India. Hindustan Publishing Corporation (India), Delhi: 1-666pp.
14. Khanna DR and Bhutani R. (2003), Limnological Status of Satikund Pond at Hardiwar. Indian J. Environ. Sci 7(2): 131-136pp.
15. Pathak SK., Mudgal LK., (2005), Limnology and Biodiversity of Fish Fauna in Virla Reservoir, MP India. J. Comp. Toxicol. Physiol. 2(1) 86-90pp.
16. Pearson, D.L., (1994), Selecting Indicator Taxa for the Quantitative Assessment of Biodiversity. Philosophical Transactions of the Royal Society B., 345: 75-79pp.
17. Ribera, I. and G.N. Foster, (1993), Uso de los Coleopteros acuaticos como indicadores biologicos (Coleoptera). Elytron, 4: 61-75.
18. Ribera, I., (2000), Biogeography and Conservation of Iberian Water Beetles (Coleoptera). Biological Conservation, 92: 131-150.
19. Royer T.V. Tank J.L David M.B. (2004), Transport and Fate of Nitrate in Headwater Agricultural Streams in Illinois. J.Environ.Qual. (33): 1296-1304pp.
20. Sharma D. and Jain R. (2001), Duirnal Variation in Some Aspects of Limnology of Gopalpura Tank of District Guna (M.P.) India Environ. Cons. J. 2(1): 41-44pp.
21. Sharma A., Mudgal L. K., Sharma A., Sharma S. (2004), Fish Diversity of Yashwant Sagar Reservoir Indore M.P. Him J. Environ. Zoology. 18(2) 117-119pp.
22. Sharma M. P., Sharma S., Goel V., Sharma P., Kumar A. (2006), Water Quality Assessment of Behta River Using Benthic Macro Invertebrates. Life Sc. Journal, 3 (4) pp. 68-74.
23. Sharma S., Tali I., Pir Z., Siddique A., Mudgal L.K. (2012), Evaluation of Physico-chemical Parameters of Narmada River, MP, India Researcher 4(5): 13-19pp. (ISSN: 1553-9865) http://www.science pub.net/researcher
24. Uniyal V.P., Sivakumar K, Padmawathe R, Kittur S, Bhargav VK, Bhardwaj M, Dobhal R (2007), Ecological Study of Tiger Beetles (Cicindelidae) as Indicator for Biodiversity Monitoring in the Shivalik Landscape. DST Project Completion Report. Wildlife Institute of India, Dehradun.

25. Welch P.S. (1998): Liminological Methods Mcgran Hill Book Co. New York.
26. Wetzel R.G., Likens G.E. (2006): Limnological Analysis. 3rd ed. Springer-Verlag, New York, 391pp.
27. World Health Organization (1993): Guidelines for Drinking Water Quality-I, Recommendations, 2nd Ed. Geneva.
28. Yogesh S. and Pendse D. C. (2001): Hydrological Study of Dahikhura Reservoir. J. of Environmental Biology. 22(1) 67-70pp.

Pages: 17-34

LIMNOLOGY AND AQUATIC SCIENCE
Edited by: Dr. Shailendra Sharma; Dr. Pawan Kumar 'Bharti'
ISBN: 978-93-5056-735-7
Edition: 2015
Published by: Discovery Publishing House Pvt. Ltd., New Delhi (India)

2

Benthic Community in an Urban Pond of Aligarh, INDIA

Habeeba A. Kabeer* and **Saltanat Parveen**

INTRODUCTION

Water is the mother of life and it is the most precious gift of the nature. About 71 percent of earth's surface is covered with water 97.3 percent of global water exists in ocean and remaining 2.7 percent in glaciers, lakes, rivers and wetlands. The total surface area of lakes accounts to roughly 1.8 percent of the land area, or about 2.5 million km^2, the volume of water contained in them is 2.80×10^3 (Schwoerbel, 1987). The organisms associated with solid liquid interface are ordinarily termed as Benthos (Haeckel, 1891).

The usefulness of benthic organisms, especially the benthos in pollution monitoring programme to ascertain the health of estuarine and marine environments has been re-emphasized. Studies made on benthos led to the development of the indicator organism concept, which is the presence of a particular species or a group of species in a given locality reflecting the status of the environment. Among benthos, polychaetes are ideal indicator organisms, since they constitute well over half of the total number of

Limnology Laboratory, Department of Zoology, Aligarh Muslim University, Aligarh - 202 002 Uttar Pradesh, India.

organisms in and on the bottom and thus give a good indication of health conditions of the aquatic environment.

The distribution of the diverse fauna within water body is extremely heterogenous. Benthic organisms either possesses adaptive mechanisms to cope with these changes, either relatively dormant stages until more physiologically amenable conditions return, move, or die. The adaptive capabilities of the benthic animals to the dynamics of environmental parameters are basic to their distribution, growth and reproductive potential (Wetzel, 1983).

Among the invertebrate taxa, benthos is sensitive to pollutants such as metals and organic waste. Mayflies, stone flies and caddis flies are generally intolerant of pollution but some species can survive in good oxygen concentration in moderately polluted water body. Benthos are sensitive to watershed condition and exhibit sufficient stability in assemblage structure over time to make them useful as long term monitor of stream health (Richards and Minshell, 1992) and indicator of water quality (Gauffin and Tarwell, 1952).

The benthic Cladocera comprise a suite of species that occupy various littoral and profundal habitats. The importance of cladocera in the trophic dynamics of freshwater systems, being the main component of benthos, has long been recognized (Sinha and Khan, 1998). They are the consumers of first order, directly drawing energy from primary producers of the ecosystem viz. phytoplankton. In turn, they form the food for planktivorous fishes and other invertebrates, transferring energy to higher trophic levels. Besides, they have also been reported to be reliable indicator of eutrophic nature of water bodies (Sharma, 2001).

Copepods are significant primary and secondary consumers in aquatic food chains. Their grazing contributes to the transfer of algal primary production to higher trophic levels. In other words, copepods can make organic material available to higher trophic levels in a larger pellet form thus saving the foraging energy of their predators.

Due to unique hydrological properties, the aquatic ecosystem has supported the development of a very complex biotic community on the earth. Virtually every form, composition, altitude and latitude are populated with organisms both plant and animal, although the composition differs greatly with differences in the various waters. With few exceptions, all the major groups of plants and animals are represented, often by a great array of species. Aquatic ecosystem is thus important sustainers of biodiversity which encompasses freshwater ecosystems, including lakes, ponds and reservoirs, rivers and streams, groundwater and wetlands. Aquatic biodiversity has enormous economic and aesthetic value and is largely responsible for maintaining and supporting overall environmental health. Human has long depended on aquatic resources for food, medicines and materials as well as for recreational and commercial purposes. Other organisms also rely upon the great diversity of aquatic habitats and resources for food materials and breeding grounds.

The organisms of lake are conveniently grouped ecologically into those associated with the free water, those associated with solid-water interface and those at the surface in film and can undertake swimming movements in any direction in spite of turbulence. Gams (1918) have given systematic classification suitable for all organisms living in aquatic environment. India is one of the most recognized country facing water pollution problems, predominantly due to untreated sewage. Rivers such as Ganga, Yamuna, kaveri and much another water body all flowing through high populated area and these are highly polluted. If we don't do anything to safe our water then we will face a great problem.

Many organisms adapted to deep-water pressure cannot survive in the upper parts of the water column. Dead and decaying matter from higher up in the water column drifts down to the depths sustains the benthic food chain. Most organisms in the benthic zone are scavengers or detritivores. The depth of water, temperature and salinity, and type of local substrate all affect what benthos is present. In coastal waters and other places where light reaches the bottom, benthic photosynthesizing diatoms can proliferate. Filter feeders, such as sponges and bivalves, dominate hard, sandy bottoms. Deposit feeders, such as polychaetes, populate softer bottoms. Fish, sea stars, snails, cephalopods, and crustaceans are important predators and scavengers.

The littoral benthos is extremely varied when compared with that of deeper region. Protozoan, sponges, coelenterates, rotifers, nematodes, bryozoans, crustaceans, molluscs, insects, annelids, echinoderms and many lower vertebrates are abundant in the shallow waters. Biglow (1928) divided the littoral benthic micro-organisms of Nipigon lake, Canada into ecological groups. The ooze films group comprises those micro-organisms living in and on the film oozes which form the upper surface of the lake bottom. The assemblage was found to contain following microscopic organisms e.g. bacteria, green algae, diatoms, protozoans, rotifers, several entomostracan (mostly cladocera), tardigrada and certain water mites.

"Pollution free water is everyone's dream. Benthos is pollution indicator organism, with the help of these organisms we can determine pollution level of water. The term Benthos is derived from two Greek words "*Ben*" meaning 'the collection of organisms living in or on the sea or lakes' and "*Thos*" 'the bottom of sea or lakes".

According to Brinkhurst (1974), the community of benthic invertebrate in lake has been used as indicator of lake fertility and even been used as a basis for lake classification (Johnson *et al.*, 1993). Knowledge of littoral benthos also becomes more important because of the increasing human influence on the aquatic ecosystem. Moreover, the effect of pollution or even more the effect of the regulation of water level cannot be understood or even cannot be predicted without knowledge of the natural state of the littoral zone. Despite the great importance of benthic communities in general, relatively fewer studies have been carried out as compared to plankton and nekton.

The need for comprehensive studies on benthic fauna is important for better understanding of benthic community and also in evaluating their role as fish food.

DESCRIPTION OF THE STUDY AREA

Aligarh district is a part of Central Ganga Plain of the state covering an area of 5498 square kilometer. and lies between North latitudes 27°28′ and 28°10′ and East longitudes 77°29′ and 78°36′ with total population of 4,32,37,60 as per 2001 census (density: 786 persons/sq.km.). The district is bounded by river Ganga in the west and the river Yamuna in the east. The entire district falling in Upper Ganga Doab represents flat topography.

Climatic factors control organic production in lakes and rivers by affecting circulation and exchange of essential nutrients (Rawson, 1939).

Ponds directly or indirectly have an enormous ecological, commercial and socio-economic importance. They are rich in the components of bio-diversity like, flora and fauna of local, national and regional significance.

Aligarh and its adjoining areas are richly well off with hundreds of derelict ponds (>0.2 ha) which are used as drainage basin and support an extensive and regular fisheries of various kind.

Urban Pond is also a perennial sewage fed, eutrophic pond, situated at distance of 1.5 km from department of Zoology in South-west of Aligarh Muslim University campus. The shoreline is somewhat irregular. The depth of the pond varies from 0.5 to 3 meters at different place. The main source of its water supply is sewage water from adjoining colonies in addition to surface run-off from surrounding areas.

This pond is also used occasionally by washermen for washing clothes, thereby adding detergents and certain chemicals that bring change in its flora and fauna. The pond is characterized by rich growth of macrophytes especially water hyacinth (*Ecchornia crassipes*) which covers about 70% of the surface during the months of June and July. Other macrophytes like *Trapa, Baccopa, Polygonum* , *Wolfi*a etc.

The main fish fauna of the pond include *Heteropneutes fossilis, Clarias batrachus Channa punctatus* etc. The bottom of the pond contains loose mud, stones, parts of dead plants and decayed litter. In the distribution of benthic flora, light plays a very important role when the water is sufficiently shallow. Light reaches the bottom sediments in plenty and as a result of it, benthic algae and macrophytes grow in greater abundance.

METHODOLOGY

Sampling of sediment was performed from February, 2009 to January, 2010. At each sampling site sediment sample was collected using Ekman-dredges and water sample in bottle after collection labeled and bring to laboratory. The collected sediment was washed and sieved on a mesh screen of 0.5 mm, and sorted in Petri dishes, using a stereomicroscope. The benthic communities were identified using identification keys Edmondson (1959), Pennak (1978) and Tonapi (1980) and density determined per meter square area (ind/m^2).

RESULT AND DISCUSSION

Due to eutrophic nature of Dipteran larvae, they have been used as reliable indicators of organic pollution and related perturbation. The high abundance of *Chironomus* sp. at all the selected ponds in present study indicates that these water bodies are highly eutrophic.

The abundance of benthic insect group e.g. Ephemeroptera, Plecoptera, Trichoptera and Chironomidae indicates the balance of the community, since Ephemeroptera, Plecoptera, Trichoptera are considered to be more sensitive and Chironomidae less sensitive to environmental stress (Plafkin *et al.*, 1989). A community considered to be in good biotic condition will display an even distribution among these four groups, while communities with disproportionately high numbers of Chironomidae may indicate environmental stress (Plafkin *et al.*, 1989). If we examine pollution level of water time to time with the help of benthic organisms then not completely but a part of pollution can be control by treatment of sewage and we can safe our water and human health.

CLADOCERA

The benthic Cladocera comprise a suite of species that occupy various littoral and profundal habitats. In Lake Myvatn, Iceland, which is renowned for its abundance of wildlife, a large proportion of the secondary production is channeled through the zoobenthos where chironomids play a major role and Cladocera are prominent (Jọ́nasson 1979).

Total percent contribution of Cladocera was found to be ranged from 10.49 % during August, 2009 to 22.63 % in April, 2009 (Table 2.2, Fig. 2.1 & 2.2) in Urban Pond.

Benthic Cladocera distribution and abundance in these ponds have showed wide fluctuations in response to favorable and unfavorable conditions. The littoral and limnetic cladocerans contribute significantly to biological productivity and energy flow in freshwater environs because of their rapid turnover rates and capability to build up substantial populations within short periods of time. Presence of detritus of all kinds, bacteria, algae and protozoans are important for their abundance as all these form the bulk of the ingested material of benthos (Pennak, 1978).

Table 2.1: Monthly Distribution and Abundance of Benthic Community (No/m²) in Urban Pond

Months Genera	February' 09	March	April	May	June	July	August	September	October	November	December	Jan' 10
CLADOCERA												
Daphnia pulex	215	115	298	276	198	162	129	218	206	237	312	297
Bosmina sp.	272	198	291	256	314	165	125	162	271	173	215	292
Moina micrura	217	125	197	298	203	146	75	97	272	172	338	319
Total	704	438	786	830	715	473	329	477	749	582	865	908
COPEPODA												
Cyclops viridis	89	63	54	79	73	97	79	87	95	68	159	186
Diaptomus sp.	73	48	75	92	43	38	83	61	152	89	115	128
Total	162	111	129	171	116	135	162	148	247	157	274	314
ROTIFERA												
Brachionus calyciflors	393	183	193	195	193	73	225	57	372	321	413	516
B. bidentata	495	225	376	63	372	223	82	67	129	223	249	519
B. angularis	133	118	128	95	252	86	173	97	115	129	326	117
Keratella tropica	133	85	149	173	183	67	84	98	54	98	219	112
K. quadrata	86	219	115	196	95	83	82	72	94	28	92	45
Asplanchna priodonta	58	130	95	215	73	135	145	75	87	305	95	67
Filinia longiseta	101	35	98	59	253	215	54	97	83	145	120	225
Notholca sp.	59	72	85	191	95	85	68	63	71	74	53	88
Hexarthra sp.	83	197	87	52	102	153	78	123	101	52	79	38
Total	1541	1264	1326	1239	1618	1120	991	749	1106	1375	1646	1727

(Table Contd...)

Months Genera	February' 09	March	April	May	June	July	August	September	October	November	December	Jan' 10
OSTRACODA												
Heterocypris	194	325	248	349	141	193	285	318	159	386	433	593
Stenocypris sp.	73	67	56	87	108	72	91	61	73	91	87	75
Centrocypris	42	71	51	108	92	53	31	67	40	76	98	54
Total	309	463	355	544	341	318	407	446	272	553	618	722
OLIGOCHAETA												
Tubifex	87	63	47	65	73	82	92	53	65	43	34	52
Chaetogaster	54	83	63	53	73	95	49	56	53	47	73	86
Nais	39	83	72	92	85	93	83	87	53	63	54	67
Aelosoma	57	62	59	67	64	63	67	57	53	62	63	73
Total	237	291	241	271	295	333	291	253	224	217	224	278

(Table Contd…)

Months Genera	February' 09	March	April	May	June	July	August	September	October	November	December	January
DIPTERA												
Chironomus larva	690	154	170	450	243	139	197	262	105	238	790	1014
Chironomus pupa	5	2	5	4	30	21	13	22	35	24	43	78
Helius larva	15	18	3	9	7	4	3	9	11	13	17	27
Culex larva	31	59	28	60	87	53	92	105	40	147	93	124
Pentanura	67	29	42	85	195	132	95	63	79	112	97	158
Total	808	262	248	608	562	349	400	461	270	534	1040	1401
HEMIPTERA												
Notonecta insulata	139	28	85	53	91	11	97	65	43	65	121	186
Coroxid	48	12	50	75	103	58	64	89	127	73	173	97
Belostoma	16	7	13	9	7	15	19	32	27	2	68	87
Hebrus sp.	7	15	9	28	3	7	24	12	19	11	39	19
Sigara	7	2	6	14	47	3	13	8	3	21	15	37
Hesperocorixa	78	17	72	46	33	24	89	43	28	56	148	97
Total	295	81	235	225	284	118	306	249	247	228	564	523
COLEOPTERA												
Hydrophilus	17	14	38	98	25	68	79	53	32	67	54	92
Dytiscus	45	9	23	23	21	52	37	64	33	52	87	89
Berosus	98	23	49	51	62	87	56	72	98	43	125	117
Haliplus	173	82	33	31	59	24	67	35	52	65	52	105
Total	333	128	143	203	167	231	239	224	215	227	321	403

(Table Contd...)

Months Genera	February' 09	March	April	May	June	July	August	September	October	November	December	January
TRICHOPTERA												
Limnephilus larva	3	2	1	3	3	1	2	1	1	2	5	4
Phryganaea larva	3	4	3	3	2	3	3	2	3	4	2	4
Polycentropus larva	2	3	1	3	3	4	2	1	1	2	2	2
Total	8	9	5	9	8	8	7	4	5	8	9	11
EPHEMEROPTERA												
Baetis hiemalis nymph	3	1	2	5	3	2	2	3	2	4	3	3
Caenis nymph	2	1	2	3	2	2	3	2	5	5	4	5
Total	5	2	4	8	5	4	5	5	7	9	7	8
Grand Total	4328	3049	3473	4114	3111	3089	3137	3016	3418	3886	5570	6296

Table 2.2: Percent Contribution and Maximum Minimum Value of Benthic Community of Urban Pond

Groups	Max %	Min %
Cladocera	22.63	10.49
Copepoda	7.32	2.82
Rotifera	41.45	24.83
Ostracoda	15.18	7.01
Oligochaeta	10.78	4.02
Diptera	22.25	7.14
Hemiptera	10.12	2.65
Coleoptera	10.12	4.06
Trichoptera	5.76	0.132
Epemeroptera	0.23	0.065

Daphnia pulex: It showed minimum density (115 No/m^2) during March, 2009 and maximum density (312 No/m^2) during December, 2009 (Table 2.1).

Bosmina sp.: In URBAN Pond, its density ranging from 125 to 314 No/m^2 during August, 2009 and June, 2009 respectively (Table 2.1).

Moina sp.: It ranged from 75 to 338 No/m^2 during August, 2009 and December, 2009 (Table 2.1).

COPEPODA

Copepods are very ancient arthropods and the diminutive relatives of crabs and shrimps. In terms of their size diversity and abundance they are often called "water fleas" (Reddy, 2001).

Copepods were represented by two genera *Cyclops viridis* and *Diaptomus sp.* The population density of Copepods ranged from 111 No/m^2 during March, 2009 to 314 No/m ^{2} in January, 2010 in Urban Pond Tables-1. Total percent contribution of copepods ranged from 2.82 % during June, 2009 to 7.39 % in October, 2009 (Table 2.2, Figs. 2.1 & 2.2) in Urban Pond.

Cyclops viridis: Its minimum density 54 No/m^2 during April, 2009 and maximum 186 No/m^2 during January, 2010 (Table 2.1).

Diaptomus sp.: The population density of *Diaptomus* ranged from a minimum of 38 No/m^2 during July, 2009 to 152 No/m^2 in October, 2009 (Table 2.1) in Urban Pond.

ROTIFERA

Rotifera, one of the oldest groups and a minor phylum of invertebrates, include animals commonly termed as "Wheel Animalcules" because of their characteristic "wheel organ" or "corona" (Sharma, 2001).

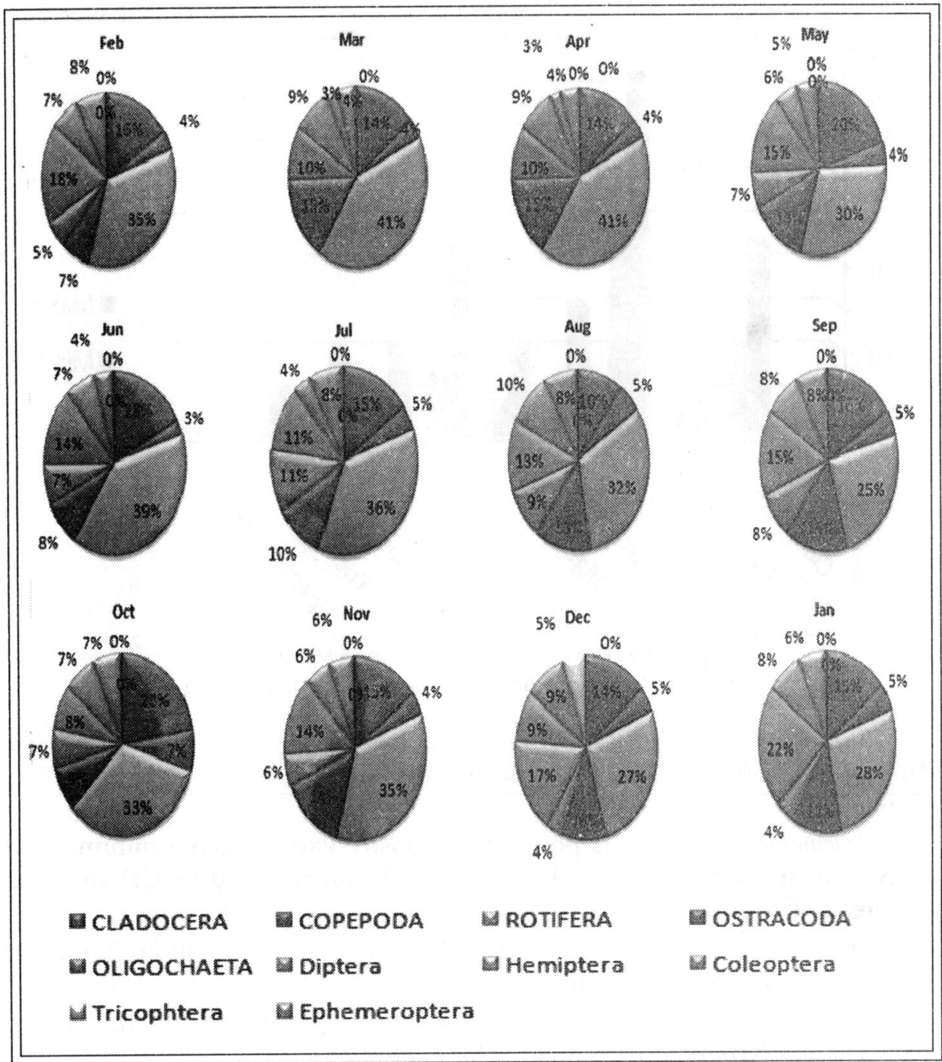

Fig. 2.1: Monthly Per cent Composition of Different Benthic Groups (No/m^2) in Urban Pond

This group was represented by six genera viz *Brachionus, Keratella, Notholca, Filinia, Hexarthra, and Asplanchna.* The monthly variations in density of various genera of Rotifers (No/m^2) in the selected water bodies are given in (Table 2.1). The population density of Rotifers ranged from a minimum of 749 No/m^2 during September, 2009 to 1727 No/m^2 in January, 2010 in Urban Pond. Total percent contribution of Rotifers ranged from 24.83 % during September, 2009 to 41.45% in March, 2009 (Table 2.2, Figs. 2.1 & 2.2) in Urban Pond.

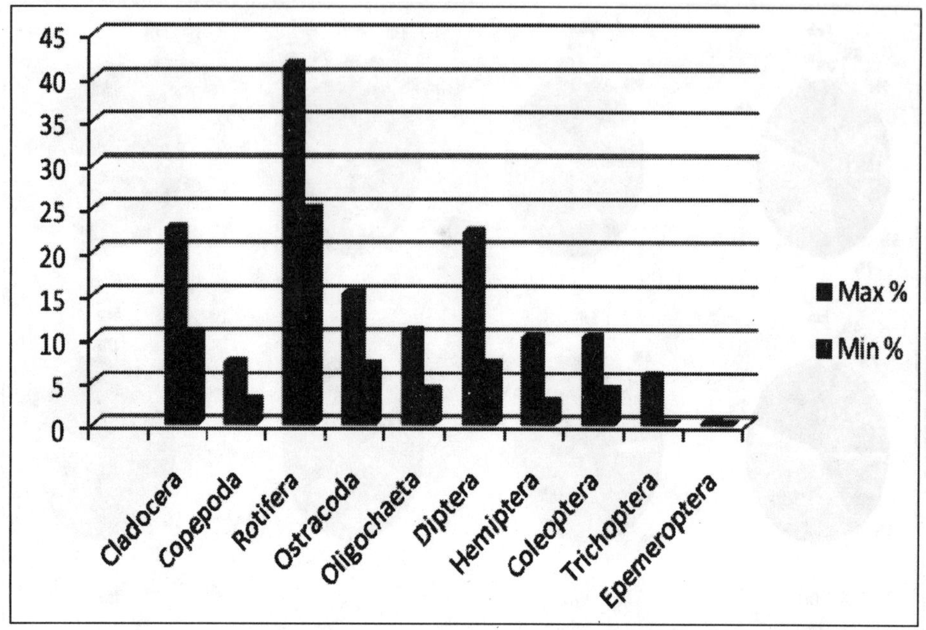

Fig. 2.2: Per cent Contribution and Maximum Minimum Value of Benthic Community of Urban Pond

Brachionus calyciflorus: In Urban Pond, it was found minimum 57 No/m^2 during September, 2009 and maximum 516 No/m^2 in January, 2010 (Table 2.1).

Brachionus bidentata: Its population density varied from a minimum of 63 No/m^2 in May, 2009 to 519 No/m^2 in January, 2010 in Urban Pond (Tables 2.1)

Brachionus angularis: Its density varied from a minimum 86 No/m^2 in July, 2009 to 326 No/m^2 December, 2009 in Urban Pond (Table 2.1).

Keratella tropica: its density was found to vary 54 No/m^2 in October, 2009 and 219 No/m^2 in December, 2009 (Table 2.1).

Keratella quadrata: In this Pond it showed variations between 28 No/m^2) in November, 2009 maximum density (219 No/m^2) was recorded during March, 2009 (Table 2.1).

Asplanchna priodonta: whereas in Urban Pond, it ranged from minimum (58 No/m^2) in February, 2010 to maximum (305 No/m^2) in November, 2009 (Table 2.1).

Filinia sp it showed minimum density (35 No/m^2) in March, 2009 while maximum density (253 No/m^2) during June, 2009 (Table 2.1).

Notholca sp.: whereas in Urban Pond, it showed minimum density (53 No/m^2) in December, 2009 and maximum (191 No/m^2) density during May, 2009 (Table 2.1).

Hexarthra sp.: In Urban Pond, it showed minimum density (38 No/m^2) during January, 2010 and maximum density (197 No/m^2) during March, 2009 (Table 2.1).

OSTRACODA

Superficially, the members of the subclass Ostracoda resemble miniature mussels and, therefore, "mussel shrimps" is an old European vernacular name (Edmondson, 1959). They have unsegmented body enclosed in two hinged valves and resemble tiny clams (Cole, 1983).

It was represented *Heterocypris, Stenocypris* and *Centrocypris*. Population density of Ostracods varied from a minimum of 272 No/m^2 October, 2009 to 722 No/m^2 in January, 2010 in Urban Pond (Tables -1). Its percent contribution varied from 7.01 % during February, 2009 to 15.18 % in March, 2009 (Table 2.2, Figs. 2.1 & 2.2) in Urban Pond.

Heterocypris sp.: It showed minimum (593 No/m^2) during January, 2010 (Table 2.1).

Stenocypris sp.: it showed minimum density (56 No/m^2) during April, 2009 and maximum density (108 No/m^2) during June, 2009 (Table 2.1).

Centrocypris sp. It showed minimum density (31 No/m^2) during August, 2009 and maximum density (108 No/m^2) during May, 2009 (Table 2.1).

OLIGOCHAETA

Except for a relatively small number of marine species, the oligochaetes are fresh water and terrestrial animals. The body is clearly divided into segments which are separated externally by distinct grooves.

This group was represented by *Tubifex, Chaetogaster, Nais and Aelosma.* Maximum oligochaetes 333 No/m^2 in the month of July, 2009, whereas the minimum 217 No/m^2 during November, 2009 (Table 2.1) were recorded.

The total percent contribution of Oligochaeta to the overall density of benthic fauna ranged from 4.02 % during December, 2009 to 10.78 % during July, 2009 (Table 2.2, Figs. 2.1 & 2.2) in Urban Pond.

Tubifex: Its population density varied from a minimum of 34 No/m^2 in December, 2009 to 92 No/m^2 in August, 2009 in Urban Pond (Table 2.1).

Chaetogaster: Its population density varied from a minimum of 47 No/m^2 in November, 2009 to 95 No/m^2 in July, 2009 in Urban Pond (Table 2.1).

Nais: Its population density varied from a minimum of 39 No/m^2 in February, 2009 to 93 No/m^2 in July, 2009 in Urban Pond (Table 2.1).

Aelosoma: Its population density varied from a minimum of 73 No/m^2 in January, 2010 in Urban Pond (Table 2.1).

DIPTERA

Diptera have aquatic larvae and pupae with terrestrial adults. Many other aquatic insects are also commonly referred to as "flies" (e.g., mayflies, dragonflies, stoneflies, caddisflies, alderflies, fishflies), but these taxa are not true flies as they do not belong to the order Diptera.

It was represented by *Chironomus, Helius, Culex* and *Pentaneura.* The monthly variations in population density of Diptera (No/m^2) in the selected water bodies are given in Tables-1. The density of Diptera ranged from a minimum 248 No/m^2 during April, 2009 to 1401 No/m^2 in January, 2010 in Urban Pond.

The percent contribution of Diptera to the total benthos ranged from 7.14 % during April, 2009 to 22.25 % in January, 2010 (Table 2.2, Fig. 2.1) in Urban Pond.

Chironomus larva: Its density varied from a minimum 105 No/m^2 in October, 2009 to 1014 No/m^2 in January, 2010 in Urban Pond (Table 2.1).

Chironomus pupa: Its population density varied from a minimum 2 No/m^2 in March, 2009 to 78 No/m^2 in January, 2010 (Table 2.1) in Urban Pond.

Helius larva: Its density varied from a minimum 3 No/m^2 in April and August, 2009 to a maximum of 27 No/m^2 in January, 2010 in Urban Pond (Table 2.1).

Culex: Its population density varied from a minimum 28 No/m^2 in April, 2009 to 147 No/m^2 in November, 2009 in Urban Pond (Table 2.1).

Pentaneura larva: Its population density varied from a minimum 29 No/m^2 in March, 2009 to 195 No/m^2 in June, 2009 in Urban Pond (Table 2.1).

HEMIPTERA

Aquatic hemipteran adults and larvae unlike most aquatic taxa in that the adults and larvae occupy the same habitat. Aquatic and semiaquatic Hemiptera can be separated into two groups based on their antennal morphology and the habitat in which they are generally found.

Hemiptera are represented by species viz *Notonecta, Coroxid, Belostoma, Hebrus, Sigara* and *Hespercorixa*. The monthly variations in density of various taxa of Hemiptera (No/m^2) in the selected water bodies are given in Table 2.1. The population density of Hemiptera ranged from a minimum 81 No/m^2 during March, 2009 to 564 No/m^2 in December, 2009 in Urban Pond. Total percent contribution of Hemiptera ranged from 2.65 % during March, 2009 to 10.12% in December, 2009 (Table 2.2, Fig. 2.1) in Urban Pond.

Notonecta insulata: Notonecta is commonly called as Backswimmers. This group is predatory.

Its population density varied from a minimum 11 No/m^2 in July, 2009 to 186 No/m^2 in January, 2010 in Urban Pond (Table 2.1).

Belostoma sp.: These are commonly called as Giant Water Bugs. Belostomatids most commonly occur in lakes, ponds, and marshes and less commonly in pools and backwaters in streams and rivers.

It was varied from 2 No/m^2 in November, 2009 to 87 No/m^2 in January, 2010 (Table 2.1).

Coroxid sp.: Coroxid commonly called as Water Boatmen. The Feeding habitat is Collector/Gatherers. Coroxids are found in areas of standing or slow flowing water in ponds, lakes, marshes, streams, and rivers. The size of this group is small (3-11 mm).

Its population density varied from a minimum 12 No/m^2 in March, 2009 to 173 No/m^2 in December, 2009 in Urban Pond (Table 2.1).

Hebrus sp.: Hebrus is commonly called as Velvet-Water Bugs. Feeding habitat of this Group is predators. It varied from 3 No/m^2 in June, 2009 to a maximum of 39 No/m^2 in December (Table 2.1).

Sigara sp.: Its population density varied from a minimum 2 No/m^2 in March, 2009 to 47 No/m^2 in June, 2009. (Table 2.1).

Hesperocorixa sp.: The body is elongate-oval, somewhat flattened, and usually dark grey. The dorsal surface of the body is cross-line. Its population density varied from a minimum 17 No/m^2 in March, 2009 to 148 No/m^2 in December, 2009 in Urban Pond. (Table 2.1).

COLEOPTERA

Aquatic Coleoptera constitute an important part of the macro-zoobenthos of freshwater habitats. Small and temporary water bodies have more species than large and permanent ones (Larson, 1985).

This group was represented by *Hydrophilus, Dytiscus, Berosus* and *Haliplus*. The monthly variations in population density of various genera of Coleoptera (No/m^2) are given in Tables-1. The population density of Coleoptera ranged from a minimum 128 No/m^2 during March, 2009 to 403 No/m^2 in January, 2010 in Urban Pond.

The total percent contribution of Coleoptera to the overall density of benthic fauna ranged from 4.06 % during June, 2009 to 10.12 % during December, 2010 in Urban Pond.

Hydrophilus larva: Hydrophilus are commonly called as minute Moss Beetles. These are Collector/Gatherers (larvae possibly predators). Hydraenids are semiaquatic and occur just above the waterline along streams and other waterbodies.

Its density varied from a minimum of 14 No/m^2 in March, 2009 to 98 No/m^2 in May, 2009 (Table 2.1).

Dytiscus sp.: Its population density varied from a minimum 9 No/m^2 in March, 2009 to 89 No/m^2 in January, 2010 (Table 2.1).

Berosus larva: Berosus are commonly called as Water Scavenger Beetles. Larvae: Predators. Adults: Collector/Gatherers.

Its population density varied from a minimum 23 No/m^2 in March, 2009 to 125 No/m^2 in December, 2009 in Urban Pond (Table 2.1).

Haliplus sp.: Haliplus are commonly called as crawling water beetles. The feeding habitat is shredders. Haliplid beetle larvae and adults most commonly occur in standing and slow-moving waters in lakes, ponds, marshes, and streams.

Its population density varied from a minimum 24 No/m^2 in July, 2009 to 173 No/m^2 in February, 2010 in Urban Pond (Table 2.1).

TRICHOPTERA

The name Trichoptera derived from the Greek words "trichos" meaning hair and "ptera" meaning wings refer to long, silky hairs that cover most of the body and wings. They are commonly known as "caddisflies" which mean case bearer. Trichoptera possess the more primitive characteristic state, having hairs rather than scales, and this character accounts for the name Trichoptera, and meaning "hairy wings.

This group was represented by *Limnephilus, Phryganaea* and *Polycentropus.* The monthly variations in the population density of various genera of Trichoptera (No/m^2) are given in Tables-1. The population density of Trichoptera ranged from a minimum 4 No/m^2 during September, 2009 to maximum 11 No/m ^{2} in January, 2010 in Urban Pond.

Total percent contribution of Trichoptera is negligible and ranged from 0.132% during September, 2009 to 5.76% in December, 2009 (Table 2.2, Fig. 2.1) in Urban Pond.

Limnephilus larva: Limnephilus are commonly called as Northern Case-Maker Caddisflies. Its population density varied from a minimum 1 No/m^2 in April, July, September and October, 2009 to 5 No/m^2 in December, 2009 in Urban Pond (Table 2.1).

Phryganaea larva: Phryganaea are commonly called as Giant Case-Maker Caddisflies. These are belonging to feeding group: predators, herbivores.

Its population density varied from a minimum 2 No/m^2 in June, September and December, 2009 to 4 No/m^2 in March, 2009 in Urban Pond (Table 2.1).

Polycentropus larva: Polycentropus commonly called as Tube-Making and Trumpet-Net Caddisflies.

Its population density varied from a minimum 1 No/m^2 in April, September and October, 2009 to 4 No/m^2 in July, 2009 in Urban Pond (Table 2.1).

EPHEMEROPTERA (MAYFLIES)

Ephemeroptera comes from the Greek word, "ephemeros" meaning lasting a day and "pteron" means a wing. They are exoperygotes and hemimetabolus. Mayflies are all aquatic as naiads (Daly, 1998).

Ephemeroptera formed tenth and least abundant group in all the selected water bodies. This group was represented by *Baetis* and *Caenis.* The population density of Ephemeroptera ranged from a minimum 2 No/m^2 during March, 2009 to 9 No/m^2 in November, 2009 in Urban Pond. Total percent contribution of Ephemeroptera is also negligible. It ranged from 0.065 % during March, 2009 to 0.231 % in November, 2009 (Table 2.2, Fig. 2.1) in Urban Pond.

Baetis: Baetis are commonly called as small Minnow Mayflies. These belong to feeding group: collector/gatherers, scrapers. Its population density varied from a minimum 1 No/m^2 in March, 2009 to 5 No/m^2 in May, 2009 in Urban Pond (Table 2.1).

Caenis: Caenis are commonly called as Small Square-Gill Mayflies. These belong to feeding group, collector/gatherers, and scrapers. Caenis mayfly larvae occur in streams in areas of slow current, at the edges of lakes, and in wetlands.

Its population density varied from a minimum from 1 No/m^2 in March, 2009 to 5 No/m^2 in October, November, 2009 and January, 2010 (Table 2.1).

REFERENCES

Brinkhurst, R.O. and Cook, D.G. (1974), Aquatic Earthworms (Annelida, Oligochaeta). In: *Pollution Ecology of Freshwater Invertebrates* (Eds. Harl and Fuller). Academic Press, London.

Gams, H. (1918), Prinzipienfragen der Vegetationsferschung. Vjschr. *Natur. Ges. Zurich.*, 63: 293-493.

Gauffin, A.R. Tarzwell, C.M. (1952), Aquatic Invertebrates as Indicators of Stream Pollution. *Pub Health Rep*, 67: 57-64.

Haeckel, E. (1891), Plankton Studies. Jenaische Zeitschr. *F. Naturw.*, 25: 232-336.

Hutchinson, G.E. (1967), *A Treatise on Limnology*: An Introduction to Lake Biology and the Limnoplankton. Vol. 2. John Wiley & Sons Inc., New York, 115 pp.

Hynes, H.B.N. (1961), The Invertebrate Fauna of a Welsh Mountain Stream. Arch. *Hydrobiol.*, 57: 344-388.

Johnson, R.K., Wiederholm, T. and Eriksson, L. (1993), Classification of Littoral Macroinvertebrate Communities of Swedish Reference Lakes. *Int. Verh. Ver. Limnol.*, 25: 512-517.

Jónasson, P.M. (1979), Ecology of Eutrophic, Suharctic Lake Myvatn and the River Laxá. *Oikos*, 32: 1-308.

Plafkin, JL., Barbour, M.T., Porter, K.D., Gross, S.K., and Hughes, R.M. (1989), *Rapid Bioassessment Protocols for use in Streams and Rivers: Benthic Macroinvertebrates and Fish.* U.S. Environmental Protection Agency. EPA 440/4-89/001. 8 chapters, Appendices A-D.

Rawson, D.S. (1939), Some Physical and Chemical Functions in the Metabolism of Lake. In: *Problem of lake Biology*. Publ. A.A.A.S.: 9-26.

Resh V.H. (1995), Fresh Water Macroinvertebrates and Rapid Assessment Procedure for Quality of Water Monitoring in Developing and Newly Industrialized Countries. In *Bilogical Assessment and criteria* (Davis W.S., Simon, T.P. eds), Lewis Publishers, England; 167-177.

Richards, C. and Minshall, G.W. (1992), Spatial and Temporal Trends in Stream Macroinvertebrate Species Assemblages: The Influence of Watershed Disturbance. *Hydrobiologia;* 241: 173-84.

Rosenberg, D.M. and Resh, V.H. (1993), *Fresh Water Biomonitoring and Benthic Macroinvertebrates.* Chapman and Hall Publication, New York; 488 pp.

Schwoerbel, J. (1987), *Handbook of Limnology.* Ellis Hoorwood Limited Publ., *Chichester,* England: 228 pp.

Sharma, 2001.

Shekhar, S. T. R., Kiran, B. B., Puttaiah, E.T., Shivraj. Y. and Mahadevan, K.M. (2008), Phytoplankton as Index of Water Quality with Reference to Industrial Pollution. Journ. *Environ. Biol.,* 29 (2) – 233-236.

Sinha, C. and Khan, R.A. (1998), Ecology and Diversity of Cladocerans in some Calcutta Wetlands. *Proc. Nat. Seminar on Envir. Biol. on Biodiversity and Environment,* 154-164.

Warming, E. (1895), Platesamfund Grundtrak ofden okologiske plantegeographic. Kjobenhavn (German trans. 1896, English as Ocology of Plants, New ed. with Assistance of M. Vahl, trans. P. Groom and I. B. Balfour, *Oxford,* 1909).

Webber, E.C., Bayne, D.R. and Seesock, W.C. (1989), Macroinvertebrate Communities in Wheeler Reservoir (Albama) Tributaries after Prolonged Exposure to DDT contamination. *Hydrobiol.,* 183: 141-155.

Wetzel, R.G. (1983), *Limnology.* 2nd Ed. Saunders College Publishing Co., New York, 767 pp.

Pages: 35-55

LIMNOLOGY AND AQUATIC SCIENCE
Edited by: Dr. Shailendra Sharma; Dr. Pawan Kumar 'Bharti'
ISBN: 978-93-5056-735-7
Edition: 2015
Published by: Discovery Publishing House Pvt. Ltd., New Delhi (India)

3

Toxic Effects of Heavy Metals on Fish

H.A. Kaoud[1], **Ahmed H.A.**[2] and **Quratulan Ahmed**[3]

ABSTRACT

Heavy metals are non-biodegradable and once discharged into water bodies, they can either be adsorbed on sediment particles or accumulated in aquatic organisms. Fish may absorb dissolved elements and heavy metals from surrounding water and food, which may accumulate in various tissues in significant amounts, therefore, fish, might prove a better material for detecting metals contaminating the freshwater ecosystems.

Aquatic systems are considered as suitable sites for disposal of and recycling the sewage and toxic wastes and drain off the excess to the sea. However, the increasing pollutant load and the over exploitation of the water resources for potable supplies, irrigation, industries and thermal power plants to meet the

1 Department of Veterinary Hygiene and Environmental Pollution, Faculty of Veterinary Medicine, Cairo University, Egypt.
2 Researcher of Pharmacology, Cairo University, Egypt.
3 Department of Zoology, University of Karachi, Karachi, Pakistan.

requirements of the ever-increasing population, significantly reduces their assimilative capacity. Thus, the dual stress exerted on the watercourses is ultimately faced by the biological communities inhabiting them. of this fish is the most important aquatic community concerning the man.

Key words: Heavy metals, Pollution, Histopathological effect, Bioaccumulation.

INTRODUCTION

Heavy metals have a great ecological consideration due to their toxicity and accumulation [3]. Fish may accumulate significant concentrations of metals in water in which those metals are below the limit of detection in routine water samples [4].

Essential metals such as Cu, Zn and Fe have normal physiological regulatory functions [2], but may bioaccumulate and reach toxic levels. Non-essential metals are usually potent toxins and their bioaccumulation in tissues lead to intoxication, decreased fertility, tissue damage and dysfunction of a variety of organs [5, 6]

Heavy metals are non-biodegradable and once discharged into water bodies, they can either be adsorbed on sediment particles or accumulated in aquatic organisms. Fish may absorb dissolved elements and heavy metals from surrounding water and food, which may accumulate in various tissues in significant amounts [7] and are eliciting toxicological effects at critical targets. Also, fish may accumulate significant concentrations of metals even in waters in which those metals are below the limit of detection in routine water samples [8], therefore, fish might prove a better material for detecting metals contaminating the freshwater ecosystems. Intensive studies were conducted on the levels of heavy metals in different water bodies [9-14].

The increase in concentration of a chemical in an organism resulting from tissue absorption levels exceeding the rate of metabolism and excretion. Bioconcentration factor (BCF) - used to describe the accumulation of chemicals in organisms, primarily aquatic, the Bioconcentration factors (BCFs) are used to relate pollutant residues in aquatic organisms to the pollutant concentration in ambient waters. The bioconcentration factor (BCF) is related to biomagnification effects. Toxic agents contamination in aquatic ecosystems due to discharge of industrial effluents may pose a serious threat to human health. Many chemical compounds, especially those with a hydrophobic component partition easily into the lipids and lipid membranes of organisms and bioaccumulate. If the compounds are not metabolized as fast as they are consumed, there can be significant magnification of potential toxicological effects up the food chain.

BIOACCUMULATION FACTOR (BAF)

The bioaccumulation factor (BAF) is the ratio between the accumulated concentration of a given pollutant in any organ and its dissolved concentration in water.

$$\text{Bioaccumulation factor (BAF)} = \frac{\text{Pollutant concentration in fish organ (mg/kg)}}{\text{Pollutant in water (mg/l)}}$$

The contamination of fresh waters with a wide range of pollutants has become a matter of concern over the last few decades [15-18]. The natural aquatic systems may extensively be contaminated with heavy metals released from domestic, industrial and other man-made activities [19, 20].

SOURCES OF METAL CONTAMINATION

Metals and metalloids occur naturally in the Earth's crust, and are released to soils and the hydrologic cycle during physical and chemical weathering of igneous and metamorphic rocks. The background concentrations of these elements are mainly controlled by the geologic characteristics of the watershed. Some metals are naturally abundant and have high background concentrations (*e.g.* aluminium and iron). Other metals are rare and have low background concentrations (*e.g.* mercury, cadmium, silver and selenium) [21]. The rarer metals are referred to as 'trace metals', 'trace elements' and 'trace constituents'. At low concentrations many of these metals are 'micronutrients' and as such are essential for life. However, many metals or metalloids can be toxic at high concentrations, hence the term 'toxic metals'. There are also some metals with as yet no identified biological functions such as mercury and lead.

Significant amounts of heavy metals are eventually carried into estuarine and coastal water systems. Heavy metals important trace components of the sea water, may function in both the regulation and stimulation of biological processes. Some metals have known biological functions such as copper, zinc, manganese, magnesium, etc. and are required in varying concentrations for growth and metabolism of all organisms. Many of these metals are found in organisms in concentrations that are high in comparison to the surrounding medium. Hence, the biota concentrates many heavy metals relative to their environment. The invertebrates appear to have a particularly high capacity for concentrating metals from the environment when they filter plankton during feeding. Because of the ability of many metals to form complexes with organic substances, there is a tendency for them to be fixed in the tissue and not to be excreted. Some of these elements have no apparent biological function and it appears that organisms have little capability for selective uptake or excreting. Such metals may not be toxic to the host organisms, such as zinc or copper in oysters, but they may be passed up the food chain to higher organisms including man.

Human activities can increase metal concentrations to higher than background levels. Anthropogenic sources of metals include industrial and municipal waste products, urban and agricultural runoff, fine sediments eroded from catchments, atmospheric deposition, CCA treated wood walkways, antifouling paints from ships (mainly tin and copper), metals from pipes in sewage treatment plants and drainage from acid sulfate soils and mine sites. Mine drainage, in particular, can significantly increase the concentrations of some metals. Metal contamination tends to be localized to areas situated in close proximity to mine sites, industrial installations and large cities. In Australia, the latter are mainly coastal sites.

ENVIRONMENTAL SIGNIFICANCE

Metals tend to accumulate in animals and plants (including mangrove vegetation [22] and sea grasses [23]. They enter aquatic organisms through body and respiratory surfaces, and by ingestion of particulate matter and water. Toxicity manifests as impairment of metabolic function, with possible changes to the distribution and abundance of populations [24]. Sublethal effects may include changes in morphology, physiology, biochemistry, behaviour and reproduction [25]. Massive fish kills can occur when aluminum and iron are mobilized with drainage from acid sulfate soils [26]. The extent of metal uptake, toxicity and bioaccumulation varies depending on the organism, and can be modified by temperature, pH, turbidity, dissolved oxygen and the concentrations of other metals in solution. Accumulation of metals by aquatic organisms (*e.g.* bivalves and crabs [27] can be a useful indicator of the presence of metals in biologically available forms. If metal levels in organisms are too high for human consumption, shell fishing waters are closed.

Heavy metal contamination may have devastating effects on the ecological balance of the recipient environment and a diversity of aquatic organisms [28- 30].Among animal species, fishes are the inhabitants that cannot escape from the detrimental effects of these pollutants [31]. Fish are widely used to evaluate the health of aquatic ecosystems because pollutants build up in the food chain and are responsible for adverse effects and death in the aquatic systems. The studies carried out on various fishes have shown that heavy metals may alter the physiological activities and biochemical parameters both in tissues and in blood [32]. The toxic effects of heavy metals have been reviewed, including bioaccumulation [33]. The organisms developed a protective defense against the deleterious effects of essential and inessential heavy metals and other xenobiotics that produce degenerative changes like oxidative stress in the body [34]. Cichlidae species are the most popular and highly economic fish.

EFFECT OF HEAVY METALS ON FISH

Heavy metals, such as copper, zinc, lead, mercury and cadmium, are among the most dangerous and abundant inorganic environmental pollutants, arising from industrial discharges and mining practices [35]. They enter aquatic systems via natural and anthropogenic sources, including industrial, agricultural, and mining activities. The aquatic environment is more susceptible to the harmful effects of heavy metal pollution because aquatic organisms are in close and prolonged contact with the soluble metals. What's more, unlike toxic organic compounds, metals cannot be degraded but undergo bioaccumulation through the food chain [36, 37].

Heavy metals can cause dermatological diseases, skin cancer, and cancer of vital organs like the liver, kidney, lung and bladder, cardiovascular disease, diabetes, and anemia, as well as reproductive, developmental, immunological and neurological affects in the human body [38].

When fish are exposed to elevated levels of metals in a polluted aquatic ecosystem, they tend to take these metals up from their direct environment [39]. Heavy metal contamination may have devastating effects on the ecological balance of the recipient environment and the diversity of aquatic organisms [28].

The presence of pollutants have been associated with decreased fertility and other reproductive abnormalities in birds, fish, shellfish and mammals, as well as altered immune function (Colborn *et al.*, 1993). Heavy metals like mercury and cadmium are known to accumulate in marine organisms, and cause rapid genetic changes [40, 41].

It is also possible that environmental toxicants may increase the susceptibility of aquatic animals to various diseases by interfering with the normal functioning of their immune, reproductive and developmental processes [42].

Prolonged exposure to water pollutants even in very low concentrations have been reported to induce morphological, histological and biochemical alterations in the tissues which may critically influence fish quality. It was reported that aquatic organisms showed high capability to accumulate heavy metals and was often regarded as an effective bioindicator of the environmental contamination.

Hematological Effect

The hemoglobin percent, total erythrocyte count and mean cell hemoglobin in *Labeo rohita* exposed to 96h LC50 concentration of chromium for 24h and 96h are given in. The decrease in hemoglobin per cent and TEC from control are significant at the end of both 24 and 96h exposure periods. Further this decrease in the hemoglobin percent and TEC is relatively highly significant at the end of96h when compared to the 24h. Hematological indices are very important parameters for the evaluation of fish physiological status under metallic stress.

Earlier works reported a fall in RBC count, hemoglobin percent and packed cell volume and decrease in MCH, MCHC and MCV in freshwater fishes exposed to cadmium, zinc and nickel indicating anemia, erythropenia and leucopoiesis [26-28]. The TEC, hemoglobin per cent and mean cell hemoglobin (MCH) were appreciably declined in *Labeo rohita* exposed to chromium reflecting the anemic state of the fish which could be possibly due to iron deficiency and its consequent decreased utilization for hemoglobin synthesis. This is in accordance with a similar study on *Labeo rohita*, which also reported hypo chromic microlytic anemia under lead chloride stress [29]. Anemia in fish is an early manifestation of acute and chronic intoxication of chromium. Further, a significant decrease in TEC, hemoglobin per cent, MCH and hematocrit were also reported in *Channa punctatus* exposed to both copper and chromium and this decrease is more pronounced in fishes exposed to chromium suggesting that the metal induces acute anemia.

Biochemical Effect

Acute exposure to hexavalent chromium proved to be highly toxic to *Labeo rohita* and induced cumulative deleterious effects at various vital functional sites like metabolic rate, hematological indices and biochemical profiles. The metal induced decrease in the total protein content could possibly affect the enzyme mediated bio defense mechanisms of the fish, which pose a serious threat to human beings by secondary poisoning through food chain.

Histopathological Changes and Alterations

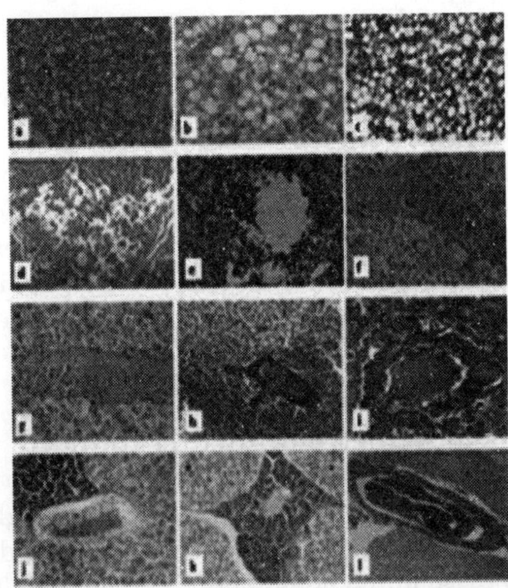

Fig. 3.1: *Liver of fish showing the normal (a) (X400), vacuolar degeneration (b) {L. niloticus}, (c) {O. niloticus})(X400), focal areas of necrosis (d) {X100}, (e) {X400}{O. niloticus}), haemorrhage and haemolysis between the hepatocytes (f,g) {O. niloticus}{X400}), intravascular haemolysis in blood vessels (h) {X100}, (i) {X400}{L. niloticus}), haemosiderin around central vein and hepatoportal blood vessel (j,k) {O. niloticus}{X400}), thrombosis formation in hepatoportal blood vessel (l) {L. niloticus}{X100}.*

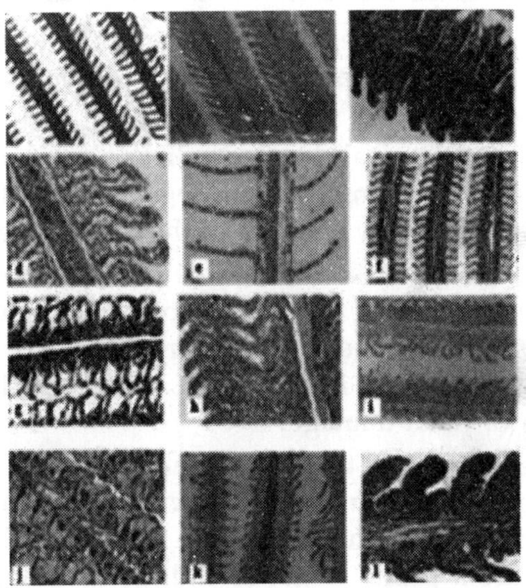

Fig. 3.2: *Gills of fish showing the normal (a) (X100), proliferation in the epithelium of gill filaments and secondary lamellae (b {X100}, c {X400}{O. niloticus}), degenerative and necrotic changes in the epithelium of gill filaments and secondary lamellae (d,e {X400}{L. niloticus}),edema in secondary lamellae (f {X100}, g{X400}{O. niloticus}), proliferation of mucous cells (h {X400}{O. niloticus}), curling of secondary lamellae (i{X100}{L. niloticus}), haemorrhage between gill filaments (j {X400}{O. niloticus}), dilation in blood vessel of gill filament (k {X100}{L. niloticus}), telangiectasis in secondary lamellae (l {X400}{O. niloticus}){Source: (Fatma ,2008) Fatma A. S. Mohamed, (2008): Bioaccumulation of Selected Metals and Histopathological Alterations in Tissues of Oreochromis niloticus and Lates niloticus from Lake Nasser, Egypt. Global Veterinaria 2 (4): 205-218, 2008}.*

CADMIUM

Cadmium is an industrial and environmental pollutant that affects adversely a number of organs in humans. Cadmium is a metal from group II B that has an atomic weight of 112.41; the ionic form of cadmium (Cd2+) is usually combined with ionic forms of oxygen (cadmium oxide, CdO2), chlorine (cadmium chloride, CdCl2), or sulfur (cadmium sulfate, CdSO4). There are estimates that30; 000 tons of cadmium are released into the environment each year, with an estimated 4000–13,000 tons coming from human activities. Natural as well as anthropogenic sources of cadmium, which include industrial emissions and the application of fertilizer and sewage sludge to farm land, increased cadmium environmental levels. It has been established that, although cadmium occurs in the aquatic organism and marine environment only in trace concentrations, the salinity can affect the speciation of this metal, and bioaccumulation is affected both by temperature and salinity. Cadmium has been reported to exert deleterious effects in terms of nephrotoxic, cytotoxic, genotoxic, immunotoxic and carcinogenic.

Cadmium in high doses induce structural and function alterations in various vital organs including liver, kidney, gill and intestine of fishes.

Cadmium accumulates in liver of fishes in high concentrations. It also induces various pathological changes in liver tissues including engorgement of blood vessels, congestion, vacuolar degeneration of hepatocytes, necrosis of pancreatic cells and fatty changes in the peripancreatic hepatocytes.

Cadmium accumulates in kidney of fishes in maximum concentration. Cadmium has been reported to posses' nephrotoxic action in man and various animals. In fact, kidney is the principle target organ of cadmium toxicity and chronic cadmium exposure in almost all animal species is characterized by varying degree of renal damage.

Gills are also reported to act as storehouse of cadmium in experimental studies. In scanning electron microscopic an augmentation of microbridges in pavement cells and an increase in the apical membrane of chloride cells (chloride cells are a prime target of cadmium toxicity, resulting into fish hypocalcaemia).

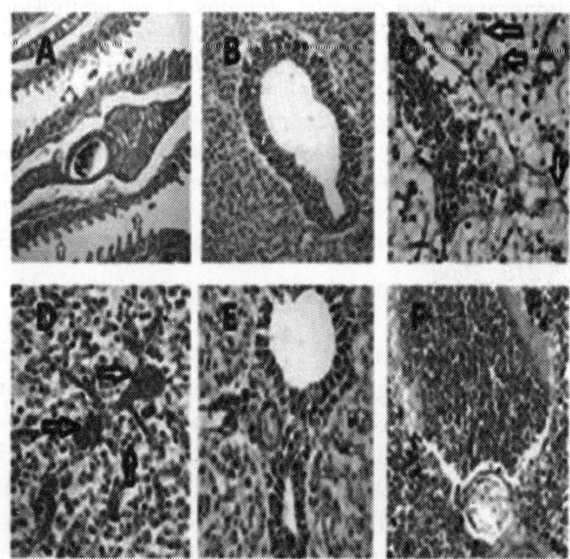

Fig. 3.3: ***A.*** *Gills of tilapia treated with cadmium showing atrophy and necrosis of gill lamellae (arrows) (H & E X 400).* ***B.*** *Liver of tilapia treated with cadmium and Plant-ext showing apparently healthy liver tissue (H & E X 200).* ***C.*** *Liver of tilapia treated with cadmium showing congestion (C) with severely degenerated and necrosed hepatocytes (arrows) (H & E X 200).* ***D.*** *Liver of tilapia treated with cadmium showing congested sinusoids with necrosed hepatocytes (arrows) (H & E X 200).* ***E.*** *Liver of tilapia treated with cadmium and Plant-ext showing normal portal tract with slightly degenerated hepatocytes (arrows) (H & E X 400).* ***F.*** *Spleen of tilapia treated with cadmium and Plant-ext showing apparently normal spleen (H & E X 200).*

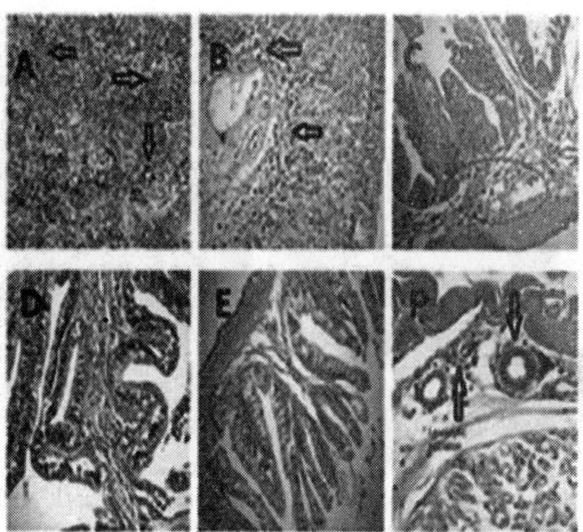

Fig. 3.4: ***A.*** *Spleen of tilapia treated with cadmium showing hyperplasia in the melanomacrophage cells (arrows) (H & E X 200).* ***B.*** *Stomach of tilapia treated with cadmium showing leucocytic infiltration in the sub mucosa (arrow) together with congestion (C) (H & E X 400).* ***C.*** *Intestine of tilapia treated with cadmium showing necrosed mucosa (n), sub mucosal haemorrhage (arrow) (H & E X 200).* ***D.*** *Intestine of tilapia treated with cadmium showing higher power of the previous lesion (H & E X 400).* ***E.*** *Intestine of tilapia treated with cadmium and Plant-ext showing apparently intestinal tissue (H & E X 200).* ***F.*** *Muscles of tilapia treated with showing congestion (C) and leucocytic infiltration (arrow) (H & E X 200).*

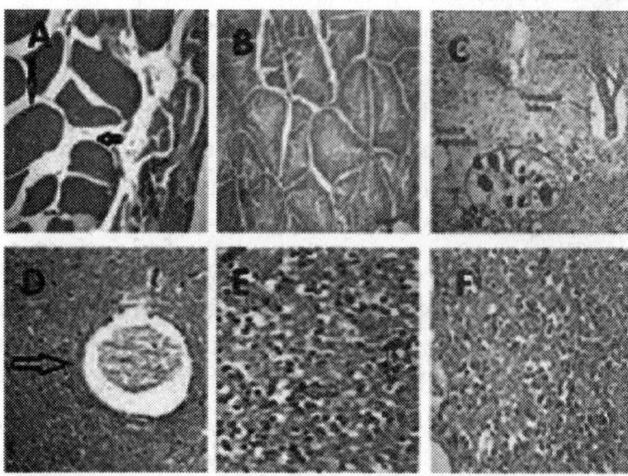

Fig. 3.5: ***A.*** *Muscles of tilapia treated with cadmium showing hyalinised muscles tissue (arrow) (H & E X 200).* ***B.*** *Muscles of tilapia showing apparently healthy muscular tissue (H & E X 200).* ***C.*** *Brain of tilapia treated with cadmium showing congestion (C), perivascular edema (e) and neural degeneration (n) (arrow) (H & E X 200).* ***D.*** *Brain of tilapia treated with cadmium showing osteomalacia (arrow) (H & E X 200).* ***E.*** *Brain of tilapia treated with cadmium showing intracellular brain edema (arrow) (H & E X 200).* ***F.*** *Brain of tilapia treated with cadmium showing apparently healthy tissue (H & E X 200).*

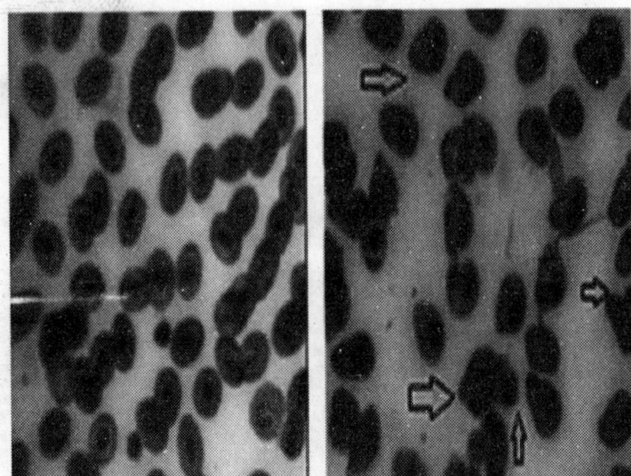

Fig. 3.6: *Tilapia showing apparently healthy blood cells (X 1000).Tilapia treated with cadmium showing abnormal blood cells (Amioscytosis) (X 1000). Kaoud H. A. and Mekawy M. M. 2011. Bioremediation the Toxic Effect of Mercury-Exposure in Nile Tilapia (Oreochromis Niloticus) by using Lemna gibba L. Journal of American Science;7(3):336-343. Kaoud H.A., Zaki M. M., El-Dahshan A.R., Saeid S. and El Zorba H.Y.2011. Amelioration the Toxic Effects of Cadmium-Exposure in Nile Tilapia (Oreochromis Niloticus) by using Lemna gibba L. Life Science Journal. 2011;8(1):185-195.*

MERCURY

Mercury (Hg) is one of the most toxic heavy metals in our environment including the lithosphere, hydrosphere, atmosphere and biosphere. A series of complex chemical transformations allows the three-oxidation states of Hg cycle in the environment.

Observed lesions in the gills of intoxicate fish were mucus coagulation and accumulation of cellular debris in the epithelium of lamellae and inter-lamellar regions, hemorrhage, lamellar edema, hyperplasia, epithelial cell necrosis and congestion.

Liver of tilapia showed degeneration of the hepatocytes with nuclear pyknosis in the majority of the cells, hepatocellular vacuolation as well as the accumulation of the metal binding proteins in their nuclei. Intravascular hemolysis is seen in blood vessels and sinusoids with necrosed hepatocytes.

Muscular tissues showed degeneration in muscle bundles with aggregations of inflammatory cells (leucocytic infiltration) between them with focal areas of necrosis; atrophy and edema of muscle bundles as well as splitting of muscle fibers were observed.

Intestine of tilapia manifested necrosed mucosa, sub-mucosal hemorrhage, loosely arranged muscle fibers with the degeneration of sub-mucosal tissue and each villus facing the lumen showed cell degeneration and the cells did not show distinct nuclei and cytoplasmic boundaries. There was a distortion of basement membrane of the villi and blood vessel, and lymphocytes were fully distorted and there was a degeneration of columnar epithelium of the intestine.

Kidney showed hydropic swelling of the renal tubules, sometimes with pyknotic nuclei and many necrotic areas as well as swollen proximal epithelial cells with necrotic nuclei.

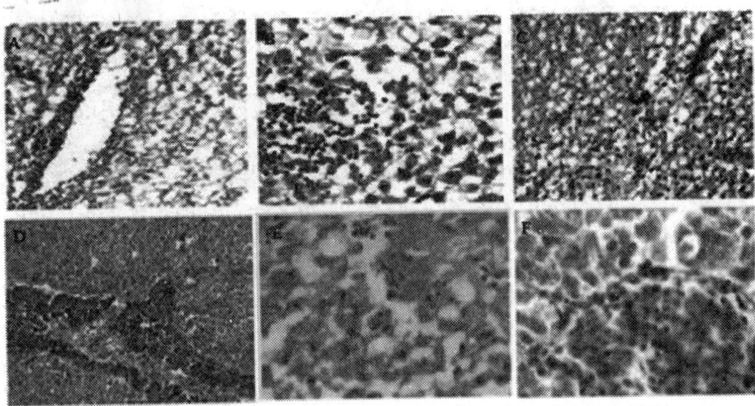

Fig. 3.7: *Histopathology of liver tissue in Nile tilapia, Oreochromis niloticus,exposed to mercury toxicity.* ***A:*** *Liver showing perivascular aggregation of mononuclear cells with hepatocellular necrosis (H&E, 200X).* ***B:*** *Liver showing dissociation of hepatocytes with focal mononuclear cells aggregation (H&E, 400X).* ***C:*** *Liver showing vaculation of hepatocytes and lymphocytic infiltrations (H&E, 400X).* ***D:*** *Hepatic parenchyma of Hg intoxicated fish showing hemorrhages (H&E, 400X).* ***E:*** *Hepatic parenchyma of Hg intoxicated fish showing degeneration (H&E, 400X).* ***F:*** *Hepatic parenchyma of Hg intoxicated fish showing congestion (H&E, 400X). [Source: H.A.Kaoud, . Mahran Khaled M.A, Rezk . A. and Khalf, M. A. (2012); Bioremediation the toxic effect of mercury on liver histopathology, some hematological parameters and enzymatic activity in Nile tilapia, Oreochromis niloticus.[Researcher. 2012;4(1):60-69].*

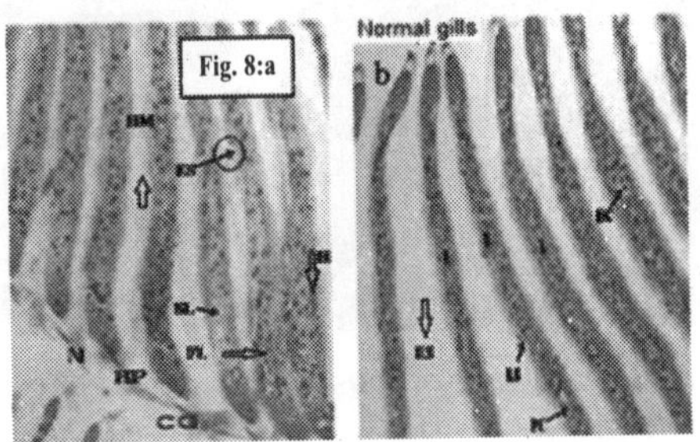

Fig. 3.8: *Cross-sections of gill lamellae of M. rosenbergii after 96 h of exposure to a control solution and Hg. Control prawn showing normal lamellae (L) with uniform interlamellar spaces (ILS), the lamellar sinus (LS), and pillar cell (PC) and hemocyte (HC) in the lamella. Mercury exposed prawn showing hemocytic infiltration (HI), swollen (SL) and fused (FL) lamellae, enlargement of the lamellar sinuses (ES) and hyper-mucus (HM) in the interlamellar spaces, necrosis (N) and hyperplasia (HP) tip of lamellae. H&E stain, (x200).*

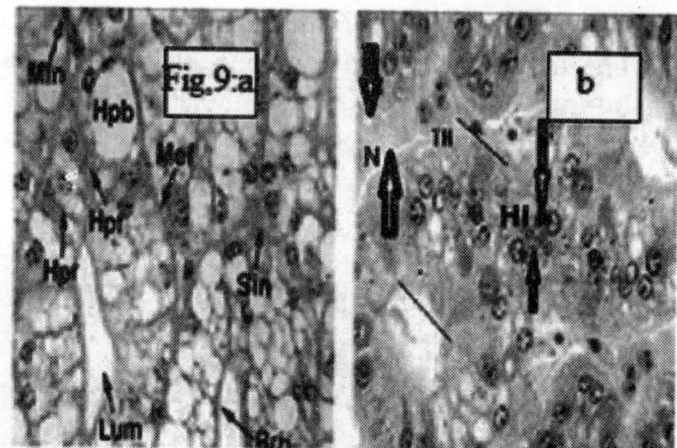

Fig. 3.9-a: *Cross sections of hepatopancreatic tubules: normal lumens (Lum), tubule tissues (Hpf: F-cell; Hpb: B-cell; Hpr: R-cell; Mfn: myoepithelial cell nuclei; Mef: myoepithelial layer; Brb: microvillus brush borders) and hemal sinuses (Sin) between tubules.*

Fig. 3.9-b: *Cross sections of hepatopancreatic tubules: showed hemocytic infiltration (HI) in the interstitial sinuses, an increased number of hemocytes, thickening (TH) and ruptures of the basal laminae, and necrosis (N) of the tubules (arrowheads). H&E stain, (x200).[Source: Kaoud H. A., Manal M .Zaki1 ,Mona M. Ismail(2011): Effect of Exposure to Mercury on Health in Tropical Macrobrachium Rosenbergii. Life Science Journal. 2011;8(1):154-163].*

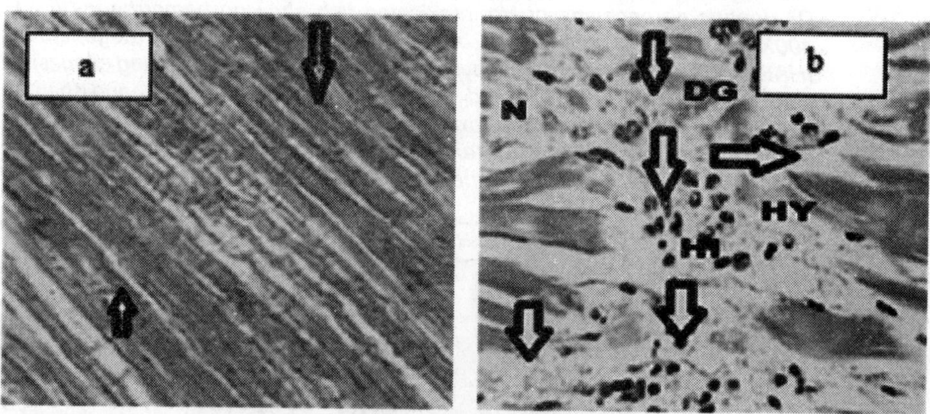

Fig. 3.10-a: *Longitudinal sections of muscle tissue Healthy prawn tissue showing normal muscle fibres.*

Fig. 3.10-b: *Cross section showing degeneration (DG), focal areas of necrotic musculature (N) infiltrated by hemocytes (HI) (arrowheads). Also, atrophy of muscle bundles, edema, hyaline degeneration (HY) and splitting of muscle fibers were seen. H&E stain, (x200). [Hussein A. Kaoud, Manal M. Zaki, Mona M. Ismail. Effect of Exposure to Mercury on Health in Tropical Macrobrachium Rosenbergii. Life Science Journal. 2011; 8(1):154-163]*

ARSENIC

The primary toxicity mode of inorganic As+3 is through reaction with sulfhydryl groups of proteins and subsequent enzyme inhibition; inorganic pentavalent arsenate does not react as readily as As+3 with sulfhydryl groups, but may uncouple oxidative phosphorylation (Howard et al. 1984; EPA 1985). Inorganic As+3 interrupt oxidative metabolic pathways and sometimes causes morphological changes in liver mitochondria. Arsenite in vitro reacts with protein-SH groups to inactivate enzymes such as dihydrolipoyl dehydrogenase and thiolase, producing inhibited oxidation of pyruvate and beta-oxidation of fatty acids (Belton et al. 1985). Inorganic As+5 may also exert toxic effects by the reaction of arsenous acid (HAsO) with the sulfhydryl (SH) groups of enzymes. In the first reaction, arsenous acid is reduced to arsonous acid (AsOH2), which then condenses to either monothiols or dithiols to yield dithioesters of arsonous acid. Arsonous acid may then condense with enzyme SH groups to form a binary complex.

Fig. 3.11 Fig. 3.12

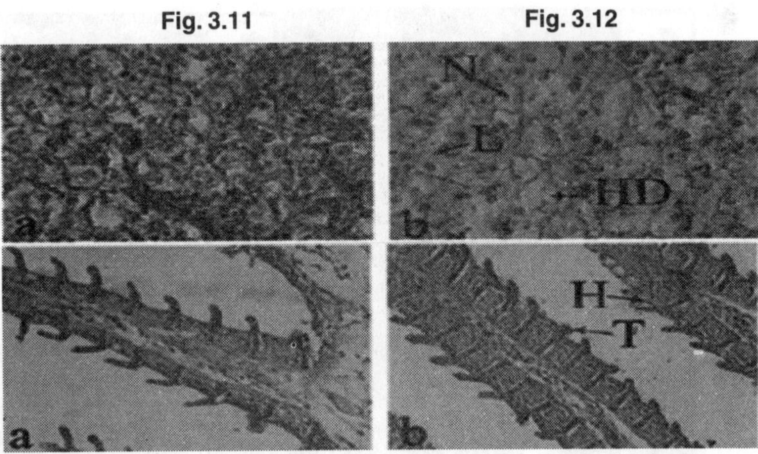

Fig. 3.11: *Photomicrograph of the liver section (6 ìm) of C. Gariepinus stained with haematoxylin and eosin (400X): (a) Fish exposed only to water (control); (b) Fish exposed to 1/10 LC50 of As, showing necrosis (N), enlarged hepatocyte (L) and hepatocyte degeneration.*

Fig. 3.12: *Photomicrograph of the liver section (6 µm) of C. Gariepinus stained with haematoxylin and eosin: (a) Fish exposed only to water (control) showing normal structure (100X); (b) Fish exposed to 1/10 LC50 of As, showing hyperplasia (H), of the gills epithelium and telangiectiasis (T) (40X). Exposure to arsenic levels, the liver cells were found to lose their regular shape due to partial precipitation of both cytoplasmic and nuclear material, resulting shape deformation, vacuolization, necrosis and even cell damage. Also, the gill hyperplasia was found the most induced branchial changes due to arsenic exposure (The DTC values recorded for the liver of arsenic exposed fish were significantly higher than those recorded for the control group, mg/L) than those subjected to arsenate only 56 mg/L.{Source: A Protective Effect of Calcium Carbonate Against Arsenic Toxicity of the Nile Catfish, Clarias gariepinus Turkish Journal of Fisheries and Aquatic Sciences 9: 191-200 (2009}.*

CHROMIUM

Earlier works reported a fall in RBC count, hemoglobin percent and packed cell volume and decrease in MCH, MCHC and MCV in freshwater fishes exposed to cadmium, zinc and nickel indicating anemia, erythropenia and leucopoiesis. The TEC, hemoglobin per cent and mean cell hemoglobin (MCH) were appreciably declined in *Labeo rohita* exposed to chromium reflecting the anemic state of the fish which could be possibly due to iron deficiency and its consequent decreased utilization for hemoglobin synthesis. This is in accordance with a similar study on *Labeo rohita,* which also reported hypo chromic microlytic anemia under lead chloride stress. Anemia in fish is an early manifestation of acute and chronic intoxication of chromium. Further, a significant decrease in TEC, hemoglobin per cent, MCH and hematocrit were also reported in *Channa punctatus* exposed to both copper and chromium and this decrease is more pronounced in fishes exposed to chromium suggesting that the metal induces acute anemia.

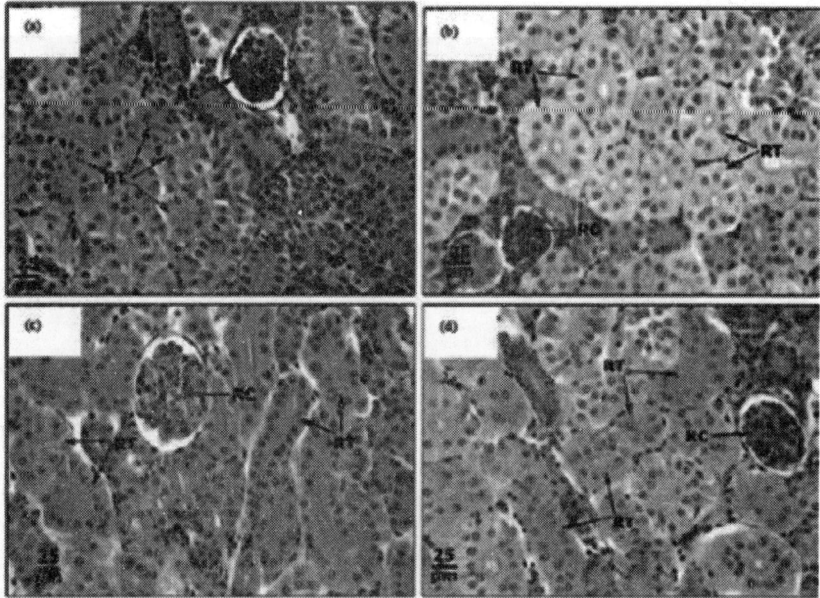

Fig. 3.13: *Transverse sections of control and treated fish kidney for 30 days showing Renal Corpuscles (RC) and Renal Tubules (RT). (H and E x400),* ***(a)*** *Control,* ***(b)*** *Lycopene treatment,* ***(c)*** *Vitamin E treatment and* ***(d)*** *Vitamin E and lycopene simultaneous treatment[Source: Imam A.A. Mekkawy, Usama M. Mahmoud, Ekbal T. Wassif and Mervat Naguib, 2013. Effects of Cadmium on Some Histopathological and Histochemical Characteristics of the Kidney and Gills Tissues of Oreochromis niloticus (Linnaeus, 1758) Dietary Supplemented with Tomato Paste and Vitamin E. Journal of Fisheries and Aquatic Science, 8: 553-580.*

COPPER

Copper is an essential trace metal in small concentrations for several fish metabolic functions. Essentiality of copper arises from its specific incorporation into a variety of enzymes which play important roles in physiological processes (e.g. enzymes involved in cellular respiration, free radical defense, neurotransmitter function, connective tissue biosyntheses and other functions), as well as, into some structural proteins.

Although the crucial role of copper in several enzymatic processes, this heavy metal can exert adverse toxicological effects, when present in high concentrations in water . In fact, it is potentially toxic when the internal available concentration exceeds the capacity of physiological detoxification processes.

Copper salts (copper hydroxide, copper carbonate and copper sulphate) are widely used in agriculture as fungicide, algaecide and nutritional supplement in fertilizers. They are also used in veterinary practices and industrial applications. Copper sulphate is released to water as a result of natural weathering of soil and discharge from industries, sewage treatment plants and agricultural runoff. Copper sulphate is also intensively introduced in water reservoirs to kill algae. Thus excessive amount of copper accumulates in water bodies and cause toxicity to aquatic fauna and flora and ultimately to man. Copper and its compounds have been designated as priority pollutants by EPA (1975).

Present study was carried out on the fresh water prawns *Macrobrachium rosenbergii* (Crustacean - Decapods) to evaluate the LC_{50} values of copper sulphate and its effect on immunity as well as the histopathological alterations in this tropical prawn.

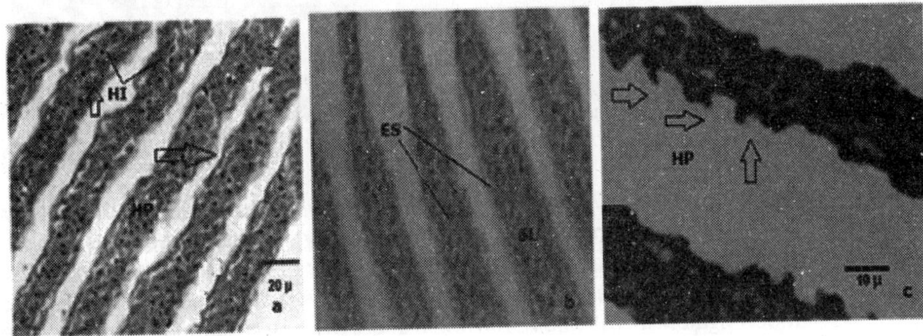

Fig. 3.14: *Exposed prawn shown hemocytic infiltration (HI), had swollen (SL) and enlargement of the lamellar sinuses (ES) and hyper-mucus (HM) in the interlamellar spaces, necrosis and hyperplasia (HP) of lamellae. H&E stain, (x200), c :(x400). Gills: showed hyper mucus, mild congestion, swelling and edema at low doses of Cu^{2+} intoxication. Severe edema, hyperplasia, haemolymph cell infiltration as well as thickened and enlarged gill chambers & lamellar sinuses at highest doses were observed.*

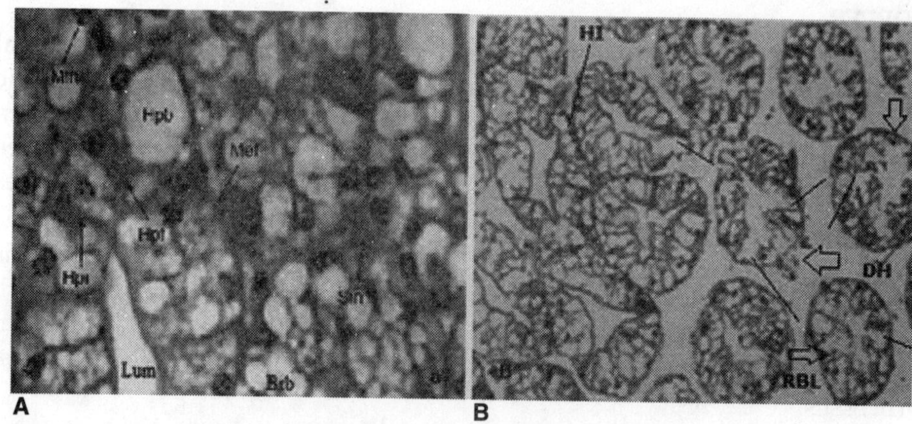

Fig. 3.15-a: *Cross sections of hepatopancreatic tubules: normal lumens (Lum), tubule tissues (Hpf: F-cell; Hpb: B-cell; Hpr: R-cell; Mfn: myoepithelial cell nuclei; Mef: myoepithelial layer; Brb: microvillus brush borders) and hemal sinuses (Sin) between tubules. Hepatopancreas: showed dissolving of the hepatocytes, haemolysis, haemocytic infiltration in the interstitial sinuses, thickening and ruptures of the basal laminae.*

Fig. 3.15-b: *Cross sections of hepatopancreatic tubules: showed hemocytic infiltration (HI) in the interstitial sinuses, an increased number of hemocytes, thickening and ruptures of the basal laminae, and necrosis of the tubules (arrowheads). H&E stain, (x200).*

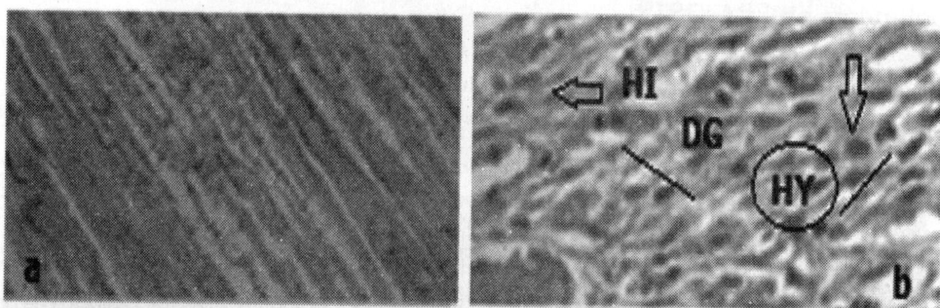

Fig. 3.16-a: *Longitudinal sections of muscle tissue, healthy prawn tissue showing normal muscle fibers.*

Fig. 3.16-b: *Cross section showing degeneration (DG), focal areas of necrotic musculature infiltrated by hemocytes (HI) . Also, atrophy of muscle bundles, hyaline degeneration (HY) and splitting of muscle fibers were seen. H&E stain, (x200). Muscles: Muscular tissues showed pathological alterations; included degeneration in muscles with infiltration and aggregations of hemocytes between them and focal areas of necrosis. Also, atrophy of muscle bundles, edema, hyaline degeneration and splitting of muscle fibers. A; splitting of muscle fibers, B: hyaline degeneration, C: infiltration of hemocytes, D: focal areas of necrosis, E: atrophy of muscles bundles and edema.[Source: H.A.Kaoud and Quratulan Ahmed (2013): Copper intoxication in tropical freshwater prawn, Macrobrachium rosenbergii. International Journal of Engineering and Innovative Technology (IJEIT) Vol., 3(4): 289- 307].*

LEAD

Lead (Pb) is one of the most ubiquitous and useful metals known to humans and it are detectable in practically all phases of the inert environment and in all biological systems. Environmental levels of lead have increased more than 1000-fold over the past three centuries as a result of human activity; the greatest increase occurred between the years 1950 and 2000. Lead is a naturally occurring element; it is a member of Group 14 (IVA) of the periodic table, has an atomic weight of 207.2 and exists in three states: Pb (0), the metal; Pb (II); and Pb (IV). Lead is a bluish-gray heavy metal and it is usually found combined with two or more other elements to form lead compounds. Lead reaches the aquatic system because of superficial soil erosion and atmospheric deposition. The concentration of lead in deep ocean waters is about 0.01–0.02 g/l, but in surface ocean waters is about 0.3 g/l.

Lead is a potentially toxic chemical that may be directly ingested by man or indirectly through aquatic animals like fish and shellfish .The effects of lead on man include mental retardation, learning dysfunction, and loss of coordination (Goodman and Gilman, 1992). Though the effect of lead toxicity is well elucidated in man, there is paucity of information on its effects on fish, which are eaten by man.

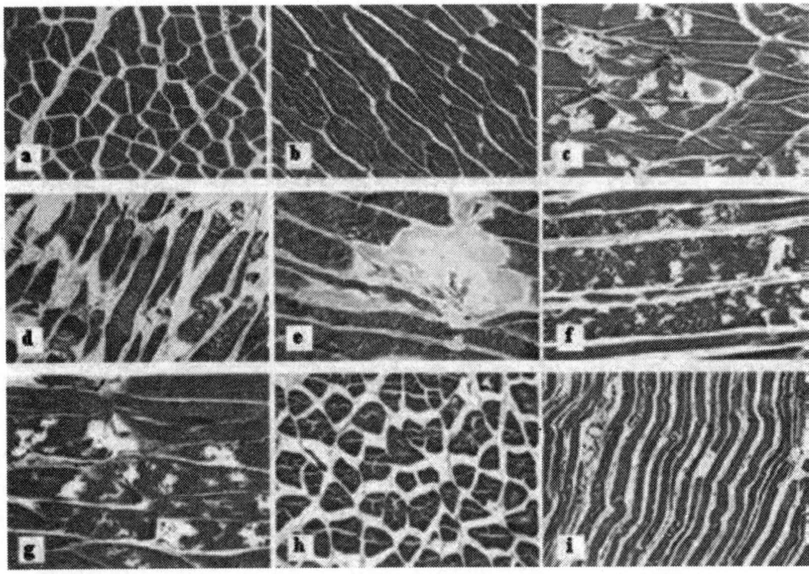

Fig. 3.17: *Muscles of fish showing the normal (a,b)(X400), degeneration in muscle bundles (c,d{O. niloticus}{X400}), focal area of necrosis (myolysis) (e {L. niloticus}{X400}), vacuolar degeneration in muscle bundles (f {O. niloticus}, g {L. niloticus}{X400}), splitting of muscle fibers (h {O. niloticus}{X400}), atrophy of muscle bundles (i{O. niloticus}{X400}); [Source:Bioaccumulation of Selected Metals and Histopathological Alterations in Tissues of Oreochromis niloticus and Lates niloticus from Lake Nasser, Egypt Fatma A.S. Mohamed Global Veterinaria 2 (4): 205-218, 2008].*

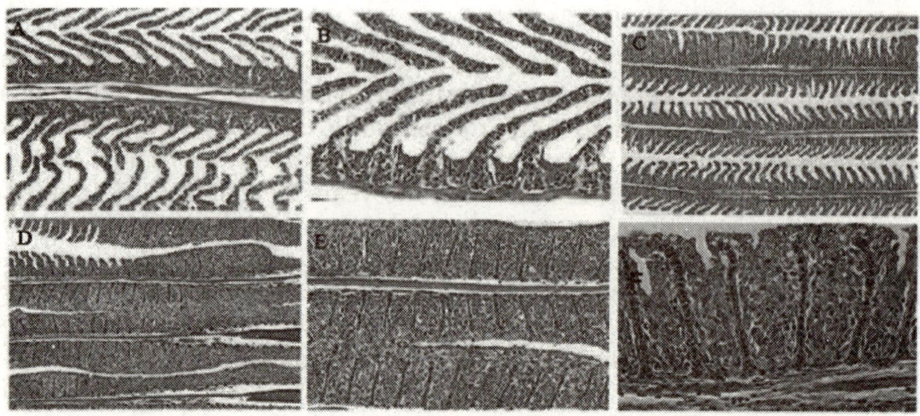

Fig. 3.18-a: *Normal primary lamellae of Oreochromis niloticus gill arch with a central hyaline cartilage, secondary lamellae perpendicular to the primary lamellae with abundant vascular spaces and a multi-layered interlamellar epithelium. Original magnification X100.* **3.18-b:** *Secondary lamellae perpendicular to the primary lamellae and a multi-layered interlamellar epithelium in the normal gill of Oreochromis niloticus. Original magnification X400.* **3.18-c:** *Gill lamellar epithelial hyperplasia, hypertrophy, shortening of secondary lamellae and with some lamellar fusion in nickel-exposed Oreochromis niloticus. Original magnification X40.* **3.18-d:** *Severe gill lamellar epithelial hyperplasia, hypertrophy, shortening of secondary lamellae and with most lamellar fusion and adjacent filaments in nickel-treatedOreochromis niloticus. Original magnification X40.* **3.18-e:** *Severe gill lamellar epithelial hyperplasia, hypertrophy, shortening of secondary lamellae, complete lamellar fusion and most adjacent filaments in Oreochromis niloticusintoxicated with nickel. Original magnification X100.* **3.18-f:** *Severe gill lamellar epithelial hyperplasia, hypertrophy, shortening of secondary lamellae and with complete lamellar fusion in Oreochromis niloticus subjected to nickel. Original magnification X400 [Source: Atef M. Al-Attar, 2007. The Influences of Nickel Exposure on Selected Physiological Parameters and Gill Structure in the Teleost Fish,Oreochromis niloticus. Journal of Biological Sciences, 7: 77-85.].*

Lead is not necessary for the biological functions of animals even at low concentrations. It is being discharged to aquatic systems mainly from petroleum, chemistry, dye and mining industries, which has toxic effects and can cause mortality to aquatic animals. Chronic lead poisoning has similar toxic effects in fish as in mammals. These include hematological and neural disorders and tetanic spasms together with some morphological changes such as darkening in caudal fin, deformation of vertebrate, anomalies in pigment formation and covering of the gills by a mucus layer.

The main mechanisms of lead toxicity are the activation of cellular functions due to this metal's calcium mimicking effect, and the inhibition of the activity of different proteins through its binding to sulfhydryl groups.

NICKEL

Nickel is widely used in industry and is a common aquatic pollutant. In natural waters Ni2+ is the dominant chemical species. In aquatic ecosystems nickel interacts with numerous inorganic and organic compounds and occurs as soluble salts adsorbed onto substances of different chemical origin. Some of these interactions are additive or synergistic in producing adverse effects, and some are antagonistic.

Signs of nickel poisoning in fishes include surfacing, rapid mouth and opercular movements and, prior to death, convulsions and loss of equilibrium. Destruction of the gill lamellae by ionic nickel decreases the ventilation rate and may cause blood hypoxia and death. Other signs of nickel poisoning in fishes include decreased concentrations of glycogen in muscle and liver with simultaneous increases in levels of lactic acid and glucose in blood, depressed hydrogen peroxide production in tissues and a reduction in superoxide dismutase, and contractions of vascular smooth muscle signs similar to those associated with hypertension in mammals. Recent investigations confirmed that toxic effect of nickel is related to effects on respiration rather than iono-regulatory disruption.

CONCLUSION

Water pollution as well as all aquaculture operations for drugs, biologics, and other chemicals, collectively can cause immediate damage to aquatic food and to humans.

Organic aquaculture aims to provide fish and other products that are ecologically, economically and socially sound. It has become more important as consumers have become more environmentally aware and concerned about sustainability and harmful impacts of aquaculture.

REFERENCES

1. Purves, D., (1985). Trace Elements Contamination of the Environment. El-Sevier, Amsterdam.
2. Mason, C.F., (1987). A Survey of Mercury, Lead and Cadmium in Muscle of British Fresh Water Fish. Chemosphere, 16: 901-906.
3. Hogstrand, C. and C. Haux, (2001). Binding and Detoxification of Heavy Metals in Lower Vertebrates with Reference to Metallothionein. Comparative Biochemistry and Physiology, 100: 137-141.
4. Oliveira Ribeiro, C., E. Pelletier; W. Pfeiffer and C. Rouleau, (2000). Comparative Uptake, Bioaccumulation and Gill Damages of Inorganic Mercury in Tropical and Nordic Freshwater Fish. Environmental Research, 83: 286-292.
5. Damek-Proprawa, M. and K. Sawicka-Kapusta, (2003). Damage to the Liver, Kidney and Testis with Reference to Burden of Heavy Metals in Yellownecked Mice from Areas Around Steel Works and Zinc Smelters in Poland. Toxicology, 186: 1-10.
6. Eiman, M. and H. Zamzam, (1996). Effect of Selenium-mercury Interaction on *Clarias lazera* Fish. Proceeding of the 3rd Congress of Toxicology in the Developing Countries, Cairo, Egypt, 19-23, Nov. 1995, pp. 379-392.

7. Barak, N.A. and C.F. Mason, (1990). Mercury, Cadmium and Lead in Eels and Roach. The Effects of Size, Season and Locality on Metal Concentrations in Flesh and Liver. Science of the Total Environment, 92: 249-256.
8. Radwan, A.M., (2005). The Levels of Heavy Metals in Lake Burullus Water Compared with the International Permissible Limits. Journal of Egyptian Academic Society for Environmental Development, 6: 11-26.
9. Samanta, S., K. Mitra, K. Chandra, K. Saha, S. Bandopadhyay and A. Ghosh, (2005). Heavy Metals in Water of the Rivers Hooghly and Haldi at Haldia and their Impact on Fish. Journal of Environmental Biology, 26: 517-523.
10. Soltan, M., S. Moalla, M. Rashed and E. Fawzy, (2005). Physicochemical Characteristics and Distribution of Some Metals in the Ecosystem of Lake Nasser, Egypt. Toxicology and Environmental Chemistry, 87: 167-197.
11. Toufeek, M.E., (2005). Distribution of Some Heavy Metals in Lake Nasser Water, Egypt. Egyptian Journal of Aquatic Biology and Fisheries, 9: 131-148.
12. Authman, M.M. and H.H. Abbas, (2007). Accumulation and Distribution of Copper and Zinc in Both Water and Some Vital Tissues of Two Fish Species (*Tilapia zillii* and *Mugil cephalus*) of Lake Qarun, Fayoum Province, Egypt. Pakistan Journal of Biological Science, 10: 2106-2122.
13. Yilmaz, A. and M. Dogan, (2007). Heavy Metals in Water and in Tissues of Himri (*Carasobarbus luteus*) from Orontes (Asi) River, Turkey. Environmental Monitoring and Assessment, (In Press).
14. Van Dyk, J., G. Pieterse and J. Van Vuren, (2007). Histological Changes in the Liver of *Oreochromis mossambicus* (Cichlidae) after Exposure to Cadmium and Zinc. Ecotoxicology and Environmental Safety, 66: 432-440.
15. Vutukuru S.S., (2005). Acute Effects of Hexavalent Chromium on Survival, Oxygen Consumption, Hematological Parameters and Some Biochemical Profiles of the Indian Major Carp, *Labeo rohita*. Int. J. Environ. Res. Public Health., 2 (3), 456-462.
16. Dirilgen, N., (2001). Accumulation of Heavy Metals in Freshwater Organisms: Assessment of Toxic Interactions. Turk. J. Chem., 25 (3), 173-179.
17. Voegborlo R.B., Methnani A.M.E., Abedin M.Z., (1999). Mercury, Cadmium and Lead Content of Canned Tuna Fish. Food Chem., 67 (4), 341-345.
18. Canli M, Ay O and Kalay M. (1998). Levels of Heavy Metals Cd, Pb, Cu, Cr and Ni) in Tissues of *Cyprinus carpio, Barbus capito* and *Chondrostoma regium* from the Seyhan River, Turkey. Turk. J. of Zool. 22: 149-157.
19. Velez, D.; Montoro, R., (1998). Arsenic Speciation in Manufactured Seafood Products: A Review. J. food. Protect., 61 (9), 1240-1245.
20. Conacher, H.B., Page, B.D., Ryan, J.J., (1993). Industrial Chemical Contamination of Foods [Review]. Food Addit. Contam., 10 (1), 129-143.
21. Roden, E.E. and Edmonds, J.W. 1997. Phosphate Mobilization in Iron-rich Anaerobic Sediments: Microbial Fe(iii) Oxide Reduction Versus Iron-sulphide Formation. *Arch. Hydrobiol.* 139, 347-378.
22. Melville, F. and Burchett, M. (2002). Genetic Variation in *Avicennia marina* in Three Estuaries of Sydney (Australia) and Implications for Rehabilitation and Management. *Marine Pollution Bulletin* 44, 469-479.
23. Prange, J.A. and Dennison, W.C. (2000). Physiological Responses of Five Seagrass Species to Trace Metals. *Marine Pollution Bulletin* 41(7-12), 327-336.
24. Elder, J.F. (1988). Metal Biogeochemistry in Surface-Water Systems - A Review of Principles and Concepts. U.S. Geological Survey Circular 1013.

25. Connell, D.W., Miller, G.J. (1984). Chemistry and Ecotoxicology of Pollution. John Wiley & Sons, N.Y.
26. Sammut, J., White, I., and Melville, M.D. (1996). Acidifcation of an Estuarine Tributary in Eastern Australia due to Drainage of Acid Sulphate Soils. *Marine and Freshwater Research* 47, 669-684.
27. Mortimer, M.R. (2000). Pesticide and Trace Metal Concentrations in Queensland Estuarine Crabs. *Marine Pollution Bulletin* 41, 7-12.
28. Farombi, E.O., Adelowo, O.A., Ajimoko. Y.R., (2007). Biomarkers of Oxidative Stress and Heavy Metal Levels as Indicators of Environmental Pollution in African Cat fish (*Clarias gariepinus*) from Nigeria Ogun River. Int. J. Environ. Res. Public Health., 4 (2), 158-165.
29. Vosyliene M.Z., Jankaite A., (2006). Effect of Heavy Metal Model Mixture on Rainbow Trout Biological Parameters. Ekologija., 4, 12-17.
30. Ashraj, W., (2005). Accumulation of Heavy Metals in Kidney and Heart Tissues of *Epinephelus microdon* Fish from the Arabian Gulf. Environ. Monit. Assess., 101 (1-3), 311-316.
31. Olaifa, F.G., A.K. Olaifa and T.E. Onwude, (2004). Lethal and Sub-lethal Effects of Copper to the African Cat Fish (*Clarias gariepnus*). Afr. J. Biomed. Res., 7: 65-70.
32. Rani U.A., Ramamurthi R.,(1989). Histopathological Alteration in the Liver of Freshwater Teleost *Tilapia mossambica* in Response to Cadmium Toxicity. Ecotoxicology and Environmental Saftey. 17(2), 221-216.
33. Waqar A., (2006). Levels of Selected Heavy Metals in Tuna Fish. Arab. J. Sci. Eng., 31 (1A), 89-92.
34. Raspor B.and Filipoviæ V (2003): Metallothionein and Metal Levels in Cytosol of Liver, Kidney and Brain in Relation to Growth Parameters of Mullus Surmuletus and Liza aurata from the Eastern Adriatic Sea. Water Res. 37(13): 3253-62.
35. Nriagu, J.O. and J.M. Pacyna (1988): Quantitative Assessment of Worldwide Contamination of Air, Water and Soils by Trace Metals. *Nature*, 333, 134-139.
36. Hickey, C.W; Quinn, J.M.; Davies-Colley, R.J.(1989b). Effluent Charcteristics of Domestic Sewage Oxidation Ponds and Their Potential Impacts on Rivers. *New Zealand Journal of Marine and Freshwater Research* 23: 585-600.
37. Kong, I.C.; Bitton, G.; Koopman, B. and Jung, K.H. (1995). Heavy Metal Toxicity Testing in Environmental Samples. Reviews of Environ. Contamination and Toxicol., 142: 119-147.
38. Taiz L, Zeiger E. (1998). Plant Defenses: Surface Protectants and Secondary Metabolites. In: Taiz L and Zeiger E (eds.). Plant Physiology. Sinauer Associates, Massachusetts. pp. 347-377.
39. Seymore T, DU Preez hh, Van Vuren JHJ, Deacon A and Strydom G (1994) Variation in Selected Water Quality Variables and the Metal Concentrations in the Sediment of the Lower Olifants and Selati Rivers, South Africa. *Koedoe* 37(2) 1-18.
40. Nimmo DR, Rigby RA, Bahner LH, Sheppard JM. (1978). The Acute and Chronic Effects of Cadmium on the Estuarine Mysid *Mysidopsis bahia*. Bulletin of Environmental Contamination and Toxicology 19: 80-85.
41. Nevo E, Noy R, Lavie B, Beiles A, Muchtar S. (1986). Genetic Diversity and Resistance to Marine Pollution. Biological Journal of the Linnean Society 29: 139-144.
42. Couch, J.A. 1978. *Fish. Bull.,* 76: 1-44. Couch, J.A. (1978). Diseases, Parasites and Toxic Responses of Commercial Penaeid Shrimps of the Gulf of Mexico and Atlantic Coast of.North America. Fishery Bulletin. 76: 1-44.

Pages: 56-64

LIMNOLOGY AND AQUATIC SCIENCE
Edited by: Dr. Shailendra Sharma; Dr. Pawan Kumar 'Bharti'
ISBN: 978-93-5056-735-7
Edition: 2015
Published by: Discovery Publishing House Pvt. Ltd., New Delhi (India)

Impact of Thyroxine and Thiouracil on the Oxygen Consumption in an Air Breathing Fish, *Channa gachua*

Qaisur Rahman and **D.N. Sadhu**

ABSTRACT

In the present investigation an attempt has been made to study the impact of thyroxine and thiouracil on the oxygen consumption in an air breathing fish *Channa gachua*. The oxygen consumption under the surfacing prevented condition was measured to whether the gills are more efficient and adequate supply of oxygen in *Channa gachua* when the air breathing organ were not allowed to function or the fish die due to asphyxiation. It was found that in *Channa gachua* the gills are most efficient and fish does not die for several days even if it is not allowed to breathe air. A good correlation was established between the increase in oxygen consumption and the increasing epithelial cell height of the thyroid follicle. The extent of thyroidal activity was determined from the range of cell height (2.78 - 4.98 μm) corresponding to minimum 102.0 (ml/kg/hr) and maximum 165.0 (ml/kg/hr) rate of oxygen consumption.

Department of Zoology, Vinoba Bhave University, Hazaribag – 825 301, Jharkhand, India.

This shows a direct relationship between thyroid follicles and oxygen consumption respectively. The coefficient of correlation was very high 0.97 which shows a high degree between these two parameters and the statistical analysis of the data revealed that (98.48%) of an increase in epithelial cell height of thyroid follicles, i.e. effects of L-thyroxine and thiouracil on oxygen consumption. During the first and second and third doses of thyroxine as compared to control one but from fourth doses on ward oxygen uptake decreases rapidly. When total dose i.e. (2.5 mg/120gm) of thiouracil was given to the fish for 8 days the oxygen consumption significantly decreased. However, the thyroid gland is an important regulator of oxygen consumption and thyroxine at higher dose shows pathological effects. The details will be discussed in this paper.

Key words: Thyroxine, Thiouracil, oxygen consumption, *Channa gachua*.

INTRODUCTION

The thyroid gland is genetically programmed to be regulators in all vertebrates. The metabolic activities of fishes is expressed in terms of oxygen uptake depends on many factors including hormones Qaisur and Sadhu (2010). Hormones are chemical agents released from one group of cells and travel i.e. the blood stream to affect one or more different groups of cell Baylis and Starling (1904). Endocrine glands through their actions on development, growth, metabolic rate and reproduction help the ectothermic animal to adapt successfully to change in their external environment. The oxygen in fish is a valid measurement of its metabolic activity which is influenced by a number of external internal factors Fry (1971). Numerous workers have tried to demonstrate the fundamental calorigenic action of the thyroid which is obvious in the higher vertebrates, but the results have often contradictory and thus precise action of the thyroid in the regulation of respiratory metabolism that remained obscure Root and Etkin (1947) Matty (1954, 1957) and Hoar (1958) believed that oxygen consumption in fishes is not influenced by thyroid hormones while Smith and Mathews (1948) Gabos Pora and Race (1973) hold the views that thyroid hormones have calorigenic effects in fishes. Most of the previous investigators in this regard have been restricted to water breathing species. Hence, in the present investigation an attempt has been made to study the oxygen consumption in *Channa gachua* with the view to assess whether or not the thyroid gland plays an important role in the regulation of oxygen consumption. *Channa gachua* lives in shallow rivers, ponds or ditches with muddy bottoms and can survive in ponds of low oxygen content. Besides respiring through its gills and skin it has supra branchial chamber for aerial respiration and thus it has bimodal breathing habits. This fish comes to the surface of water frequently to engulf air.

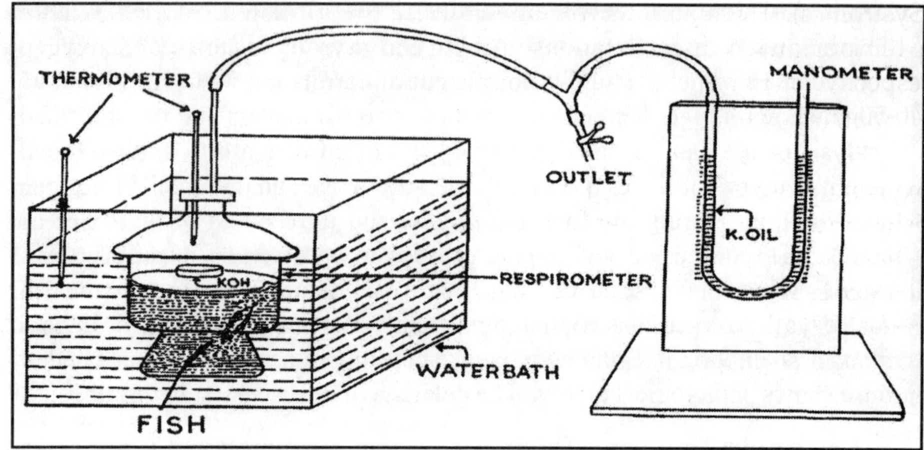

Fig. 4.1: Experimental set up for the Measurements of Dual mode of Oxygen uptake in *Channa gachua*

MATERIALS AND METHODS

Live specimens of *Channa gachua* were procured from local fish dealers at Hazaribag (Latitude 25° 59′N and Longitude 85° 22′E) and maintained in large glass aquaria size (90x60x60cm) with continuous flow of water. The specimens were fed on chopped goat liver daily during a minimum acclimation period of 15 days in the laboratory. Routine oxygen consumption from air and still water was measured in a closed glass respirometer containing 3 litres of water (initial O_2 content = 6.5 mg O_2/Iitre; pH = 7.2) and 0.51 ML of air (Fig. 4.1). The fish had free access to air through a small semi circular hole (10 cm diameter) in a disc float. Carbosorb (B.D.H) or KOH in a petridish placed on the float absorbed CO_2. Thus the fish could exchange gases with water by way of its gills as well as with the air using the suprabranchial chamber. The air phase of respirometer was connected to a differential manometer. Movement of the manometer fluid follow uptake of oxygen when the CO_2 is absorbed by "Carbosorb" (KOH). The fish were acclimatized to the respirometers for at least 12 hours before the readings were taken. The concentration of dissolved oxygen in the water was estimated by Winklers volumetric method (Welch, 1948).The oxygen uptake through gills was calculated from the difference between the oxygen levels of the ambient water in the respirometer before and after the experiment and the reading of volume of water in the respirometer. The oxygen uptake from air was measured and calculated from the reading of volume change in the manometer and by the use of the combined gas law equations and vapour pressure (Dejour's 1975). Mean values of oxygen consumption in a series of observations, on each fish at standard temperature pressure dry and standard errors were calculated. The experiments were conducted at 29.0 ± 1.5°C. The pH of the ambient water was measured by an electronic pH meter

(Systronics). The respiratory chambers were thermostated by immersion in a temperature controlled water bath Qaisur and Sadhu (2009, 2010) respectively. However, sexually mature fishes of almost same weight group (40-50g) were used.

Five fishes were used for each set of experiment and mean values of oxygen uptake of all the fishes were taken and compared. The experimental fishes including controls were divided into six groups each containing ten fishes. To study the effects of hormones on oxygen consumption at different doses of L-thyroxine (Sodium salts) at pH 8.0 and was injected slightly anterior to the pelvic fin and the powder form thiouracil was dissolved in distilled water and were fed orally with the help of catheter rubber pipe. The animals of control group having ten fishes got the treatment of normal saline. The hormones were purchased from local stockists. For every experiment the effective doses of different hormones were standardized and oxygen consumption of animals treated with different hormones was measured in every 24 hours.

For thyroidal activity every month the pharyngeal tissue with thyroid follicles of four fishes was fixed in aqueous fluid Bouins fluid. Dehydration, cleaning and embedding of the thyroid cut at 5-6µ were stained in eosin haematoxyline. The histometry has been taken for assessing the activity of the thyroid. The cell height of thyroid follicles was measured directly by calibration of an ocular micrometer. The cell height of thyroid follicles in different months of year were compared with the oxygen consumption of the corresponding conditions (surfacing allowed or surfacing prevented). The difference of significance if any between the control and experimental groups of fish was calculated by student 't' test at the level of 5%.

RESULTS AND DISCUSSION

The results showing the different doses of L-thyroxine and thiouracil on oxygen consumption are summarized in table (4.1 and 4.2). This reveal that at first and second dose (0.031 and 0.062 mg/100 gm) of thyroxine injection the oxygen consumption increased significantly as compared to control one being almost equal to control group at third dose (0.078 mg/100 gm). From the fourth to last dose the oxygen consumption of the thyroxine injected group decreased significantly as compared to control ones. The total dose (2.0 mg/100gm) of thyroxine causes (100%) mortality of fish whereas total dose of (2.5 mg/100 gm) thiouracil brought significant decrease in oxygen consumption in *Channa gachua*. A good correlation was established between the increase in oxygen consumption and the increasing epithelial cell height of thyroid follicles of thyroidal activity as determined from the range of epithelial cell height (3.69-6.36 µm) correspond to minimum 102.0 (ml/kg/hr) and maximum 165.0 (ml/kg/hr) rate of oxygen consumption. The coefficient of correlation was very high (0.97) showing a high degree of correlation between these two parameters. Statistical analysis of the data reveals that (98.48%) coefficient determination increased the oxygen consumption that was associated with an increase in epithelial cell height of thyroid follicles.

Table 4.1: Effects of L-thyroxin and thiouracil on Oxygen Consumption in *Channa gacha*

Sl. No.	Condition	Doses (mg/100gm)	Treatment in No. of Days	Oxygen Consumption (ml/kg/hr)
1.	Control	–	–	–
2.	Thyroxine	0.031	1	114.0
3.	DO	0.062	2	126.0
4.	DO	0.078	3	141.0
5.	DO	0.093	4	152.0
6.	DO	0.187	5	165.0
7.	DO	0.374	6	155.0
8.	DO	1.5	10	152.0
9.	Thiouracil	2.5	8	138.0

Table 4.2: Average Water Temperature, Epithelial Cell Height of Thyroid Follicles and Oxygen Consumption in *Channa gachua* N = 6, ± = S.E.M

Sl. No.	Months	Av. Water Temp. (°C)	Cell Height of Thyroid (μm)	Oxygen Consumption (ml/kg/hr)
1.	January 2010	22.5	3.04±0.12	106.0
2.	February	25.4	3.34±0.12	114.0
3.	March	29.3	3.69±0.19	126.0
4.	April	29.8	4.01±0.15	141.0
5.	May	31.4	4.52±0.31	152.0
6.	June	31.5	4.98±0.28	165.0
7.	July	30.6	4.62±0.10	155.0
8.	August	30.4	4.01±0.21	152.0
9.	September	29.8	3.86±0.31	138.0
10.	October	28.2	3.61±0.18	120.0
11.	November	26.5	3.52±0.26	116.0
12.	December	21.6	2.78±0.09	102.0

The thyroid gland in *Channa gachua* is compact, being situated in the sub-pharyngeal region Srivastav and Sathyanesan (1971). It extends anteriorly in front of the first afferent branchial artery and posteriorly it extends over the fourth afferent branchial artery. However, besides the main compact group of follicles overlying the sinus scattered groups or individual follicles are also found away from the pharyngeal sinus. The oxygen consumption under surfacing prevented condition was measured to ascertain whether the gills are most efficient for adequate supply of oxygen to this fish when their air breathing organs was not allowed to function or the fish die due to asphyxiation (Ghosh, 1931) respectively. The role thyroid in oxygen consumption in teleostean fishes is contradictory several investigators using either thyroid stimulants or depressants have claimed that such treatment has no significant effect on the rate of oxygen consumption in gold fish (Etkin, Root and Mofsin (1940) Hasler and Mayer (1942) Hoar (1958) Qaisur and Sadhu (2010, 2011). In *lebistes reticulatus* (Smith and Everret,1943) *Scyllium canalicula* (Matty, 1954) *Pseudoscarus gaucamia* (Matty, 1957) *Rhodeas amarus* (Punt and Jungbloed, 1963) and *Salmo gairdneri* (Baraduc, 1963) respectively. Smith and Mathews (1948) using *Bathystoma* Gabos *et al.*, (1973) in carp and Pandey and Munshi (1976) in *Heteropneustes fossilis* have reported a calorigenic effect of fish thyroid and our findings in *Channa gachua* is similar with the above investigators. It is very difficult or premature to make any comment at this stage unless a detailed investigation is made in number of species at cellular level that's why such specific differences exists in different species of fish.

In *Channa gachua* a high correlation was found between the increased in oxygen consumption and the increase in cell height of thyroid follicles. It seems probable that the thyroid hormones are important regulator of oxygen consumption in this fish and similar with the findings of Chavin and Rosmoore (1956) Gabos *et al.*, (1973) and Pandey and Munshi (1976) respectively. The results were further confirmed by the administration of L-thyroxine or thiourea. The injection of L-thyroxine caused a significant increase ($p<0.05$) in oxygen consumption whereas in thiouracil treated fish was significantly depressed ($p< 0.01$) respectively. Chavin and Rosmoore (1956) obtained an increase of (222%) of the oxygen consumption i.e. results of injection of thyroid stimulating hormones into hypo-physectomised immature gold fish. Muller (1953) reported that injection of (1.0 mg) of thyroid into gold fish (6.0 gm) produce an increase in metabolic rate. Pritchard and Gorbman (1960) have also found that injection of tri-iodothyroacetic acid (10 µm) every second day into the late embryo of *Squalus suckleyi* increases oxygen consumption. Osborn (1951) had reported a decrease of oxygen consumption in *Campastoma* and Pandey and Munshi (1976) in *H. fossilis* when treated with thiouracil (anti thyroidal drug) and Ruhland (1971) had also observed a significant decrease in oxygen consumption after radio thyroidectomy in *Acquidens latifrons.* Hence, the results obtains from the above discussion in *Channa gachua* is similar with the treatment of thyroxine and thiourea confirm the findings of the above investigators. Thyroxine at higher dose shows pathological effects as reported by Martin (1969) Qaisur and Sadhu (2012) respectively. The following precautions are advisable to the fore investigators: Thyroxine and thiouracil at different dosage must be injected carefully as the present study suggests that the third dose proved to be neutral dose which has no significant differences. The oxygen consumption of control and experimental fishes must be measured at same temperature and there must be provision inside the respirometer to minimize the locomotor activity of the fish. The body weight of the control experimental fish must be same because the oxygen consumption differs greatly with respect to body size. Fish must be acclimatized properly inside the respiratory chambers before conducting any experiments.

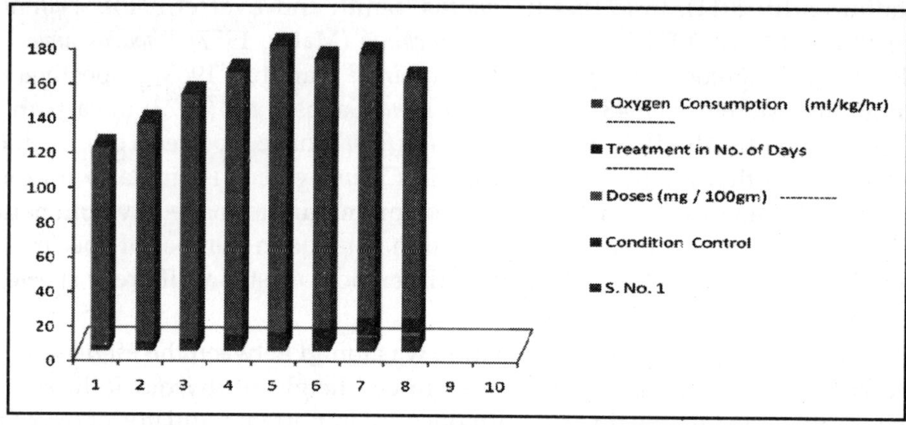

Graph 4.1: Showing the Effects of L-thyroxine and Thiouracil in *Channa gachua.*

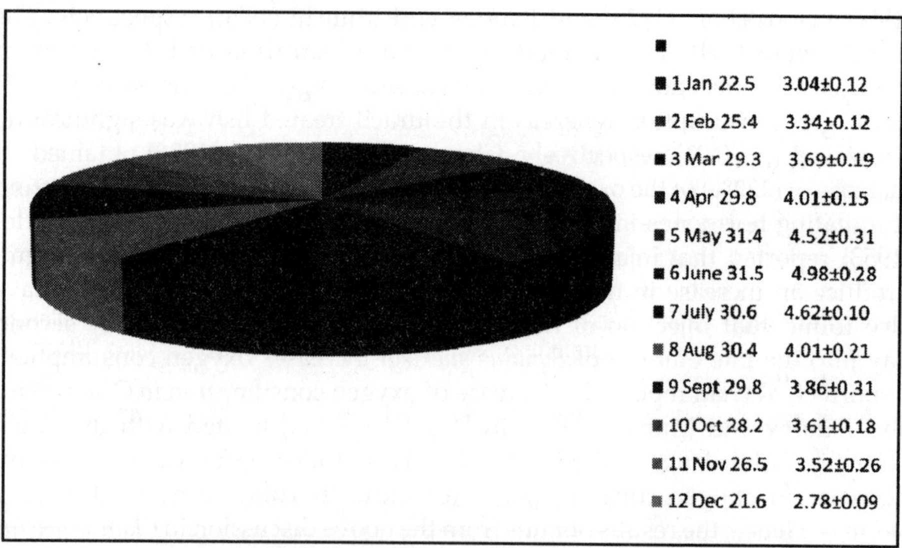

Graph 4.2: Showing the Average Water Temperature, Epithelial Cell Height of Thyroid Follicles in *Channa gachua.*

REFERENCES

Bayliss, W.M. and Starling, E.H. 1904, The Mechanisms of Pancreatic Secretion *J. Physiol.* 28: 325-1903.

Barduc, M.M. 1963, Quoted by A. Gorbman (thyroid hormones). *In* Comparative Endocrinology *Eds.* U.S. Von Euler and H. Heller, New York. Academic Press Vol. 1, pp. 291-324

Chavin, W. and Rosmoore, H.W. 1956, Pituitary Thyroid Regulation of Respiration in the Fold Fish *Carassius auratus Anat. Rec.* 125, 559.

Etkin, M.N. Root, R.W. and Mofsin, B.D. 1940, The Effect of Thyroid Feeding on Oxygen Consumption of the Gold Fish *Physiol. Zool.* 13: 415-429.

Gabos, M.E. Pora, A. and Race, L. 1973, Effect of Thyroxine (T4) TSH and Thiourea (TU) Treatment on the Oxygen Consumption of the Carp *Stud. Cerlet. Biol. Zool.* 25(1): 39-43

Gorbman, A. and Bern, H.A. 1962, "A Text Book of Comparative Endocrinology" John Willey and Sons New York.

Ghosh, E. 1934, An Experimental Study of the Asphyxiation of some Air Breathing Fishes of Bengal. *J. Asia. Soc. Bengal.* 29: 327-332.

Hasler, A.D. and Meyer, R.K. 1942, Respiratory Responses of Normal and Castrated Gold Fish to Teleost and Mammalian Hormones. *J. Exp. Zool.* 91: 391-404.

Hoar, W.S. 1958, Effect of Synthetic Thyroxine and Gonadal Steroids on the Metabolism in Gold Fish *Can. J. Zool.* 36: 113-121.

Kaya, M.K. 1973, Effects of Temperature on Response of the Gonads of Green Sunfish *lepomia cynellus* to Treatment with Carp Pituitaries and Testosterone propionate *Fish. Res. Bd. Can.* 30: 905-912.

Krantz, J.C. Jr and Carr. 1958, Pharmacological Principles of Medical Practice William and Wilkins Co. Baltimore 1260 pp.

Matty, A.J. 1954: Thyroidectomy of the Dog Fish *Scyllium canalicula* and the Effect of Dog Fish Thyroid upon the Oxygen Consumption of Rats. *J. Mar. Biol. Assoc.* United Kingdom. 33: 689-697.

Matty, A.J. 1957, Thyroidectomy and its Effect Upon Oxygen Consumption of Teleost Fish *Pseudoscarus gaucamia J. Endocrinol.* 15: 1-8.

Muller, J. 1957, Metabolic Effects of Thyroxine on Gold Fish *Anabas testudineus* (Bloch) *Acta Physiol.* 44: 113-123.

Osborn, P.E. 1951, Some Experiments on the Use of Thiouracil as an aid in Holding and Transporting Fish. *Progr. Fish. Cult.* 13: 75-80.

Pandey, B.N. and Munshi, J.S.D. 1976, Role of the Thyroid Gland in the Regulation of Metabolic Rate in a Air Breathing Siluroid Fish *Heteropneustes fossilis* (Bloch) *J. Endocrinol.* 69: 421-425.

Pandey, B. N. Prasad,S. and Sinha, D.P 1985, Cyclic Variations in the Activity of Internal Tissue and Oxygen Consumption in the Fresh Water Mud eel *Macrognathus aculeatum Ad. Bios.* 4II 87-91.

Pandey, B.N. Prasad, S. Singh, B.K. and Umesh Prasad 2002, Thyroidal Control of Respiratory Metabolism in Fresh Water Mud eel *Macrognathus aculeatum* (Bloch) *Proc. Zool. Soc. India.* I (1 & 2): 53-58.

Prasad, S. 1979: Ph.D. Thesis Entitled "Cyclic Activity of Endocrine Glands" Magadh University, Bodh Gaya, Bihar.

Prichard, A.W. and Gorbman, A.S 1960, Thyroid Hormone Treatment and Oxygen Consumption in Embryos of the Spiny Dog Fish Biol. Marine. *Biol. lab. Wood. Hole Mass.* 119: 109-119.

Punt and Jungbloed 1963, Quoted by A Gorbman (Thyroid Hormones) *In* Comparative Endocrinology *Ed.* W.S. Von Euler and H Heller New York London Vol. I. pp. 219-324.

Qaisur Rahman and Sadhu, D.N. 2010, Effects of Body Weight and Sex on Oxygen Consumption in an Air Breathing Murrel Fish, *Channa gachua. J. Ecobiol.* 26 (1): 195-200.

Qaisur Rahman and Sadhu, D.N. 2009, Effects of Seasonal Variations of Ambient Water Temperature on Oxygen Consumption in an Air Breathing Murrel fish, *Channa gachua. Columban. J. life Sci.* 10 (2): 23-27.

Qaisur Rahman and Sadhu, D.N. 2010, Effects of Hormones on Oxygen Consumption in an Air Breathing Murrel Fish, *Channa gachua. Biospectra.Org.* 5 (2): 45-50.

Qaisur Rahman and D N Sadhu. 2011, Effects of Heavy Metals on Oxygen Consumption in an Air Breathing Murrel Fish, *Channa gachua. Environ. Ecol.* 29 (2A): 818-821.

Qaisur Rahman and Sadhu, D.N. 2012, Factors Affecting Aerial and Aquatic Respiration in an Air Breathing Murrel Fish, *Channa gachua. J.Ecotoxicol. Environ. Monit.* 22 (1): 17-30.

Qaisur Rahman 2012, Studies on Some Factors Affecting Aerial and Aquatic Respiration in an Air Breathing Fish, *Channa gachua* (Ham.) Ph.D. thesis Vinoba Bhave University, Hazaribag, Jharkhand.

Root, R.W. and Etkin, W. 1947, Effect of Thyroxine on the Oxygen Consumption of Toad fish, *Proc. Soc. Exp. Biol. Med.* 37: 174-175

Ruhland, M.L. 1971, Radio Thyroidectomy and its Effect on Oxygen Consumption in cichlid *Acquidens latifrons Can. J. Zool.* 49: 423-425.

Singh Ranjana and Vijay Kumar 2008, Effect of Adrenocortical Hormones on the Oxygen Uptake in an Air Breathing Fish *Channa punctatus* (Bloch) *Proc. Zool. Soc. India* 7(1): 135-137.

Smith, D.C. and Everett, G.M. 1943, The Effect of Thyroid Hormone on Growth Rate, Time in Sexual Difference and Oxygen Consumption in the Fish, *Lebistes reticulatus J. Experimental. Zool.* 94, 229-240.

Smith, D.C. and Mathews, S.A. 1948, Parrot Fish Thyroid Extract and its Effect upon the Oxygen Consumption in the Fish *Bathystoma. Am. J. Physiol.* 153: 215-221.

Srivastav, S.S. and Sathynesan, A.G. 1971: Structure of Thyroid of Some Teleosts having Accessory Respiratory Organs. *Zeits. Micros. Ana. Forsch.* 153: 215-221.

Van Oordlt, G.J. 1963, Quoted *In* "Comparative Endocrinology" *Ed.* by U.S. Von Euler and H. Heller Vol. I. A.P.N.Y.

Welch, P.S.1948, Limnological Methods Mc Graw Hill Book Co. Inc New York, London. pp. 206-213.

Pages: 65-78

LIMNOLOGY AND AQUATIC SCIENCE
Edited by: Dr. Shailendra Sharma; Dr. Pawan Kumar 'Bharti'
ISBN: 978-93-5056-735-7
Edition: 2015
Published by: Discovery Publishing House Pvt. Ltd., New Delhi (India)

5

Rotifer Diversity in most Polluted Areas (Mandideep and Nayapura) of River Betwa, Madhya Pradesh, India

Santosh Vishwakarma[1]; **Alok Varma**[2] and **Geeta Saxena**[1]

ABSTRACT

The aim of the study was to find out rotifers diversity in most polluted areas (Mandideep and Nayapura) of river Betwa. Survey and sampling took place between October-2011 to September- 2012, and two major stations and ten sampling sites were selected for the study. Thirty-four rotifers taxa were identified (34 species, 11 genera). In all members of rotifer most dominant species were *Brachionus* (18 species) and *Keratella* (06 species). Rotifers reached peak in density in the summer season, while minimum were in winter season. Physico-chemical parameters of river water Temperature, pH, Dissolve oxygen, Biological oxygen demand and Chemical oxygen demand were also measured and the correlation coefficient of physic-chemical parameter with rotifers were established, The rotifer significant relation with pH (0.810), inverse

1 Department of Biotechnology, Institute for Excellence in Higher Education, Bhopal, Madhya Pradesh, India.

2 Department of Zoology, Raja Bhoj Govt. College, Mandideep, District Raisen, Madhya Pradesh, India.

relation with dissolve oxygen (-0.314) while significant relation with BOD (0.430) and COD (0.220). The abundance of rotifers with various physico-chemical indicate that the selected sites station I and II is polluted from various industrial, domestic and municipal waste and the present of rotifers species at this sites shows indicator of pollution.

Key words: Rotifera, zooplankton, Mandideep, Biomonitoring, Betwa.

INTRODUCTION

Aquatic pollution in India has now reached at a critical point. Almost every river system in India is now polluted to a considerable extent. In developing countries 1.8 million people, mostly children, die every year as a result of water-related diseases (WHO, 2004). According to an estimate; about 80% of the total population in India is deprived of pure and safe drinking water. A recent study revealed that there were 1, 53,000 village in India, which had infected water supply. 90% of total drinking water is severally polluted. Ganga is the most polluted river in the world. Other Indian rivers include Damoder, Hoogly, kulu, which have almost the same story to reveal.

The word plankton is derived from the Greek *planktos*, meaning wandering. It is used to describe the small, usually immotile, freely floating organisms living in aquatic habitats (Powell *et al.* 1975). Plankton drives energy cycling in aquatic ecosystems as they are the productive base of food webs, converting basic forms of energy into forms usable by higher trophic levels (Vilar *et. al.*, 2003). Plankton growth and dynamics depends on the characteristics of their environment – light and nutrient availability, temperature, salinity, pH, currents, turbulence, and predation intensity.

Rotifers (Rotatoria) are the microscopic pelagic living mostly in fresh water, and characterized by the presence of an anterior wheel like rotating structure called corona. Rotifers are important zooplankton and biotic component in fresh water ecosystem, comprising integral links of aquatic food-webs (primary as fish food) and contributing significantly to secondary productivity. The cosmopolitan distribution and occurrence in relation to water quality have been the attention of many planktologists (Cajander, 1983; Edmondson, 1959; Pennack, 1953; Sladecek, 1983). Rotifers are considered as most sensitive indicator of water quality (Ali *et al.* 1990).

As a group, the rotifers display an amazing range of morphological variation and adaptation. Among the zooplankton, rotifers respond quickly to the environmental stress so they can be used as a bioindicators of pollution, Bahura *et. al.*, (1993) reported that *Brachionus* and *Keratella* were indicators of eutrophication. There have been only limited investigations on the rotifer fauna of the Indian reservoirs and lakes which confined mainly on the systematic, seasonal occurrence and the spatiotemporal variations (C. George, 1961; Singhal *et al.*, 1989). Only a few Indian workers have reported the seasonal abundance of rotifers.

The river Betwa plays a significant role in the human life of the villages located in Mandideep, Nayapura and Bhojpur areas. It has become polluted at some places of Mandideep due to industrial activities and the confluence of sewage, domestic wastes and industrial effluents of many big and small enterprises with various types of organic compounds and heavy metals deterioted to human health and aquatic organisms. Urban areas, farms, factories and individual households – all contribute to the contamination of this river. The water quality in the stretch of the river Betwa extending from its origin near Mandideep industrial area up to Bhojpur remains poor because of the regular inflow of domestic waste of the Bhopal city through the Kaliyasot river and industrial/domestic waters from Mandideep (Kori *et. al.*, 2006).

The present work is aim to understanding various types of pollution in River Betwa at selected sites, and observes the impact of pollution on different sites of River Betwa, both biologically as well as chemically; bio-assessment will be done by using zooplankton as bio-indicator of pollution.

MATERIAL AND METHODS

Study Area (Sampling Sites)

The Betwa is a river Northern India, and tributary of the Yamuna originating in the Kumra (Jhirri) village in Raisen district of Madhya Pradesh, India, the river basin lies between the latitudes of 22° 54′ N and 26°00, N and the longitudes of 77°10′ E and 80°20′ E. The total length of the river from its origin to confluence with the Yamuna is 590 km. out of which 232 km. in Madhya Pradesh and the rest 358 km. in Uttar Pradesh (fig. 5.1).

After the intensive survey of river Betwa ten sites were selected. The selected sites (Mandideep and nayapura) were affected with anthropogenic and industrial activities.

Major Station I Nayapura (1 to 5 sampling sites)

It is a village near Mandideep, the Betwa touches the boundary of this village near Road Bridge where it confluences with the Kaliyasot tributaries.

Major Station II Mandideep (6 to 10 sampling sites)

Mandideep is the municipality in Goharganj district Raisen in MP. Mandideep is 20 km away from Bhopal and popular as Industrial Township which came in to existence in late 1970s. It has an industrial area, the major industries that are closer are Hindustan Electro Graphite (HEG), Procter & Gamble, Eicher tractors Ltd, Lupin laboratories, and national and international level companies have their manufacturing units at Mandideep. It is located near River Betwa. River Betwa encircle this industrial area, thus, Mandideep was also selected as a study site in the present research work.

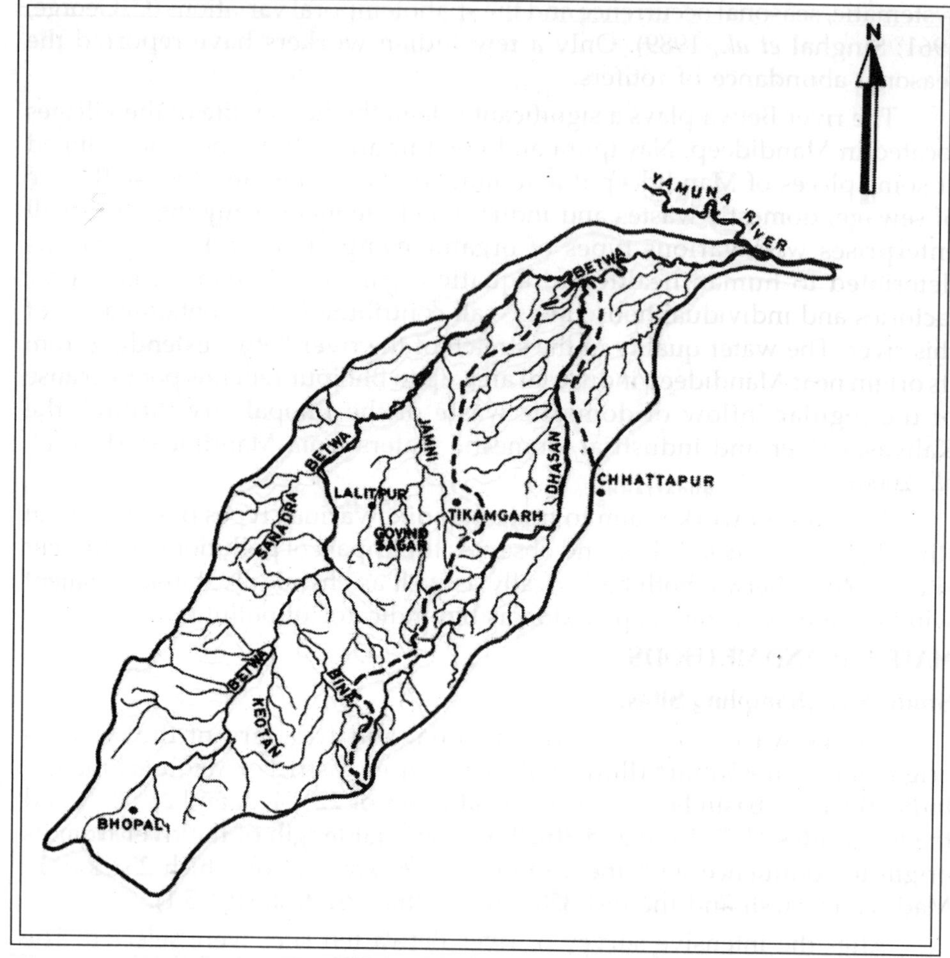

Fig. 5.1: Index Map of Betwa Basin

Measurement of physico-chemical parameters: The physico-chemical parameters temperature, pH, dissolved oxygen, Biological oxygen demand and Chemical oxygen demand were measured as per detail follows (APHA 1995).

Temperature:	Systronic Labtronics laboratory digital thermometer (An iso 9001: 2008 certified)
pH:	Systronic Labtronics laboratory digital pH meter (An iso 9001: 2008 certified)
Dissolved oxygen:	Winklar's method (Titrometric method)
Biological oxygen demand:	5 days incubation method
Chemical oxygen demand:	Reflux index method (Titrometric method)

Biodiversity of rotifers (Analysis of zooplankton)

Collection of zooplankton: Plankton samples were collected from the surface water of the river. Each sample was collected by filtering 50 liters of water through mesh size 60-65μm plankton net.

Preservation: Plankton preserved in 5% formaline. Slide was prepared by using stain with fuschin acid.

Quantitative analysis (counting): The quantitative enumeration of the zooplankton was carried out with the help of a Sedgwick-Rafter (S-R) counting cell which is 50 mm long, 20 mm wide and 1 mm deep. Before filling the SR cell with sample, the cover glasses were diagonally placed across the cell and then samples were transferred with a large bore pipette so that no air bubbles in the cell covers were formed. The S-R cell was let stunned for at least 15 minutes to settle zooplankton. Then plankton on the bottom of the S-R cell was enumerated by compound microscope. By moving the mechanical stage, the entire bottom of the slide area was examined carefully. To achieve a random sampling, each time 3 fields were examined for each sample and an average of the counts had been recorded. The organisms thus counted, were expressed as cells per liter (cells) of the sample. From each sample 20 cells counts in 3 slides have been made to achieve random counts and an average of the counts has been recorded. Number of plankton (Zooplankton) in the S-R cell was derived from the following formula (Gosh, *et.al.*, 2011).

$$No./ml = \frac{C \times 1000\text{mm}^3}{L \times D \times W \times S}$$

Where, C = Number of Organisms Counted; L = length of each strip (S-R cell length) in mm; D = depth of a strip (whipped grid image width) in mm; S = number of strips counted. The number of cells per mm was multiplied by a correction factor to adjust the number of organisms per liter (APHA 1976).

Identification: The zooplanktons were identified with the help of standard books and monographs as follows:

- **Needham, J G. Needham, P. R. (1962):** A guide to the study of freshwater biology.
- **Pennak, W. R. (1953):** Freshwater Invertebrates of the United States.
- **Edmonson, W. T. (1965)**: Fresh water biology.United State of America.
- **Ward, H. B. and Whipple, G. C. (1959)**: Freshwater biology, New York
- **Altaff, K. (2003)**: A manual of zooplankton.
- **Battish, S.K. (1992)**: Fresh water zooplankton of India.

- **Dhanapathi, M.V.S.S.S (2000)**: Taxonomic notes on the Rotifers from India.
- **Digital documentation:** Images of zooplankton or digital documentation were prepared by the Magnus (mips) live 2.0 usb camera attached with computer with 10X and 100 X magnification.
- **Statically analysis:** The correlation between rotifers and abiotic (physico-chemical) parameters was done by using coefficient of correlation Karl Pearson's formula:

$$r = \frac{\sum d_x d_y}{\sqrt{\sum d_{x^2} \sum d_{y^2}}}.$$

Rotifers are economically and ecologically important group, they occupy a wide range of habitat existing in aquatic ecosystem. Recently it has shown that diversity abundance of rotifers is sensitive to change in water variables. During the period of study, Thirty-four rotifers taxa were identified (34 species, 11 genera). In all members of rotifer most dominant species was *Brachionus* (18 species) and *Keratella* (06 species). Thirty four species of Rotifers which is includes 18 species of *Brachionus,* 06 species of *Keratella,* 02 species each of *Euchionus* and *Ascomorpha* and 01 species of *Chromogaster, Harringia, Mikrocodides, Tetramastix, Notholca* (Graph. 5.1 & Table. 5.1).

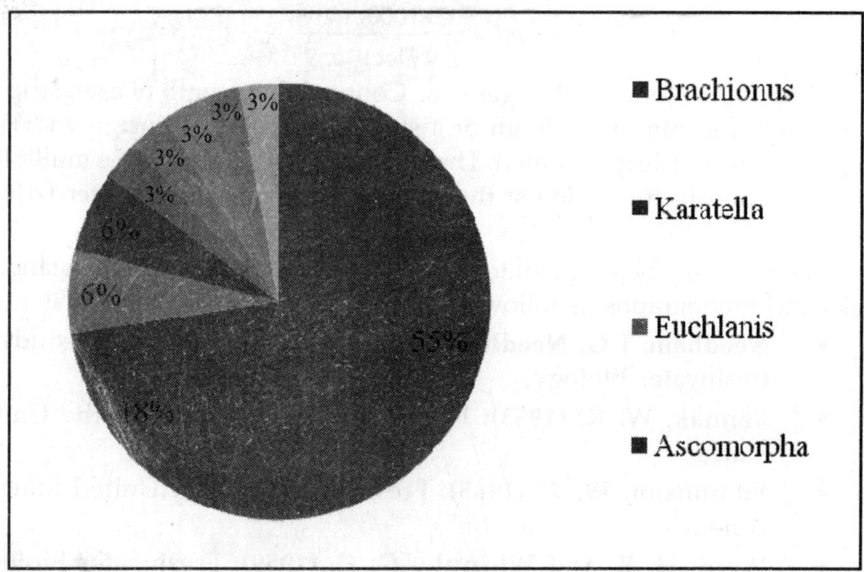

Graph 5.1: Percentage Composition of Different Species of Rotifers

Table 5.1: List of Rotifers at Station-1 Nayapura and Station-2 Mandideep

Brachionus bidentata	*Brachionus murrayi*	*Keratella serrulata*
Brachionus Rotundiformis	*Brachionus plicatilis*	*Keratella tropica*
Brachionus calyciflorus	*Brachionus quadridentata*	*Keratella valga tropica*
Brachionus caudatus	*Brachionus rubens*	*Euchlanis dialatata*
Brachionus diversicornis	*Brachionus variabilis*	*Euchlanis deflexa*
Brachionus calyciflorus f	*Branchionus urceolaris*	*Asplanchna priodonta*
Brachionus durgae	*B. dichotomus reductus*	*Ascomorpha ecaudis*
Brachionus falcatus	*Keratella hiemalis*	*Ascomorpha saltans*
Brachionus forficula	*Keratella cochlearis*	*Chromogaster*
Brachionus havanaensis	*Keratella quadrata*	*Harringia eupoda*
Mikrocodides chlaena	*Tetramastix opoliensis*	*Notholca acuminate*

In addition the influence of biotic on abiotic parameters is correlated in order to understand ecological relationship. During the study period, minimum temperature 17° C was measured in the month of February and the maximum temperature was 31° C in the month of June, the hydrogen ion concentration (pH) value was ranged 5.3 to 6 at Nayapura and Mandideep. Dissolved oxygen mean value was maximum 3.1 mg/L. in winter season, while the lowest mean value of dissolved oxygen as 1.7. BOD value ranges between 12.2 mg/L. to 15.5 mg/l. at Nayapura and Mandideep. In Betwa river maximum value of COD (62 mg/L.), and minimum value of COD (55.5 mg/L.), have been recorded Highest value of COD indicates that most of pollution in study zone in Betwa river in caused by industrial effluents discharged by industrial units (Table 5. 2).

In this study, pH ranged 5.3 to 6. The pH showed positive correlation (0.810) in relation to the population of rotifers in all ten study area. The population density and biodiversity of most rotifers genera showed inverse relation (-0.314) with DO of water in all the study areas. BOD ranged were 12.2 to 15.5 mg/L in the present study, the population of rotifers showed significantly positive correlation (0.430) with BOD of water in all the study area. In the present study minimum COD 55.5 mg/L. and maximum COD value 62mg/L. the rotifers population of rotifers showed positive correlation (0.220) with COD of river water (Table 5.3).

DISCUSSION

Zooplankton organisms occupy central position in the food webs of aquatic ecosystem. They do not only form an integral part of the lentic community but also contribute the biological productivity of the fresh water ecosystem (Wetzel, 2001). Due to short life cycle, zooplankton communities often respond quickly to environmental changes Sharma *et. al.*, (2007). Rotifera are the most important soft bodied metazoans among the zooplankton. Species diversity was highest at station – II and III in river Betwa at Nayapura and Mandideep (Table 5.1).

Table 5.2: Values of Physico-chemical Parameter at Different Sites of River

Months	Sites										
	1	2	3	4	5	6	7	8	9	10	M
Temperature											
October	21	20	20.5	21	21.4	22	20	21.1	22	22.4	21
December	19	18	19.4	19	17.3	18.3	19.2	20	20.5	17.7	18.6
February	16.3	17.5	17.2	18	16.5	18.5	19.2	17	19	18.5	17.5
April	23	23.5	24.3	22	23	24	21	23	23.2	23.5	23
June	30	30.2	31.3	29.5	32	31	31.6	30.2	32.2	31.2	31
August	24	24.3	23	22	24	23	21	23.2	23	24.3	23.1
pH											
October	6.3	6.1	6.2	6.4	6	5.8	5.5	5.7	5.9	6	5.8
December	6.4	5.8	5.5	6	6.2	6.3	5.4	5.3	5.8	5.5	5.5
February	6.2	6	6.3	6.5	5.7	5.3	5.2	5	5.8	5.1	5.3
April	6.1	6.4	6.2	6.1	6	5.5	5.6	5.7	5.3	5.2	5.7
June	6	6.2	6.4	6.3	6.1	6	5.7	5.4	5.2	5.5	6
August	5.8	5.4	5.6	5	5.3	5.5	5.1	5.4	5.8	5.2	5.7
Dissolved Oxygen											
October	2.4	2.2	2.6	2.8	2	1.8	1.6	2	2.2	1.5	2.1
December	2.2	2.3	2.4	2	2.1	2.5	2	2.7	1.8	1.7	1.9
February	2.8	2.9	2.6	2.5	3	3.1	3.2	2.2	2	2.4	2.7
April	2.1	2.2	2.4	2.3	2.4	2.1	2.8	2.3	2.5	2.1	2.2
June	1.8	1.9	1.5	1.3	1.6	1.3	1.2	1.9	1.5	2.1	1.7
August	2.8	2.5	2.8	2.9	3.2	3.4	2.6	2.8	2.6	3.5	3.1
Biological Oxygen Demand											
October	6.4	6.5	7.4	7.5	6.3	18.6	16.5	16.4	16.2	18.4	15.5
December	8.4	8.2	8	8.5	8.2	16.3	16.7	17.4	16.8	16.5	12.2
February	8.5	9.9	8.5	8	9	18.5	18	18.3	18.4	17.5	13.5
April	10.2	10.4	10.5	10.2	9.8	19.4	19.5	19.8	19	19.2	14.5
June	10.4	10.2	11	10.5	10.6	19.8	20.1	18.8	19.5	18.5	15
August	9.5	9.8	9.4	9.2	9.1	18.6	18.5	19.5	18.4	18.2	14
Chemical Oxygen Demand											
October	41.1	40.4	42.3	42.2	40.5	71.2	70.5	72.2	70.6	71.5	56.2
December	38.4	38.5	38.6	38.2	38.9	72.5	71.3	73.5	72.2	73.8	55.5
February	39.5	39.8	39.2	40	40.6	74.2	75.6	73.5	75.8	76.4	57.5
April	41.5	40.5	42.5	40.3	40.2	78.5	76.4	72.3	78.5	72.2	58.2
June	42.5	41.2	43.3	41.4	42.5	82.2	80	81.4	80.5	82.4	62
August	41.5	40.3	42.8	40.6	40.8	81.8	82.5	80.4	83.2	80.6	61.4

Table 5.3: Correlation of Rotifers with Abiotic Parameters

Parameters	Rotifera	Co-efficient of Corre.	Comments
Temperature	Rotifera	0.110	Significant
pH	Rotifera	0.810	Significant
DO	Rotifera	-0.314	Inverse relation
Biochemical Oxygen Demand	Rotifera	0.430	Significant
COD	Rotifera	0.220	Significant

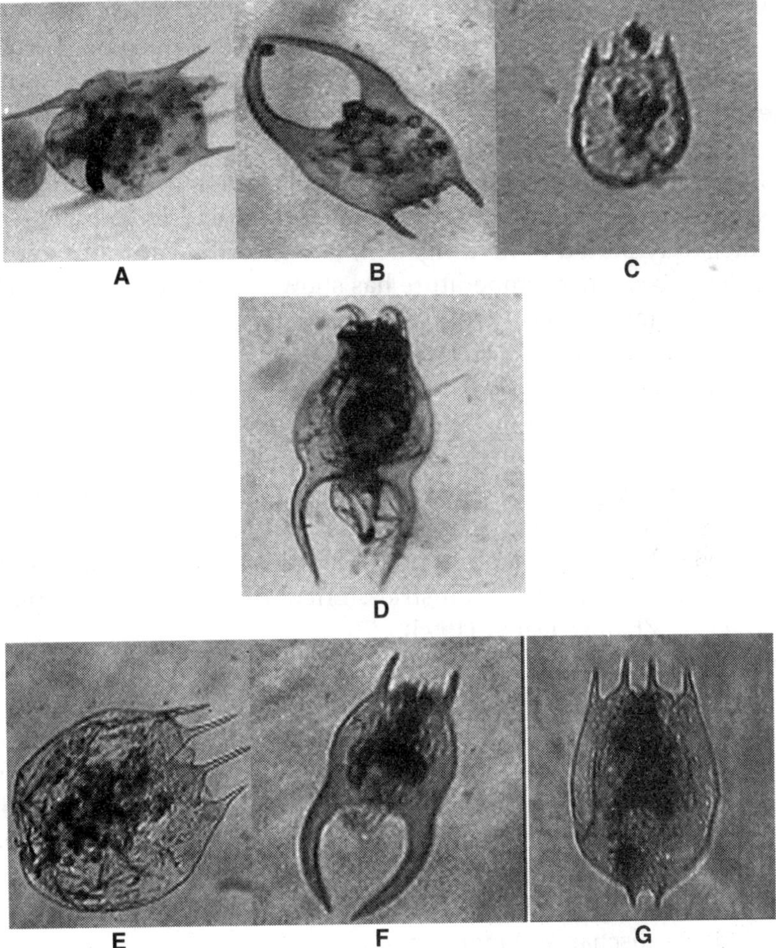

Fig. 5.2 (A-G): Different species of rotifers

A- *Brachionus bidentata;* B- *Brachionus diversicornis*
C- *Keratella cochlearis;* D- *Brachionus falcatus*
E- *Brachionus murrayi;* F- *Brachionus forficula*
G- *Brachionus plicatilis.*

Brachionus and *Keratella* genus was abundant at station- II and III. The genus *Brachionus* is considered as a biological indicator for the eutrophication, and *Keratella* species has been indicated as an indicator of pollution Nogueira,2001; Sampath *et. al.*, 1978; Bahura *et. al.*,1993).. Similar observation was also noticed by various workers Arora, (1996) and Patil *et. al.*, (2006). *Brachionus angularis, B. calyciflorus* and *B. diversicornis* are indicative of the mesosaprobic condition and *B. angularis* and *B. calyciflorus* are also having strong affinity to alkaline waters (Sladecek, 1983). The dominance of *Brachionus* and *Keratella* is the general trend in freshwater bodies in India (Singhal *et al.*, 1989; Sharma, 1988, Sukumaran and Das, 2003).

Temperature is very important in controlling the population density and diversity of rotifers. The surface of water directly receives solar radiation, suitable for the growth of plankton. The seasonal variation in the temperature of river water were observation all sampling stations. The seasonal variation showed a similar trend at all the stations. The temperature at station No.I & II was slightly higher because of mixing of sewage and industrial effluents. During the study period of investigation, due to shallowness of river Betwa at Mandideep, the water temperature has show a tendency to follow closely the atmospheric temperature. The findings were common with the observations of Malhotra *et. al.*, 1986; and Das *et. el.*,(2003).

The *pH* of a solution refers to its hydrogen ion activity and is expressed as the logarithm of the reciprocal of the hydrogen activity in moles per liter at a given temperature (APHA.1992). The pH expresses the intensity of acidity or alkalinity of an aquatic environment. The present finding reveal that in river Betwa pH fluctuate in station I Nayapura and station II Mandideep, In the present study low pH value were found may be due to industrial effluent of nearby industries. Effect of low pH on zooplankton was studied by Zhaung Dehvi (1995).

Dissolved oxygen (DO) levels in natural and waste water are dependent on the physical, chemical and biochemical activities prevailing in the water body. Running water contain relatively high concentration of dissolved oxygen. In the present finding, the volume as well as rate of flow of water decreases, while the disposal of waste water, industrial effluents and sewage remain virtually the same at station- II Nayapura and station- III Mandideep showed lowest value of dissolved oxygen. The same results were reported by Verma and Mathur (1971), Baruah *et.al.*, 1996. Minimum dissolved oxygen due to effluents discharge, Emongor *et. al.*, 2005.

Biological oxygen demand (*BOD*) is an important parameter which is widely used to determine the pollution load of waste water. Biological oxygen demand is the amount of oxygen required by microorganism for stabilizing biologically decomposable organic matter (carbonaceous) in water under aerobic condition. In the present finding the highest BOD value was recorded station I, and station –III Mandideep. Seasonal fluctuations in the hydro biological factors revealed higher value of BOD were observed during late summer (May-June). These were due to higher rate of decomposition of organic matter at higher temperature, turbidity and less water current (Sanap *et.al.*, 2006) . Similar observation recorded Sachidanandamurthy and Yajurvedi, (2004), and Pratima (2008).

Chemical oxygen demand is a test which is used to measure pollution of domestic and industrial waste. COD gives us reliable parameter for judging the extent of pollution in water (Shrivastava and Patil 2002). This makes COD useful as indicators of organic pollution in surface water (King *et. al.*, 2003). The chemical oxygen demand (COD) was higher than the NESREA (2011) and WHO (1993) values recommended for good water quality. High COD value at the discharge point could be due to high organic load of total solid and total suspended solid from industries. This could probably explain the linear relationship between solid and COD (Osibanjo and Adie, 2007). Highest value of COD indicates that most of pollution in study zone in Betwa river in caused by industrial effluents discharged by industrial units. Similar results were also reported by Pande and Sharma (1998). The population of rotifers seemed to be positive correlation (0.110) with temperature. The rotifer significant relation with pH (0.810), inverse relation with dissolve oxygen (-0.314) while significant relation with BOD (0.430) and COD (0.220) (Table No.3), These findings similar to various investigators (Das *et. al.*, 2003; Rim- Rukeh *et.al.*, 2006; Arimoro *et al.*, 2007; Pratima 2008; Osibanjo and Adie, 2007).

Species Composition	(S-1 Nayapura)	(S-2 Mandideep)
Rotifera (34species)		
Brachionus bidentata	+	–
Brachionus Rotundiformis	–	+ +
Brachionus calyciflorus	+	+
Brachionus caudatus	+	+
Brachionus diversicornis	–	+
Brachionus quadridentatus var.	+	–
Brachionus calyciflorus f.	–	+ +
Brachionus durgae	+	–
Brachionus falcatus	–	+
Brachionus forficula	–	+
Brachionus havanaensis	+	+
Brachionus murrayi	–	+
Brachionus plicatilis	+ +	–

(Table Contd...)

Brachionus quadridentata	+	–
Brachionus rubens	–	+
Brachionus variabilis	–	+
Branchionus urceolaris	+	–
B. dichotomus reductus	–	++
Keratella hiemalis	–	+
Keratella cochlearis	++	–
Keratella quadrata	+	+
Keratella serrulata	–	+
Keratella tropica	–	+
Keratella valga tropica	–	+
Euchlanis dialatata	+	–
Euchlanis deflexa	+	–
Asplanchna priodonta	+	–
Ascomorpha ecaudis	–	+
Ascomorpha saltans	–	+
Chromogaster	+	–
Harringia eupoda	–	+
Mikrocodides chlaena	+	+
Tetramastix opoliensis	–	+
Notholca acuminate	+	–

- = **Absent**

+ = Common

++ = Abundant

REFERENCES

Ali Musharraf, Asif A. Khan and Noorul Haque (1990). Population Dynamics of rotifer fauna from Tropical Ponds of Aligarh, India. *Proc. Nat. Acad. Sci.* India, 60(B) 1: 14-19.

Aoyagui A.S.M., Bonecker, C.C, (2004). *Hydrobiologia*, 522,281.

Arimoro F.O, Chukwudi M.A. and Ogheneghalome O. (2007). Effect of Industrial Waste Water on the Physical and Chemical Characteristics of a Tropical Coastal River. *Res.J.En. Sci.*, 2: 209-220.

Arora H.C.(1996). Rotifera as Indicators of Trophic Nature of Environment. Hydrobiologia. 27, 146-149.

Baruah B.K, Baruah D, and Das M, (1996). Study of the Effect of Paper Mill Effluent on the Water Quality of Receiving Wetland. Poll. Res,15 (14): 389-393.

Cajender, V.R. (1983). Production of Planktonic Rotatoria in Ormajarvi and Eutropical Lake in Southern Finland. *Hydrobiologia*, 104: 329-333.

George, M.C. (196). Observations on the Shallow Ponds in Delhi. *Curr. Sci.*, 30(7): 268-269.

Das A.C, Baryagm B.K, Baruha D. and Sengupta S. (2003). Study on Wetlands of Guwahati City: 2, Water Quality of River and Drains; *Poll. Res.* 22(1): 117-119.

Dhanapathi M.V.S.S.S (2000). Taxonomic Notes on the Rotifers from India. *Indianassociation of Aquatic Biologists* (IAAB) Hyderabad. 1-78.

Edmonson W.T, (1965). Fresh Water Biology. *2nd Ed. Wiley*, New York, pp. 420-494.

Egborge A, (1993). Biodiversity of Aquatic Fauna of Nigeria. *Abuja. Nat.Reso.Cons.Council.*, Nigeria. p. 173.

Emonger V, Kealotswe E, Koorapetse I, SanKwasa S. and Keikanestswe S, (2005). Pollution Indicators in Gaberone Effluents. J. Appl. Sci., 5, 147-150.

Kori R, Shrivastava P.K, Upadhyay N, Singh R. (2006). Studies on Presence of Heavy Metals and Halogenated Hydrocarbons in River Betwa (M.P), India No 2/3: 147-153.

King J.M, Scheepers A.C.T, Fisher R.C, Reinecke M.K. and Smith L.B. (2003). River Rehabilitation: Literature Review, Case Studies and Emergin Principles. WRC Report No. 1161/1/03.

Laxmi Narayan J.S.S. (1965). Studies on the Phytoplankton of the River Gangas. Vanarasi. India II the Seasonal Growth and Succession of Plankton Algae in the River Ganga. *Hydrobiologia.*, 25: 138-165.

Malhotra Y.R, Dutta S.P.S, and Suri S.N. (1986). Limnology of Fish Pond in Regional Research Laboratory. *Jamu. Matsya*, (12-13): 174-177.

Needham J G. Needham, P.R. (1962). A Guide to the Fresh Water Biology, *Holdend-day inc. Sanfrancisco*, California: 108 pp.

Neschuk N, Claps M, and Gabellone N, (2002). Planktonic Rotifers of a Saline-lowland River: the Salado River (Argentina). *Ann. Limnol.-Int. J. Limnol.*, 38: 191-198.

Nogueira M.G, (2001). Zooplankton Composition Dominance and Abundance as Indicators Environmental Compartmentalization in Jurumirim Reservoir (Paranapanema river), Sao Paulo, Brazil. Hydrobiologia, 455, 1-18.

Okechukwu I.O, Nwani C.D, Okoha, F.A, (2010). *J. Envior. Biol.* 31, 533.

Osibanjo O. and Adie G.U, (2007). Impact of Effluents from Bodijia Abatter on the Physicochemical Parameter of Oshunkaye Stream in Ibadan City, Nigeria. *Afr. J. Biotechno.*, 6: pp. 1806-1811.

Pande K.S. and Sharma S.D, (1998). Studies of Toxic Pollutants in Ramganga River at Moradabad India. Envtal Geo., 1(2): 93-96.

Powell T.M, Richerson P.J, Dillon T.M, Agee B.A, Dozier B.J, Godden D.A. & Myrup, L.O. (1975). 'Spatial Scales of Current Speed and Phytoplankton Biomass Fluctuations in Lake Tahoe', *Science*, Vol. 189, pp. 1088-1090.

Pennak W.R. (1953). Freshwater Invertebrates of the United States.

Pratima M, Shiddamallayya N. (2008). Impact of Domestic Sewage on Fresh Water Body. *Journal of Environmental Biology* 29(3): 303-308.

Patil S.U, mule M.B. and S.S. Kharade, (2006): Zooplankton Study of Krishna River from Walwa Taluka, District Sangli, Maharashtra. Research Hunt.1, 31-35.

Rim-Rukeh A, Ikhifa GO, Okokoyo P.A. (2006). Effects of Agricultural Activities on the Water Quality of Orogodo River, *Agbor, Nig. J. Appl. Sci. Res.*, 2(5): 256-259.

Sladecek, V. (1983). Rotifers: An Index of Water Quality. *Hydrobiologia*, 100: 169-201.

Saler S. and Sen, D, (2002). Seasonal Variation of Rotifera fauna of Cip Dam lake (Elazig-Turkey). *Pakistan J. Biol. Sci.* 5: 1274-1276.

Sharma M.S, Sharma V, and Malara H, (2007). *Biodiversity of Zooplankton in Relation to Different Types of Aquatic Pollution.* C.P. 46. NSL 2007. pp. 300-302.

Sarma, S.S.S. (1988). New Records of Rotifers (Rotifera) from Indian Waters. *Hydrobiologia*, 160: 263-269.

Sampath V, Sreenivasan A, and Ananthanarayanam (1978). Rotifers as Biological Indicators of Water Quality in Cauvery River. Abst. Symp. Environ. Biol. 5.

Singhal, S., G.M.A. Ramani, and U.S. Gupta (1989). Seasonal Variation of Rotifers in the Newly made Tawa Resrvoir, Hoshangabad, India. *Proc. Nat.Acad. Sci. India*, 59(B) II: 163-168.

Scholl K. and Kiss, A., (2008). Spatial and Tamporal Distribution Pattern of Zooplankton Assemblages (Rotifera, Cladodera, Copepoda) in the Water Bodies of the Gemenc Floodplain (Duna-Drava National park, Hungary). *Opusc, Zoo. Budapest.*, 39: 65-76.

Segers H, Nwadiro, C.S, Dumont, H.J., (1993). *Hydrobiologia*, 250, 63.

Sachidanandamurthy K.L. and Yajurvedi H.N. (2006). A Study of an Physicochemical Parameters of an Aquaculture Body in Mysore City, Karnataka, India. Journal of Environmental Biology 27(4): 615-618.

Sanap R.R, Mohite A.K, Pingle S.D. and Gunale, V.R (2006). Evaluation of Water Qualities of Godawari River with Reference to Physicochemical Parameters, Dist. Nasik (M.S.), India. Poll. Res., 25(4), pp. 775-778.

Shrivastava V.S. and P.R. Patil (2002). Tapti River Water Pollution by Industrial Wastes: A Statistical Approach. Nat. Environ. Pollut. Tech., 1, 279-283.

Sukumaran, P.K. and A.K. Das, 2003. Status of Plankton in Impoundments in Major Reservoirs of Andhra Pradesh. *Fishery Technology*, 40(1): 1-4.

Varma S.R. and Mathur R.P. (1971). Characterictics and Pollution Effect of Paper Mills Wastes on the Hindon River: Seminar on Water Supply and Sanitation.

Vilar J M.G, Sole R.V, & Rubi J.M. (2003). 'On the Origin of Plankton Patchiness', *Physica A*, Vol. 317, pp. 239-246.

Wetzell R.G. (2001). Limnology: Lake and River Ecosystem, 3rd ed. Academic Press. ISBN –12-744760-1.

Zhaung J. Yan J. Zhang ZF. (1995). National River Chemistry Trends in China: Huanghe and Chanjiang, Ambio- AJ. Hum. Enviro.,24 (5): 275-279.

Pages: 79-104

LIMNOLOGY AND AQUATIC SCIENCE
Edited by: Dr. Shailendra Sharma; Dr. Pawan Kumar 'Bharti'
ISBN: 978-93-5056-735-7
Edition: 2015
Published by: Discovery Publishing House Pvt. Ltd., New Delhi (India)

Impact of Sociobiological Activities on Narmada River Flowing from Omkareshwar to Khalghat (M.P), India

*Shailendra Sharma; **Taniya Sengupta

ABSTRACT

Predicting, quantifying and monitoring the impacts of human activities on river ecology, the environment and people's lively hoods is a very important issue. Environmental assessment is a process whereby all major components of the environment (including physical, chemical, biological and socio-economic) are considered in the planning stages of any development. The baseline conditions that describe the status of the environment before development takes place are assessed through collection and interpretation of environmental data. Predictions are then made on the potential impacts of the proposed development on these baseline environmental conditions. Monitoring programs need to be carefully planned and implemented especially those related to selection of environmental components to be monitored, and frequency of monitoring required. These may be modified over time as new information is obtained on

* Department of Biotechnology and Life Science, AIMS, Dhamnod, M.P, India.
** Department of Zoology, P.M.B Gujarati College, (M.P), India.

the impacts of the development. There are several environmental conditions for the existence of bioindicators. Therefore, by using bioindicators, we can see the environmental conditions of a certain area or the extent of pollution. Qualitative and quantitative assessment of Bacterial diversity with different physiochemical parameters can be use to determine the quality of fresh water on the basis of human health on consumption.

Keywords: *Sociobiological activities, water quality, Narmada River, Microbial Biodiversity.*

INTRODUCTION

In recent years, the environment has been put to serious threat due to the discharge of harmful and toxic chemicals of various types which are primarily the byproducts of developmental activities like industrialization, urbanization, use of chemical fertilizers as well as pesticides and burning of fossil fuel emitting green house gases. River is very rich in bacteria because of the large quantity of dissolved organic matter present in water. Bacterial population is one of the major problems with respect to fresh water pollution. Due to the effect of temperature on the rate of a chemical reaction, one would predict that all bacteria would continue grow at lower pace as the temperature is reduced, until the system freezes. Bacterial number ranges from a few too many millions in a millimetre of water depending upon the source and the level of contamination.

CONCEPT OF BIOINDICATOR

Monitoring by biological methods i.e. as "biomonitoring" is 'an ecological exercise where various kinds of biota are considered in ascertaining the extent of pollution in a water body'. These biota are known as bioindicators. Bioindicators are organisms, chemical markers or biological processes whose change point can beobserved to altered environmental conditions and can be used to identify and quantify the effects of pollutants on the environment. It can also be defined as anthropogenically induced response in biomolecular, biochemical and physiological effects on one or more organisms, population, community or ecosystem level of biological organization. Bioindicators can tell us about the cumulative effects of different pollutants in the ecosystem and about how long a problem may persist, for example: (a) abundance of large marine organism or darkening of coral pigmentation may indicate that a reef has been exposed to poor quality of water for several weeks or months; (b) reduced photosynthesis in plants or coral may indicate stress due to exposure of herbicides.

CRITERIA FOR SELECTING BIOINDICATORS

- Indicator should have casual relationship to ecological significant endpoint.

- Indicator should have specific dose responsiveness to specific stressor i.e. should be sensitive and specific.
- Indicator should have wide temporal and spatial distribution. Indicator should have casual relationship to ecological significant endpoint.
- Indicator should have specific dose responsiveness to specific stressor i.e. should be sensitive and specific.
- Indicator should have wide temporal and spatial distribution.
- Indicator should be available all the year and should have low variability to noise in the system.
- Indicator should have results which are transparent and reproducible.
- Indicator should sometime even surrogate the role of other responses.
- Indicator should be easy to collect and should be cost-effective.

Fig. 6.1: Design of a Bioindicator

Bioindicators may be of two types (Fig. 6.2), (a) accumulation bioindicator: store pollutants without any evident changes in their metabolisms; (b) response bioindicator: react with cell changes or visible symptoms of damage when taking up even small quantity of harmful substances. Types of responses observed while using them may be: (a) ecological changes: involving changes in population density, key species and species diversity; (b) behavioural changes: can be changes in feeding activities, bacterial mobility or web spinning; and (c) physiological changes: can be accumulation of heavy metal, CO2 production, BOD and microbial activity.

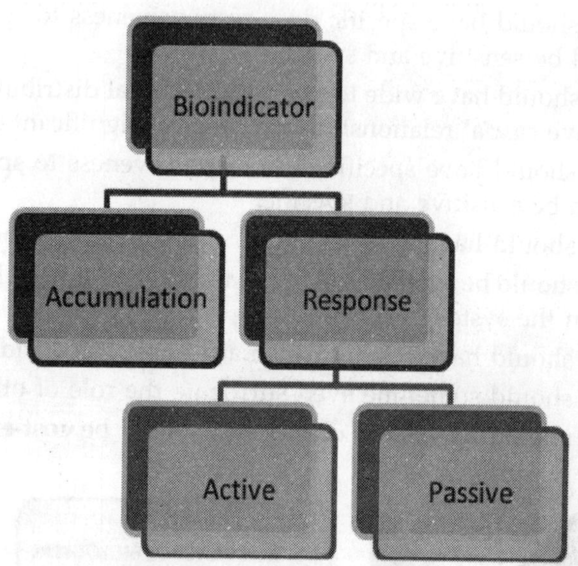

Fig. 6.2: Types of Bioindicators

Organisms including plants, animals, and microorganisms have been adopted in biomonitoring. The majority of bioassays are based on presence absence or on physiological, behavioural or genotypic expression of certain (or groups of) indicator organisms.

MICRO ORGANISMS AS BIOINDICATORS

Microorganisms are diverse group of organisms found in large quantities and are easier to detect and sample. The presence of some microorganisms is well correlated with particular type of pollution and it serves as standard indicator of pollution. Some bacteria produce stress proteins in response to contaminant like cadmium and benzene.

The main source of organic burden of sewage is human body waste, or, faeces, and micro organismsare themselves a main part of human faeces. If a person has gastrointestinal illness or is a carrier of gastrointestinal pathogen such as *Salmonella typhi*, the pathogen is excreted along with rest of microbial population. *Bacteriphage* can too be used as faecal pollution indicators of viral pollution. Two phages somatic *coliphage* which infects *E.coli* host strains and F-specific RNA *coliphage* which infects *E.coli* and related bacteria can be used as indicators. Some other microorganisms have been dealt later; here we will concentrate on bacteria as bioindicator. Ideal bacterial indicator for water analysis (contamination of faecal origin) should have following characteristics:

- The indicator bacterium should be present whenever enteric pathogens are present.
- The indicator bacterium should not reproduce in contaminated water and produce inflated values.

- It should survive longer than the hardiest enteric pathogen.
- It should have greater specificity.
- Its detection assay should be easy to perform.
- It should be harmless to humans.
- Its level in water should have some direct relationship with faecal pollution.

Some important bioindicator bacteria are:

1. Total coliforms and faecal coliforms: the coliform group includes *Klebsiella, Escherichia, Citrobacter* and *Enterobacter*. Faecal coliforms (Fc) are coliforms which respond to elevated temperature of 44.5°C within 24 hours by acid and gas production. These coliforms are derived from intestines of warm blooded animals (*E.coli*). Fc concentration less than 200/100ml indicates Salmonella occurrence ranging from 6.5 to 31% and 1000/100ml indicate double Salmonella concentration. Their presence can be detected by several morphological and biochemical methods. Their quantification is done by MPN method.
2. *Faecal Streptococci:* in water, this genus is represented by Streptococcus bovis, S. equims which are considered to be the true streptococci. It is suggested that faecal coliforms/faecal streptococci (Fc/Fs) ratio of 4 or more indicates water contamination of human origin and Fc/Fs less than 0.7 indicates contamination from animal origin.
3. *Clostridium perfringens*: Their heat and disinfection resistant hardy spores are usedas indicators for water pollution.
4. Other anaerobic bacteria such as *Bifidobacterium* and *Bacteroides* are potential indicators. *Bifidobacterium* are primarily associated with human contamination.
5. Other indicators may be *Pseudomonas spp., yeast, Aeromonas, Staphylococcus, acid fast mycobacteria.*
6. Recently, a bacterium *Vogesella indigofera* was found to respond to heavy metal quantitatively. Under conditions without pollution by metals, this bacterium produces a blue pigmentation which is so distinct that any morphological change might easily be detected visually. In the presence of hexavalent chromium, their pigment production will be obstructed, and the relationship between chromium concentrations and blue-pigment production by the bacterium can be correlated.
7. Bioluminescent bacteria: These are used to test water for environmental toxins. If there are toxins present in the water, the cellular metabolism of bacteria is inhibited or disrupted. This affects quality or amount of light emitted by bacteria. It is very quick method and takes just 30 minutes to complete but could not identify the toxin.Examples of such luminous bacteria include *Photobacterium fisceri, P. phosphoreum.*

Detection and Enumeration of Bioindicators of Water Contamination

More rapid and reliable tests for the presence of microorganisms in water are the future area of thrust. APHA (2002) has developed standard methods for microbiological examination of water. The standard technique involves three successive steps: (1) the Presumptive test (2) The Confirmed test (3) The Completed test.

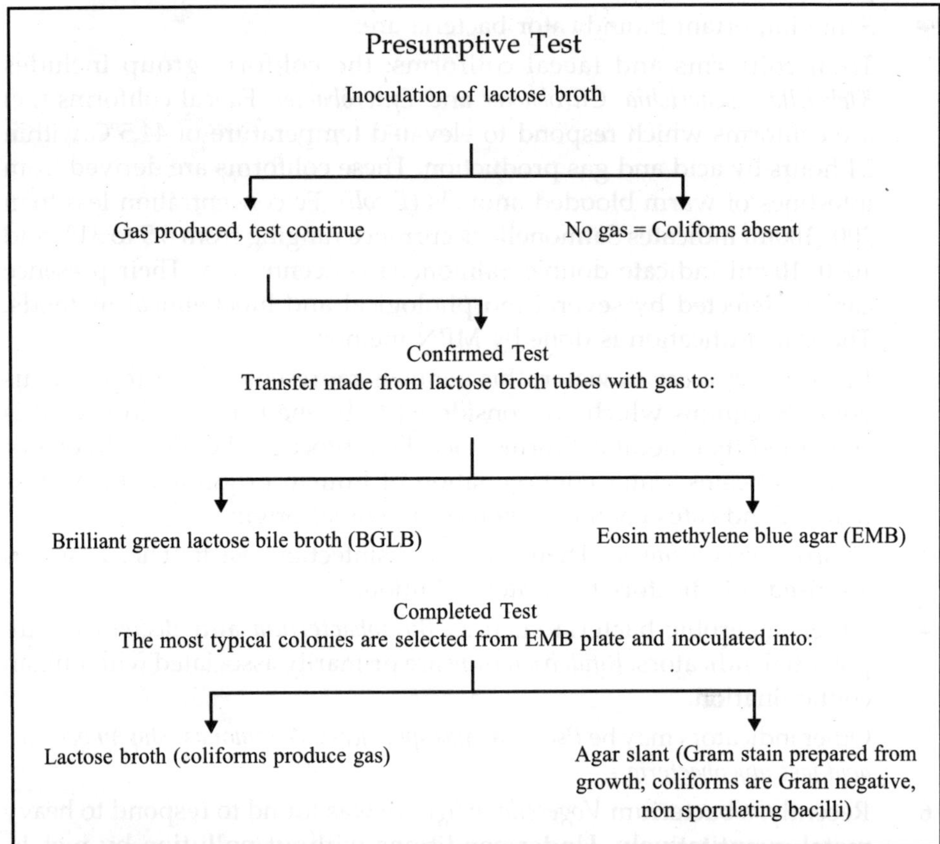

BIOCHEMICAL TESTS

IMViC: A battery of biochemical tests known as IMViC are used in the clinical lab to distinguish between enteric microorganisms. The acronym IMViC stands for indole, methyl red, Voges Proskauer and citrate. The "i" in the acronym is added for pronunciation purposes.

Tryptone broth/Indole test ("I"): Used to demonstrate the ability of a bacterium to produce the enzyme tryptophanase. This enzyme acts on the amino acid to produce "indole".

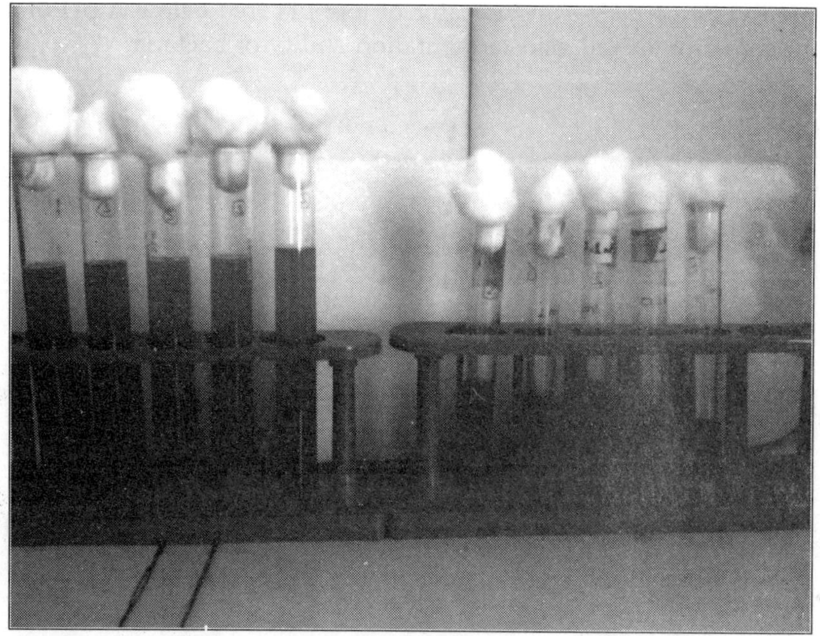

Fig. 6.3: Coliform Test

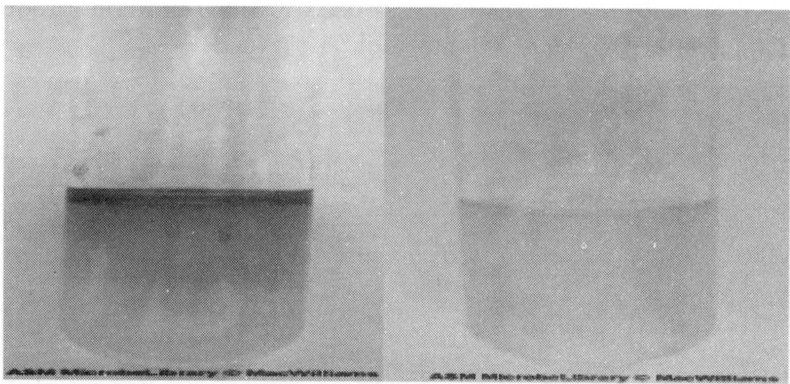

Tryptone broth/Indole – positive result	Tryptone broth/Indole – negative result

Fig. 6.4: Indole Test

Methyl Red ("M") – an indicator of low pH (red belowaa pH of 4.4) – used to show the mixed acid fermentation ability of bacteria.

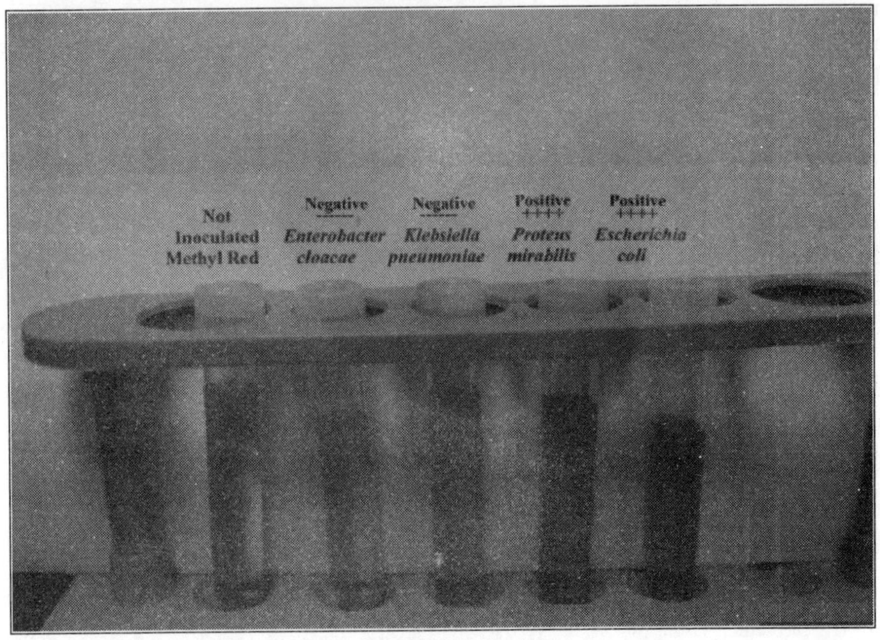

Fig. 6.5: Methyl Red Test

VP -Voges-Proskauer Test ("Vi") – used to show bacterial production of acetoin, also known as 2, 3-butanediol.

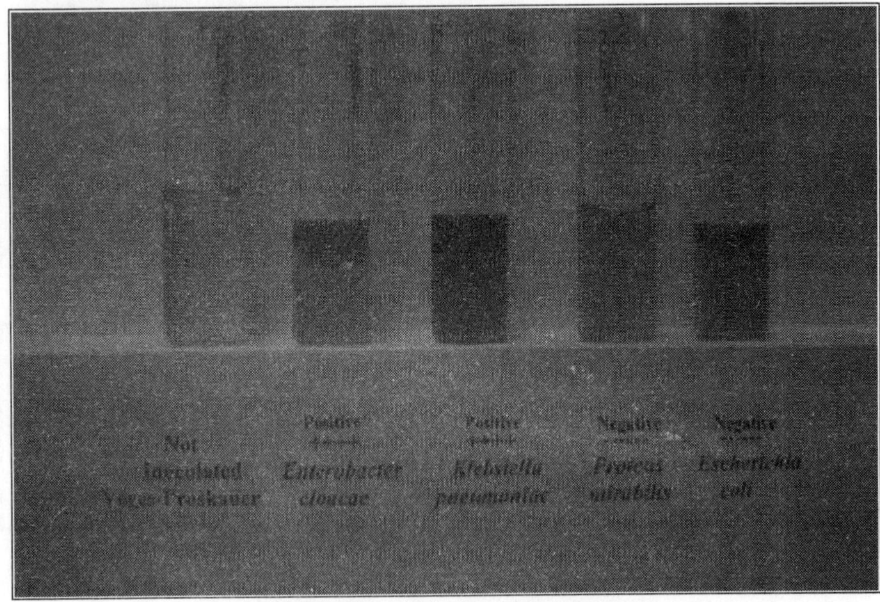

Fig. 6.6: Voges Proskauer Test

Simmons citrate slant ("C") – Simmons citrate agar tests for the ability of a gram-negative organism to import citrate for use as the sole carbon and energy source. Only bacteria that can utilize citrate as the sole carbon and energy source will be able to grow on the Simmons citrate medium, thus a citrate-negative test culture will be virtually indistinguishable from an un inoculated slant.

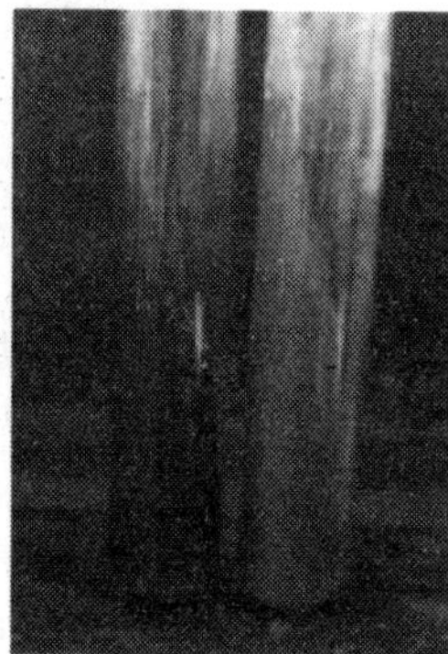

Simmons citrate – blue is a positive citrate test, while green is negative/no growth

Fig. 6.7: Simmons Citrate Test

U -Urea broth: demonstrates the ability of a bacterium to produce the enzyme urease, capable of hydrolyzing urea. Phenol red indicator is added (fuchsia above pH 8.4) to show rise in pH due to accumulation of ammonia.

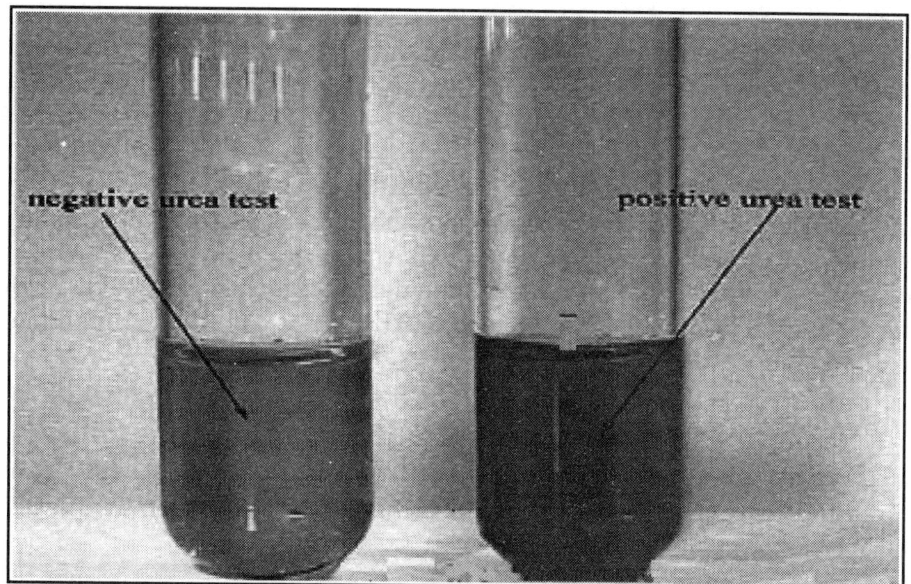

Fig. 6.8

Advantage in selecting Bacteria as Bioindicators

1. The biological methods are quite quick, economical and can be integrated with other relevant studies.
2. Much less equipments are required and large area can be surveyed in less time resulting inlarge amount of information suitable for assessment.
3. Provide cheaper option in comparison to physico-chemical assessment, where chemical analytical equipment, manpower and operational cost are very high.
4. Bacterial assessment methods do not eliminate the need for chemical analysis of water samples, however, these may provide information, which may be integrated with physico-chemical information.
5. The integration of bacterial method with physico-chemical method may provide a system, which is not too expensive and generate necessary information with maximum efficiency.

Information Generated by Bacteriological Bio-assessment

Bacteriological assessment relies on the fact that pollution of water body will cause changes in physico-chemical environment of water and that those changes will disrupt the ecological balance of the system. The measure of extent of ecological upset will depict the severity of pollution.

Bacteriological assessment of often able to indicate an effect on ecosystem arising from a particular use of the water body. It can determine and depict the general effect of anthropogenic factors on ecosystem as well as the presence and effects of common pollution problems (eutrophication, toxicity and industrial inputs etc.) Biological assessments exhibit deleterious changes in aquatic communities and provide systematic information on water quality. The pollution transformation in water and in organisms can be determined through biological surveillance. The long-term effects of polluting substances in water body may be reflected by study of bio-accumulation and bio-magnification. The biological surveillance may depict the conditions resulting from disposal of wastewater, its character and dispersion as well as assess the effectiveness of environmental protection measure. Quantify the toxicity of substances under controlled, defined laboratory conditions (e.g. toxicity studies).

1. The biological systems used as water quality indicators should have specific characteristics.
2. The sampling, sorting, identification and data processing should be as simple as possible involving minimum time and manpower.

Physiochemical Estimations

Various physiochemical parameters can be estimated with the help of Standard books of APHA (2002), Wetzel (2000), Golterman(1989), Trivedi and Goel(1989).

National Sanitation Foundation Water quality Index (NSF WQI)

A water quality index is defined as a rating reflecting the composite influence of different water quality parameters on the overall quality of water. NSF WQI is an excellent management and general administrative tool in communicating water quality information. This index has been widely tested and applied to data from a number of different geographical areas all over the world in order to calculate Water Quality Index Samantray (2009). NSF WQI has taken into consideration nine parameters and a weight was given to each factor according to its importance in water quality.

LITERATURE REVIEW

Pollution of surface and ground water is largely a problem due to rapid urbanization and industrialization. The large scale urban growth due to increase in population or migration of people from rural areas to urban areas has increased domestic effluents while industrial development manifested either due to setting up of new industries or expansion of the existing industrial establishments resulting in generation copious volume of industrial effluents. Though the point sources like domestic waste and sewage are the first order contamination sources in Narmada River. Human activity and cattle grazing also add to the river pollution. Once the contaminants enter the water source it is a difficult and expensive to remove them. Unplanned and injudicious disposal of municipal waste causing pollution of water bodies. The information pertaining to characterization of river water on the basis of several socio biological activities with reference to different physical, chemical and biological parameters are briefly reviewed.

In India, pioneering studies on limnology of river and lake ecosystems were carried out(Chakrabarty *et al.*, 1959) on River Yamuna, (David., 1963) on river Gandak, (Ray et al., 1966) on river Ganga and Yamuna, (Pahwa and Mehrotra., 1966) on river Ganga,(Vyas., 1968) on Pichhola lake, Udaipur (David et al., 1969) on Tungabhadra reservoir, (John., 1978) on the river Kallayi, Kerala, (Raina et al., 1984) on river Jhelum, (Tiwari et al., 1986) on river Jhelum and (1988) on river Subarnarekha, (Qadri et al., 1993) on river Ganga, (Das et al., 1994) on river Ganga, (Hosetti et al., 1994) on Jayanthi nalla and river Panchaganga at Kolhapur, (Rao et al., 1994) on Ooty lake, (Murugesan et al., 1994) on river Tampraparani, (Chaurasia., 1994) on river Mondakini, (Mishra et al., 1994) on river Subarnarekha, (Mitra et al., 1995) on river Mahanadi, (Choubey., 1995) on river Tawa, (Desai., 1995) on river Dudhsagar and Khandepar river, (Kataria et al., 1995) on river Kubza, (Chandra et al., 1996) on river Ramaganga, (Lal., 1996) on Pushkar.

Sarovar, (Banerjee et al., 1999) on river Tikara and Brahmani, (Gambhi., 1999) on Maithon Reservoir,(Jain., 1999) on Khnop Reservoir, (Koshy et al., 1999 ; 2000) on river Pamba, (Bhuvaneswaran et al., 1999) on river Adyar, (Patel., 1999) on Pitamahal Dam, (Sharma et al., 1999) on river Yamuna, (Singh et al., 1999) on River Damodar, (Gyananath et al., 2000) on river Godavari,(Kausik et al., 2000) on river Ghaggar, (Chatterjee et al., 2001) on river Nunia in Asansol, West Bengal, (Kaur et al., 2001) on river Satluj, (Garg et al., 2002) on western Yamuna canal from Tajewala (Haryana) to Haiderpur treatment plant (Delhi), (Abbasi et al., 2002) on Buckinghhum canal, (Martin et al., 2003) on river Tamiraparani, (Srivastava et al., 2003) on river Gaur at Jabalpur, (Sinha et al., 2004) on river Ram Ganga, (Singh et al., 2004) on river Yamuna.

Study carried out in the five rivers were chosen i.e. Alaknanda, Bhagirathi, Ganga, Mandakini and Yamuna. Water samples were collected from nine monitoring stations viz.Devprayag (2), Gangotri (1), Haridwar (2), Rudraprayag (2), Dakpathar (1) and Yamunotri (1). The samples were analyzed for physical, chemical and microbiological parameters. The sample temperatures ranged from 7.8 - 280C, pH from 7.02 - 8.16, turbidity from 1-15 NTU, DO from 6.3 – 10 mg/l and BOD from 1.4 - 4.5 mg/l. The rivers at Gangotri and Yamunotri showed nil BOD. COD ranged from 2.9 - 34.2 mg/L, total alkalinity from 32-118 mg/l and total hardness from 42 - 194 mg/L. All samples showed permissible limit except samples of Haridwar. All samples were positive for E. coli, which indicates fecal pollution of water. The result showed that Brahma Kund in Haridwar, a famous tourist places, is most polluted (Kumar et al., 2010)

Review Related to Influence of Socio biological Activities on Rivers

According to (Adekunle et al., 2004) accessibility and availability of fresh clean water is key to sustainable development and an essential element of health. Unfortunately given the prevalent appalling sanitary conditions pollution of these water sources by chemical and biological agents is not uncommon (Oluyege et al., 2009); Adesomoye et al., 2006). Human pressures on fresh water resources have seriously reduced the security of water for people and river biodiversity across the world. Study by (Vorosmarty et al., 2010) provided that almost 80% of the world's population is at high risk from threats to water security and 65% of river habitats are under threat. (Gopal and Sah., 1993) has reported the water quality and change in biota of River Yamuna during past four decades. The extraction of water through a series of barrages, extensive channelization and heavy discharge of untreated domestic and industrial waste has turned the river into a sewer at least between Delhi and Agra. The human impacts on the river extend beyond the direct use of water to all anthropogenic activities in their entire catchment. (Bhaskar et al., 2003) have studied the physico-chemical and bacteriological parameters on certain locations of the river Torsa and reported that the water was highly alkaline with high concentration of free ammonia with respect to albuminoid ammonia. Water of Kalingadaki river system in the Trans Himalayan region is found to be less polluted reported by (Sharma., 2003). The nature of rivers and their communities are determined by climate, vegetatioin and human activities (Johal., 2005). Excessive amount of such nutrients can also lead to eutrophication (Thilaga et al., 2005). (Akuskar et al., 2006) recommended treatment of water at Manjara river, Dhanegaon due to bad water quality. Khangembam and (Gupta., 2008) regarded Nambul River as one of the most polluted rivers of Manipur which receives a heavy flux of sewage, domestic and agricultural wastes and other effluent which may vary from simple nutrients to toxic and hazardous substances. (Gupta and Pankaj., 2006) reported organic pollution in River Gomati due to anthropogenic activities. Sewage from many parts of Tripur and discharged from the surrounding areas, gets into Noyyal river, which are responsible for the decreased in water quality was reported by (Magudeswaran et al., 2007). (Okendro and Mahanta., 2007) described chloride, bicarbonate alkalinity and pH are indicators of three significant component viz., animal waste, sewage and industrial discharges in to Narmada river. (Verma and Khan., 2007) reported that rapid urbanization and increased anthropogenic activities have been deteriorated the water quality parameter of Arpa river water of Bilaspur in Chhattisgarh. Majority of water characteristics of river Gomati at Sultanpur (Uttar Pradesh) were found to exceed the permissible limits due to sewage discharge and posed problems for the survival of aquatic life and human beings. The river also continuosly receiving daily sewage, domestic and municipal and industrial wastewater from the city war reported (Singh and Singh., 2007). (Shyamala et al., 2008) found pollution at the banks of Cauvery river and Kalingarayan canal in and around Erode town, Tamilnadu. The study showed increased in the pollution load due to the movement of fertilizers, agricultural ashes, industrial effluents and anthropogenic wastes at river Cauvery. (Tripathi et al., 2008) found degradation in water quality of River Rapti near Balrampur in Uttar Pradesh. (Saksena et al., 2008) indicated that Chambal river water quality in Chambal sanctuary area extending up to 600 km is pollution free and can serve as a good habitat. (Raj and Azeez., 2009) have evaluated the water quality of the effluent of river Bharathapuzha, and found that it contained the residues from soaps and detergents, phosphate from the agriculture run-off and water quality was degraded due to the anthropogenic activities such as excessive mining.

The entire array of life in water is affected due to pollution in water. The problem of water quality deterioration is mainly due to human activities such as disposal of dead bodies, discharge of industrial and sewage wastes and agricultural runoff which are major cause of ecological damage and pose serious health hazards (Meitei et al., 2004). The degree of pollution is generally assessed by studying physical and chemical characteristics of the water bodies (Duran and Suicnz., 2007).

Studies related to water pollution of rivers like Godavari, Krishna and Tungbhdra (Mitra., 1982), Cauvery (Somashekar., 1985); Batcha (1997), Jhelum

(Raina et al., 1984), Kosi (Bhatt and Negi., 1985), Morar (Kalpi) (Saksena and Mishra., 1991), Alaknanda (Tiwari et al., 1991), Brahamani (Panda et al., 1991) (Mitra., 1997) Betwa (Datar and Vashishtha., 1992), Ganga (Pandey., 1985; Singh et al., 1990; Sahu et al., 2000); Rao et al., 2000), Godavari (Rao et al., 1993;Rafeeq and Khan., 2002), Yamuna (Meenakshi et al., 2000; Anand et al., 2006), Pachin (Hussain and Ahmed., 2002), Irai (Sawane et al., 2004), Tansa (Shaikh., 2004) and Purna (Meitei et al., 2004) have received greater attention from time to time and during recent years.

Review Related to Water Quality Assessment by Different Physiochemical and Microbiological Parameters

Water quality assessment by different physiochemical and microbiological parameters were carried out by many workers in different Rivers in India such as in Song River in Dehradun (Khanna and Singh., 2007), Yamuna in Agra (Vergese, Singh and Mishra., 2005), River Ganga in Kanpur (Mishra and Sultana., 2005), Umshypri River in Meghalaya(Rajurkar., 2003), River Sanam of Keonjhar(Mohanta and Patna., 2000).

Review Related to Water Quality Assessment by Different Physiochemical Parameters

Different physiochemical parameters for water quality criteria have established (Khajuria and Dutta., 2009; Kesre, Vivek and Mudgal., 2007;Sharma et al., 2007; Hussain and Ahmed., 2002; Sharma., 2002). (Srivastava et al., 2003) reported that Jal Mahal Lake water was most polluted due to high pH, hardness, alkalinity, free carbon dioxide, zinc content, and a low level of dissolved oxygen, contrarily to Ramgarh Lake which was least polluted. Study of physicochemical properties of the Jamwa Ramgarh wetland water in Jaipur revealed that the water quality is not fit for drinking without treatment. Changes in water quality were due to use of land for agriculture after water recedes in the dried up area of the wetland, waste disposal and other polluting practices around the lake (Moundiotiya et al., 2004). (Mohanta amd Patra., 2000) stated that addition of sewage, detergents and large scale human use might be the cause of elevation of hardness. Hardness values declined during monsoon due to dilution of lake water. (Palharya et al., 1993) also recorded similar observation during summer and monsoon in the Narmada River. The peak values of BOD in monsoon were due to high concentration of dissolved and suspended solids in water (Jameel., 1998). In summer BOD values increased due to increased biological activities at elevated temperature (Palharya et al., 1993), high input of organic pollutants and reduced rate of flow (Singh and Srivastva., 1988).

Review Related to Water Quality Assessment by Different Microbiological Parameters

The most common manifestation of waterborne illness is gastrointestinal upset which is usually of short duration. However, in susceptible individuals such as infants, elderly and immuno-compromised individuals, the effects may be more severe or even fatal. *S. enteritidis* and *S. typhimurium*, affect both man and animals, generally cause gastrointestinal infections usually less severe than enteric fever in human (Velge., 2005). *Citrobacter freundii* is found in nutrient-rich waters, soil, decaying plant material as well as in drinking-water containing relatively high concentrations of nutrients. It causes infections of the urinary tract and infant meningitis (Badger., 1999).

Microbiological characteristics of different rivers have been studied by several workers in Attharabanki River (Barik and Patel., 2004), Song River (Khanna and Bhutiani., 2004), Damodar River (Singh., 2002), Alisagar Dam (Trivedi and Goel., 1986). Water pollution through various anthropogenic activities in Narmada in different regions such as Hoshangabad city (Sharma, Dixit, Shah and Vishwakarma., 2008), Mandla (Joshi and Dubey., 1991) have been studied. The excellent study on impact of socio biological activities on Gomti River was also done (Shukla and Sharma., 2009). The biological characteristics of water and wastewater are of fundamental importance to human health, in controlling diseases caused by pathogenic organisms of human origin, and because of the role that they play in the decomposition of waste (Metcalf and Eddy., 2003). Similar works were done by (Karikari et al.., 2004) in Densu River of Ghana, (Maciej Walczak.., 2008) in Vistula and Barda rivers, (Kumarasamy P. et al., 2009) in Cauvery River, South India.

Like, in gangetic river sites witness holy dip and mass bathing by a large number of pilgrims as an old age ritual in India, which is a constant source of contamination of water bodies. (Semwal and Akolkar., 2006).

Review Related to Water Quality Assessment of Narmada River

Several bacterial enteropathogens namely Salmonella, Shigella, Aeromonas, Vibrio cholerae and Escherichia coli have been isolated from the water of river Narmada (Sharma & Rajput, 1996; Sharma & Khokhale, 2005; Sharma et al., 2009). The region of India where the river Narmada flows is predominantly rural and residents rely on untreated water sources for daily water needs.

Fresh water is very important for human health and sound ecosystem, especially aquatic ecosystem.However, freshwater resources have reduced and water quality has also deteriorated throughout the world. Due to contamination of fresh water, along with population explosion, one-fifth of the world's population has no access to safe water (WAO, 2009).

Fresh water and the related microbial population in the distribution system constitute one of the most extensively studied oligotrophic systems (Lechevaller et al., 1987; Pedersen, 1990).

Water quality of Narmada river with reference to different physiochemical activities has been estimated (Sharma et al., 2011). This study provides an informative data and helps to understand the contamination of wastewater in river Narmada and the influences the ecology of river Narmada. The major source of pollutants are local anthropogenic activities, agricultural runoff and by industrial effluent. In the present study it was found that physico-chemical characteristics of a few of the river water samples crossed the maximum permissible limit, due to heavy mixing of effluent waste and domestic sewage it was noticed that the physico-chemical parameters indicates balance of the river Narmada was disturbed. The study concluded that due to discharge of untreated sewage into the Narmada, the water quality of Narmada has been severely deterioted and the potable nature of water is being lost(Sharma et al., 2011).

Narmada River water at Omkareshwar is getting slightly polluted. Informative data of Physio - chemicalParameters helps us to understand the contamination of waste water in river Narmada. Few parameters are found beyond the desirable limits. The major sources of pollution are local anthropogenic activities, agricultural run-off, pilgrim's waste & Domestic waste. The studies conclude that due to discharge of untreated sewage into the Narmada, the water quality of Narmada River is deterioting. If proper measures are taken for the treatment of sewage before discharge and restrictions are put on various anthropogenic activities, Narmada river water would remain healthy in the long run (Verma et al., 2012).

Rationales of the Work

India is a Riverine country. The Narmada is considered as one of the holiest rivers in the country. Millions of people take holy dip in the river Narmada on some auspicious occasions. An overall microbiological and physiochemical analysis in five different stations of Narmada indicate the impact of different anthropogenic and socio biological activities. This needs a regular monitoring and analysis as the river is subjected to various points and non point sources of pollution, which may adversely reduce the quality of water, used for domestic purposes such as drinking and cooking. This work is aimed at assessment of impact on Narmada water quality due to percolation of pollutant from socio biological activities and their effect on human health.

CONCLUSION

The term "biological monitoring" has been widely used in this discussion to include almost any type of data gathered to assess the environmental impact of discharges. In our opinion, biological monitoring is limited to a continue collection of data to establish whether explicitly stated quality control conditions are being met. If these conditions are not being met, there will be an immediate decision to take corrective action. Purpose of bacteriological monitoring include providing early warnings of hazards, detecting spills, detecting environmental trends or cycles, determining the best and least redundant information for monitoring, and evaluating the environmental effects associated with the introduction of genetically engineered organisms into natural systems. One design will not serve each purpose, but if the researchers have clearly defined goals for the monitoring program, powerful designs are possible.

GAP AREA

I have been registered as Research Scholar under Department of life Science (Zoology) since September 2010. By then I have completed Sampling and data collection through various methodologies for 24 months. I have also completed the data analysis and statistical calculations related to my work. At present I am dealing with the writing work for my thesis. I have completed two chapters (Introduction and Material and methods). Now I am busy with the rest chapters& writing and publication of research paper. I am trying my best to submit the thesis in the end of this year.

REFERENCES

Abbasi, S.A., Nipaney, P.C (1995). An Assessment of Drinking Water Quality of the Open Wells in Malappuram Coast, Kerala. Poll Res. 14 (3): 313-316.

Abbasi, S.A., Khan, F.I., Sentilvelan, K. and Shabudeen, A. (2002). Modelling of Backingham Canal Water Quality. Indian J. Environ. Hlth., 44(4): 290-297.

Abdo, M.H., Sabae, S.Z, Haroon, B.M, Refat, B.M and Mahammed, A.S (2010) Physiochemical Characteristics, Microbial Assessment and Antibiotic Susceptibility of Pathogenic Bacteria of Ismalia Canal Water, River Nile. Egypt. J. of Amer.Sc. 6(5): 234-250.

Abdo, M.H (2005) Physiochemical Characteristics of Abu Za'baal Ponds, Egypt. Egyptian J. of Aqua. Research.31 (2): 1-15.

Adhikari, S. and Gupta, S. K. (2002). Assessment of the Quality of Sewage Effluents from Dry Weather Flow Channel, Calcutta. Indian J. Environ. Hlth., 44(4): 308-313.

Agrawal, K. Ashok and Rajwar, S.G (2010) Physiochemical and Microbiological Study of Tehri Dam Reservoir, Garhwal Himalaya, India. J. of Amer. Sc 6(6): 65-71.

Akaninwar, J.O., Anasike, E.O., and Egwim, O. (2007) Effect of Indomic Industrial Effluent Discharge on Microbial Properties of New Calabar river. Scientific Resear. And Essay. 2(1): 1-5.

Akuskar, S.K. and Gaikwad, A.V. (2006). Physico-chemical Analysis of Manjara Dam Back Water of Manjara River Dhanegoan, Maharashtra. India. Ecol. Environ. and Conserv 12(1): 73-74.

Almasri, M.L. and J.J. Kaluarachchi (2004). Assessment and Management of Long Term Nitrate Pollution of Groundwater in Agriculture-domonated Watersheds. Journal of Hydrology, 1295 (1-4): 225-245.

Ammann, Adrian A., Eduard Hoehn and Sabine Koch (2003). Groundwater Pollution by Roof Infiltration Evidenced with Multi-tracer Experiments. Water Research 37(5): 1143-1153.

APHA (2002) Standard Method for Examination of Water, American Public Health Association Inc. Newyork 22nd Ed. 2002. pp. 10-161.

Banerjee, S.K., Banerjee, M and Agarwal, K.M. (1999). Study of Tikara and Brahmani River Ecosystems. Env Eco, 17(2): 296-305.

Barik, R.M, Patel, R.K (2004) Seasonal Variation of Water Quality of Atharabanki River Paradip, Ind. J. Env Port. 24(3): 161-166.

Barrett, P. (1953) Relationship Between Alkalinity and Absorption and regeneration of Added Phosphorus in Fertilized Trout Lakes. Trans Am. Fish. Soc., 82, 78-90.

Batcha Anvar, S.M. (1998) Studies on Hydrography and Domestic Pollution Problems in the North Bank of River Cauvery. J. Environ. Pollut., 5: 69-71.

Bauder, T.A., Cardon, G.E., Waskom, R.M., & Davis, J.G (2004) Water Quality Criteria. http://www.ext.colostate.edu/pubs/crops/00506.html.

Begum, A. and Harikrishna (2008) Study on the Quality of Water in Some Treams of Cauvery River. J.Chem., 2(5): 377-384.

Begum, A., Ramaiah, M., Harikrishna, Irfaanulla Khan and Veena, K. (2009) Heavy Metal Pollution and Chemical Profile of Cauvery River Water. J. Chem., 6(1): 47-52.

Begum,A and Harikrishna (2008) Study on the Quality of Water in Some Stream of Cauvery River. E.J. of Chem.5(2): 377-384.

Bhadauria and Seema (1997). Characterization of Agricultural Soils Irrigated with Petroleum Refinery Effluents Physicochemicala Analysis. J. Environ. Pollu., 4(4): 295-302.

Bhandari, N.S. and Nayal, K. (2008). Correlation Study on Physico-chemical Parameters and Qualitys Assessment of Kosi River Water, Uttarakhand. J. Chem., 2(5): 342-346.

Bhaskar, B., Mukherjee, S., Chakraborty, R. and Nanda, A.K. (2003). Physico-chemical and Bacteriological Investigation on the River Torsa of North Bengal. J. Environ. Biol., 24: 125-133.

Bhatt, J.P., Jain, A, Bhaskar, A. and Pandit, M.K. (2001). Pre-impoundment Study of Biotic Communities of Kistobazar Nala in Purulia, West Bengal. Curr. Sci., 81(10): 1332-1337.

Bhatt, S.D. and U. Negi (1985) Hydrology and Phytoplankton Population in River Kosi of Western Himalaya (U.P.). Ind. J. Ecol., 122, 141-146.

Bhuvaneswaran, N., G. Santhakalshmi and S. Rajeswari (1999). Water Quality of River Adyar in Chennai City – The River a Boon or a Bane. Indian J Environ Prot., 19(6): 412-415.

Badger JD, Stins MF, Kim KS (1999) Citrobacter Freundii Invades and Replicates in Human Brain Microvascular Endothelial Cells. Infect Immun 67: 4208-4215.

Chandra, R., Y. Bahadur and B. K. Sharma (1996). Monitoring the Quality of River Ramganga Waters of Bareilly. Poll Res., 15(1): 31-33.

Chatterjee, C. and M. Raziuddin (2001). Bacteriological Status of River Water in Asansol Town in West Bangal, J Env Polln, 8(2): 217-219.

Chaurasia, S. and G.K. Kanran (1994). Impact Assessment of Mass Bathing in River Mandakini during Ashwamedha Yagna April 1994. Indian J Environ Prot., 14 (5): 356-359.

Chavan, R.P., Lokhande, R.S. and Rajput, S.I. (2005). Monitoring of Organic Pollutants in Thane Creek Water. Natl. Environ. Pollu. Technol., 4(4): 633-636.

Chin D.A (2000) Water Resources Engineering. Prentice- Hall Inc. Upper Saddle River, New Jersey, 585-635.

Choubey V.K. (1995). Water Chemistry of Tawa River and Reservoir in Central India. Energy Env Monit, 11(2): 167-176.

Das, N.K. and R.K. Sinha (1994). Pollution Status of River Ganga at Patna (Bihar), India. J. Freshwater Bio, 6(2): 159-161.

Datar, M.O. and R.P. Vashishtha (1992) Physico-chemical Aspects of Pollution in River Betwa. Ind. J. Environ. Protect., 12: 577-580.

David, A. (1963). Report on Fisheries Survey of River Gandak (North Bihar). Sur. Rep.Cent. Inl. Fish Res. Inst. Barrackpore, 1: 24-39.

David, A., P. Ray, B.V. Govind, K.V. Rajgopal and R.K. Banerjee (1969). Limnology and Fisheries of Tungbhadra Reservoir, Bull Cent. Inl. Fish Res. Inst. Barrackpore, 13: 188.

Desai, P.V. (1995). Water Quality of Dudhsagar River of Dudhsagar (Gao), India. Poll Res. 14(4): 377-382.

Dugan, P.R. (1972). Biochemical Ecology of Water Pollution. Plenum Press London.

Duran, Mustafa and Menderes Suicmez (2007) Utilization of Both Benthic Macroinvertebrates and Physicochemical Parameters for Evaluating Water Quality of the Stream Cekerek (Tokat, Turkey). J. Environ. Biol., 28: 231-236.

Durfor, C.N., E. Becker (1964). Public Water Supplies of the 100 Largest Cities in the U.S. US Geol. Sur. Water Supply Paper, 1812: 364.

Ebaire Ekibe & Luo Zejiao (2010) Water Quality Monitoring in Nigeria, Case Study of Nigeria's Industrial Cities. J. of Amer. 6(4): 22-28.

Ekhaise F.O and Anyasi C.C (2005) Influence of Breweries Effluent Discharge on the Microbiological and Physiochemical Quality of Ikpoba River, Nigeria. African. J. of Biotech. 4(10): 1062-1065.

FEPA (1991) Guidelines and Standard for Environmental Control in Nigeria Published by the Federal Environmental Protection Agency Lagos. pp 15-34.

Fokmare, A.K. and Musaddiq, M. (2002). A Study on Physico-chemical Characteristics of Kakshi Lake and Purna River Wastes in Akola District of Maharashtra (India). Natl. Environ. Poll. Technol., 1: 261-263.

Fokmare, A.K. and M. Musaddiq (2002) A Study of Physico-chemical Characteristics of Kapsi Lake and Purna River Waters in Akola District of Maharastra, India. Nat. Environ. Pollut. Technol., 1, 261-263.

Francis-Floyd, R. (2003). Dissolved Oxygen for Fish Production. Fact Sheet FA 27. Florida: Department of Fisheries and Aquaculture, Florida Cooperative Extension Service, Institute of Food and Agricultural Sciences, University of Florida.

Gambhi, S.K. (1999). Physico-chemical and Biological Characteristics of Water of Maithon Reservoir of D.V.C. Poll Res., 18(4): 541-544.

Gangwar, K.K., Joshi, B.D. and Deepali (2008). Impact of Mass Bathing on Water Quality of River Ganga during Ram Navmi Festival of Ardh-kumbh, at Har ki Pauri, Haridwar. Indian J. Environ. Sci., 12(2): 107-110.

Garg, V.K, R. Gupta, A. Malik and M. Pahwa (2002). Assessment of Water Quality of Western Yamuna Canal from Tajewala (Haryana) to Haiderpur Treatment Plant (Delhi). Indian J. of Env. Protection, 22(2): 191-196.

Gunkel G, Kosmol J, Sobral M, Rohn H, Montenegro S and Australiano J (2007) Sugar Cane Industry as a Source of Water Pollution- Case Study on the Situation in Ipojuca river, Pernambuco, Brazil. Water, Air & Soil Pollution, 180, 1-4, March, 261-269.

Gupta, A.K. and Pankaj, P.K. (2006). Comparative Study of Eutrophication and Heavy Meatl Pollution in Rivers Ganga and Gomati with Reference to Human Activities. Natl. Environ. Pollu. Technol., 5(2): 229-232.

Gyananath, G, S.V. Shewdiker and S. Samiuddin (2000). Water Quality Analysis of River Godavari during 'Holi Mela' at Nanded. Poll Res. 19(4): 673-674.

Herzog, D.J. (1996). Evaluating the Potential Impacts of Mine Wastes on Ground and Surface Waters. Fuel and Energy Abstracts, 37(2): 139.

Hiware, C.J. and B.V. Jadhav (2001) Biological Studies of Manjar River Near Kallam, District Osmanabad, Maharastra, India. J. Aqua. Biol., 16, 11-13.

Horne, R.A. (1978). The Chemistry of Our Environment. Wiley Inter Science Pub. John Wiley and Sons, New York.

Hosetti, B.B., A.R. Kulkarni and H.S. Patil (1994). Water Quality in Jayanthi Nalla and Pancha Ganga at Kolhapur. Indian J Environ Hlth, 36(2): 120-127.

Hussain M.F, Ahmed. I (2002) Variability in Physiochemical Parameters of Panchin River, Itanagar. Ind. J. Environ hlth. 44(4): 329-336.

ICMR. 1975. Manual of Standard of Quality of Drinking Water Supplies. Indian Council of Medical Research. Spe. REF. Sci. 44: pp. 27-28.

IS (1991) Tolerance Limits for Inland Surface Waters Subject to Pollution (IS-1055: 1991), ISI New Delhi, India.

ISI (1974) Tolerance Limits for Inland Surface Water when Used as Water for Public Water Supplies and Bathing Ghats. Indian Standard Institute. New Delhi IS: 2296.

Jain, P.K. (1999). Assessment of Water Quality of Khnop Reservoir in Chatarpur, MP India. Eco Env Conserv, 5(4): 401-403.

Jameel, A. (1998). Physico-chemical Studies in Vyyakondan Channel Water of Cauvery, Poll. Res. 17(2): 111-114.

Jayaraman P.R, Devi T.G and Nayar T.V (2003) Water Quality Studies on Karamana River, Tiruvantapuram District, South Kerela, India. Poll. Res. 22(1): 89-100.

Johal, M.S. (2005). Biodiversity with Special Reference to Indian Freshwater Fishes. Proceeding. Natl. Sem., 'New Trends in Fishery Development in India'. (Ed.: M.S. Johal). February, 16-18, 2005. Punjab University, Chandigarh: 11-22.

Johnson, M.E.C (2004) Silica Content of Two Hyderabad Lakes, Andhra Pradesh, India. J. Aqua. Biol., 19, 61-62.

Joseph, P.V., & Claramma, J. (2010). Physicochemical Characteristics of Pennar River, a Fresh Water Wetland in Kerala, India. E-Journal of Chemistry, http://www.e-journals.net. 7(4): pp. 1266-1273.

Kar, P.K., Pani, K.R., Pattanayak, S.K., & Sahu, S.K. (2010). Seasonal Variation in Physico-chemical and Microbiological Parameters of Mahanadi River Water in and Around Hirakud, Orissa, India. J. The Ecoscan. 4(4): pp. 263-271.

Karikari, A.Y., & Ansa-Asare, O.D. (2004). Physico-chemical and Microbial Water Quality Assessment of Densu River of Ghana. West Afr. J. appl. Ecol. 1: 23-34.

Karnchanawong, S. and S.K.T. Ikeguchi (1993). Monitoring and Evaluation of Shallow Well Water Quality Near a Waste Disposal site. Environmental International, 19(6): 579-587.

Kataria, H.C. (1995). Turbidity Measurement in Groundwater of Bhopal City. J Nature Conservators, 7(1): 79-82.

Kaur, H., J. Syal and S.S. Dhillon (2001). Water Quality Index of the River Satluj. Poll Res., 20(2): 199-204.

Kaushik. A, Kumar. A, Sharma J.S, Sharma H.R (2004) Ground Water Quality Assessment in Different Land Use Area of Faridabad and Rohtak Cities Haryana Using Deviation. Intec. J. Environ. Biot. 25(2): 173-180.

Kelkar, P.S., Nanoti, M.V. (2005). Impact Assessment of Ganga Action Plan on River Quality at Varanasi, J. Indian Water Work Assoc., 37(3): 225-234.

Keramat, A.A. (2008). Environmental Impact on Nutrient Discharged by Aquaculture Waste Water at on the Haraz River. J. of Fish. and Aquat. Sci., 3(5): 275-279.

Kesre, Vivek, Mugdal L.K, Khanna D.R, Matta, Gagan and Kumar D (2007) Study of Physiochemical Parameters for a Reservoir at Khandwa District (M.P). Environ. Cons. J. 8(3): 127-132.

Khajuria M, and Dutta S.P.S (2009) Physiochemical Characteristics of Raw Water of River Tawi Near Sitlee Water Treatment Plant Jammu. Environ Conc. J.10(3): 45-52.

Khangembam, B. and Gupta, A. (2008). Limnological Studies of Nambul River with Reference to its Resources. Flora and Fauna, 12(2): 193-198.

Khanna D.R, Bhutiani R (2004) Water Analysis at a Glance. Pub. Action for Sustainable Efficacious Development and Awareness (ASEA). pp. 1-108.

Khanna D.R, Singh V, Bhutiani R, Chandra, Kumar Satish, Matta, Gagan, Kumar D (2007) A Study of Biotic and Abiotic Factors of Song River at Dehradun, Uttarakhand. Environ. Cons.J.8(3): 117-126.

Khatavakar R.S, Shah N.V, Rao K.R and Navale R.A (2004) Variation in Physiochemical Parameters in Fresh Water Tanks in and around Solapur City, Maharastra. J. Aqua Biol.19: 111-114.

Koshy M and Nayar T.V (2000) Water Quality of River Pamba at Kozhencherry. Poll. Res.19(4): 665-668.

Koshy, M. and V. Nayar (1999). Water Quality Aspects of River Pambha. Poll Res., 18(4): 501-510.

Koshy, M., T. Vasudevan Nayar (2000). Water Quality of River Pambha at Kozhencherry. Poll Res., 19(4): 665-668.

Kriubuauthy A, Kavitha B.S, Mariamma Nand Rajammal T (2005) Assesment of Water Quality of Orathupalayau Resrvoir, Erore District, Tamil Nadu. J. Ecophysoil. Occup.hlth. 5: 53-54.

Kulkarni, R.R., Sharma, R. N. and Bukari, M. (2002). Diurnal Variations of Physico-chemical Aspects of Pollution in Khushavati river at Quepem, Goa. J. Aquat. Biol., 17(1): 27-28.

Kulshrestha, H. and S. Sharma (2006) Impact of Mass Bathing during Ardhkumbh on Water Quality Status of River Ganga. J. Environ. Biol., 27, 437-440.

Kumar, A, Bisht. B.S., Joshi. V.D., Singh.A.K., Talwar.A (2010) Physical, Chemical and Bacteriological Study of Water from Rivers of Uttarakhand,J Hum Ecol, 32(3): 169-173.

Kumar, S. S, Puttaiah, E.T., Manjappa, S., Prakash, Naik, S. and Kumar, V. (2006). Water Quality Assessment of River Tunga, Karnataka. Environ. Eco., 24(5): 23-26.

Lal, A.K. (1996). Effects of Mass Bathing on Water Quality of Pushkar Sarovar. Indian J Environ Prot, 16(11): 831-836.

LeChevaller MW, Babcook TM, Lee RG, (1987). Examination and Characterization of Distribution.

Lendhe, R.S. and Yeragi, S.G. (2004). Seasonal Variation in Primary Productivity Phirangi-Kharbav Lake, Bhiwadi District Thane, Maharashtra J. Auqat. Biol., 19(2): 49-51.

Lind O.T (1979) Handbook of Common Methods in Limnology C.V Moshy Co. 2nd Ed, St Louis, Missouri, pp. 199.

Maciej Walczak (2008) Changes of Microbial Indices of Water Quality in the Vistula and Brda Rivers as a Result of Sewage Treatment Plant Operation., International Journal of Oceanography and Hydrobiology. Vol. XXXVII, No. 2: 65-75.

Magudeswaran, P.N. and Ramchandaran, T. (2007). Water Quality Index of River Noyyal at Tripur, Tamilnadu, India. Natl. Environ. and Pollu. Technol., 6(1): 51-54.

Marchese, M.R., A., Rodriguez, R., Paola J. P. and Maria, R. C. (2008). Benthic Invertebrates Structure in Wetlands of a Tributary of the Middle Parana River (Argentina) Affected by Hydrologic and Anthropogenic Disturbances. J. Environ. Biol., 29(3): 343-348.

Martin, P. and m. A. Haniffa (2003). Water Quality Profile in the South India River Tamiraparani. Indian J. of Env. Protection, 23(3): 286-292.

Maticie, B (1999). The Impact of Agriculture on Groundwater Quality in Slovenia: Standards and Strategy. Agricultural Water Management, 40(2-3): 235-247.

McLellan, S.L., Daniels,A.D., & Salmore, A.K.(2001). Clonal Population of Thermotolerant Enterobacteriaceaes in Recreational Water and Their Potential Interference with faecal Escherichia coli counts. Applied Environ. Microbiol. 6(7): pp. 4934-4938.

Meenakshi, V.K. Garg, K. Yadava, R. Gupta and M. Malik (2002) Water Quality Monitoring of Western Yamuna Canal from Tajewala to Haiderpur Treatment Plant, Delhi. Res. J. Chem. Environ., 6, 21-23.

Meitei, N.S., P.M. Patil and A.B. Bhosle (2004) Physico-chemical Analysis of Purna River for Potability. J. Aqua. Biol., 19, 103-105.

Meitei, N.S., V. Bhargava and P.M. Patil (2004a) Water Quality of Purna River in Purna Town, Maharastra State. J. Aqua. Biol., 19, 77-78.

Metcalf & Eddy. (2003) Wastewater Engineering Treatment and Reuse, Forth Edition., New York, USA: McGraw Hill.

Mikkelsen, P.S., Hafliger, M. Ochs, P. acobsen, J. C. Tjell and M. Boller (1997) Pollution of Soil and Groundwater from Infiltration of Highly Contaminated.

Mishra P.C, Pradha K.C, Patel R.K (2003) Quality of Water for Drinking and Agriculture in and Around Mines in Keonjhar District Orrisa. Indian. Environ. J. helth. 45(3): 213-250.

Mishra Pratibha, Naheed Sultana (2005) Water Quality of River Ganga at Kanpur. Indian. J. Env. Port.25(20): 938-940.

Mishra, A. and Tripathi, B.D. (2007). Seasonal and Temporal Variation in Physico-chemical and Bacteriological Characteristics of River Ganga in Varansi. Cuur. World Environ., 2(2): 149-154.

Mishra, A., J.S. Datta Munshi, M. Singh (1994). Heavy Metal Pollution of River Subarnarekha in Bihar. Part I: Industrial effluents. J Fresh Water Bio, 6(3): 197-199.

Mishra, S.R. and D.N. Saksena (1991) Pollutional Ecology with Reference to Physicochemical Characteristics of Morar (Kalpi) River, Gwalior (M.P.). In: Current Trends in Limnology (Ed.: Nalin K. Shastree). Narendra Publishing House Delhi, India. pp. 159-184.

Mitra, A.K. (1995). Water Quality of Some Tributaries of Mahanadi. Indian J Environ Hlth, 37 (1): 26-36.

Mitra, A.K., (1982) Chemical Characteristics of Surface Water at Selected Gauging Stations in the River Godavari, Krishna and Tungabhadra. Ind. Environ. Hlth., 24: 165-179.

Mitra, A.K. (1997) Impact of Waste Water Inflow on Water Quality of River Brahamani. Ind. J. Environ. Hlth., 39, 257-264.

Mohanta B.K, Patna A.K (2000) Studies on the Water Quality Index of River Sanam Acchakandan at keonjhar Garh orrisa. Poll. Res.19(3): 377-385.

Mohanta, B.K., and A.K. Patra. (2000) Studies on the Water Quality Index of River Sanmachhakandana at Keonjhar Garh, Orissa. Poll. Res. 19: 3, 377-385.

Moundiotiya C., R. Sisodia, M. Kulshreshtha, and A.L. Bhatia. (2004) A Case Study of the Jamwa Ramgar.

Murugesan, A.G., K.M.S.A. Abdul Hameed, N. Sukumaran (1994). Water Quality Profile of the Perennial river Tampraparani. Indian J Environ Prot, 14 (8): 567-572.

Nath, D. and D.K. De (1998) Preliminary Studies on the Changes in the Physicochemical Characteristics of Hooghly Estuary in Relation to Tides. J. Inland Fish. Soc. India, 30: 29-36.

Nath, D. and N.P. Srivastava (2001) Physico-chemical Characteristics of Narmada for the Stretch Sandia to Mola in M.P. State in the Context of Construction of Reservoirs on the River or its Tributaries. J. Inland Fish. Soc. India, 33, 17-24.

Negi R.K, Negi T and Joshi P.C (2008) Study of Physiochemical Parameters of Hinval Fresh Water Stream and Ganga River Water at Shivpuri in the Garhwal Region. J. Env. Biol. Sc.22(2): 203-212.

Niewoikar S (2000) Bacteriological Monitoring of River Water Quality in North Area of Wigry National park. Pol. J. of Environ studies.9(4): 291-299.

Okendro, N. Singh, S.K. and Mahanta, P.C. (2007). Multivariate Statistical Analysis of Water Quality Data in Narmada River. J. Ecopysiol. Occup. Hlth., 7: 45-53.

P. Samantray, B.K. Mishra, C.R. Panda, and S.P. Rout (2009) " Assessment of Water Quality Index in Mahaadi and Atharabanki Rivers and Taldanda Canal in Paradip Area, India", Journal of Human Ecology, 26(3): 153-161.

Pahwa, D.V. and S.M. Mehrotra (1966). Observations of Fluctuations in the Abundance of Planton in Relation to Certain Hydro-biological Conditions of River Ganga. Proc. Nat. Acd. Sc. Ind., 36 (2): 157-189.

Palharya, J.P., V.K. Siriah, and S. Malviya. (1993) Environmental Impact of Sewage and Effluent Disposal on Theriver System, Aashish Publ. House, New Delhi.

Panda, R.B., B.K. Sahu, B.K. Sinha and A. Nayak (1991) Characterization of Brahmini River Water. Ind. J. Environ. Hlth., 33, 252-256.

Pandey, N.C (1985) Pollution of River Ganga in U.P. with Specific Reference to Varanasi. Civic affairs. 32, 52-59.

Pani, B.S. (1986). "Outfall diffusers". In. Abstract of the National Seminar on Air and Water Pollution, April 1986, University College of Engineering, Burla.

Patel, R.K. (1999). Assessment of Water Quality of Pitamahal Dam. Indian J EnvironProt, 19(6): 437-439.

Pelczar J.M, Chan E.C.S, Krieg N.R (2005) Microbiology: Tata McGraw Hill Pub, 5th Ed. ISBN-0-07-462320-6: pp. 261-330.

Pesce, S.F., & Wunderlin, D.A., (2000). Use of Water Quality Indices to Verify the Impact of C´ordoba city (Argentina) on Suqu´ya River. Water Res., 34(11): pp 2915-2926.

Pillay, T.V.R. (2004). Aquaculture and the Environment. Blackwell Publishing, U.K. 16-18p.

Prasad, G. B. (2005). Assessment of Water Quality in Canals of Krishna Delta Area of Andhra Pradesh, Natl. Environ. Pollu. Technol., 4(4): 521-523.

Qadri, S.A., J. Mussarrai, A.M. Siddiqi and M.Ahmad (1993). Studies on the Water Quality of River Ganga at Narora and Kachla (UP). Cheml Environ Res, 2 (1 & 2): 101-108.

Rafeeq, M.A. and A.M. Khan (2002) Impact of Sugar Mill Effluents on the Waterquality of the River Godavari Near Kandakurthi Village, Nizamabad District, Andhra Pradesh. J. Aqua. Biol., 17, 33-35.

Raina, V., A.R. Shah and S.R. Ahmed (1984) Pollution Studies on River Jhelum I. An Assessment of Water Quality. Indian J. Environ. Hlth., 26, 187-201.

Raina, V., A.R. Shah and S.R. Ahmed (1984). Pollution Studies on River Jhelum: an Assessment of Water Quality. Indian J. Evniron. Hlth., 26: 187.

Raj, N. and Azeez, P.A. (2009). Spatial and Temporal Variation in Surface Waterchemistry of a Tropical River, the river Bharathapuzha, India. Curr. Sci., 96(2): 245-251.

Rajurkar N.S, Hongri B, Patwardhan A.M (2003) Physiochemical and Biological Investigation of River Umshrpi at Shillong Meghalaya. Indian. J. Environ helth.45(1): 45-92.

Ramamurty N, Subashini J and Raju S (2005) Physiochemical Properties of Palar River in Tamil Naidu. Indian J. Env.port.25(10): 925-928.

Rao, K.S., D. Pandmrathy and Babu Ram (1993) Monitoring the Quality of Godavari Waters during and After the 1991 Pushkaram at Rajamundry. Pollut. Res., 12, 191-195

Rao, V.N.R., R. Mohan, V. Hariprasad and R. Ramasubramanian (1994). Sewagepollution in the High Altitude Ooty Lake, Udhagamandalam Causes and Concern. Poll.Res., 13(2): 133-150.

Ray, P., S.B. Singh and K. I. Sehgal (1966). A Study of Some Aspect of Ecology of River Ganga and Yamuna at Allahbad, U. P. in 1958-59. Proc. Nat. Acad. Sci. India,36 (3): 235.

Roy P.N (2002) Studies on Hydrological Status of Stream in Santel Parganas (South Bihar) with Special Reference to Pollution. Indian J. Environ & Ecoplan.3(1): 127-130.

Sabae S.Z, Abdo M.H, Refat B.M, Horoun B.M, Hassanin M.F (2006) Evaluation of Water Quality, Microbial Diversity and Antibiotic Susceptibility of Pathogenic Bacteria in the River Nile, Egypt. Inter. J. of Lakes & Rivers. Issue No. 0973-4570, 1: 97-116.

Sabae S.Z, Emam W.M and Rabeh S.A (2008) Microbial Characteristics of Wadi E1-Raiyan Lakes, Egypt. Egypt. J. Egy. Acad. Soc. Env. Devlop. 9(2): 17-28.

Sabae S.Z, Rabeh S.A (2006) Evaluation of the Microbial Quality of River Nile Water at Dameitta brancg. Egypt.

Saha, T, Ghosh, P.B., Madal, C.C. and Bandyopadhyay, T.S. (2000). Quality Assessment of Bagjola Canal Waste Water, Calcutta. J. Inland Fish Soc. India, 32(2): 76-80.

Sahu, B.K., Rao, R.J., Behara, S.K. and Pandit, R.K. (1996). Diel Fluctualtions of Some Water Quality. Poll. Research 15(1): 61-65.

Sakhare V.B and Joshi P.K (2002) Ecology of Palas Nilegaon Reservoir in Osmanbad District, Maharastra. J. Aqua. Biol.18: 17-22.

Saksena, D.N., Garg, R.K. and Rao, R. J. (2008). Water Quality and Pollution Status of Chambal River in National Chambal Sanctuary, Madhya Pradesh. J. Environ. Biol., 29(5): 701-710.

Semwal, N., & Akolkar.(2006). Water Quality Assessment of Sacred Himalayan River of Yttarakhand. Curr. Sci., 9(1): pp. 486-496.

Shamruck, M., M. Yavuz Corapcioglu and Fayek A. A. Hassona (2001). Modeling the Effect of Chemical Fertilizers on Groundwater Quality in the Nile Valley Aquifer, Egypt. Groundwater, 39(1): 59-67.

Sharma.S., Vishwakarma.V., Dixit.S., Jain.p. (2011) Evaluation of Water Quality of Narmada River with Reference to Physcochemical Parameters at Hoshangabad City, MP, India. Res.J.Chem.Sci.1(3): 40-48.

Sharma A and Rajput S, (1996) Salmonella as an Index of Pollution of Fresh Water Environments. Environmental Monitoring Assessment 41: 67-76.

Sharma A. and Khokale D, (2005). Characterization of Aeromonads Isolated from River Narmada at Jabalpur (M.P.). Indian Journal of Microbiology 45 (4): 265-68.

Sharma A. and Rajput S, (1996). Microbial Quality and Persistence of Entero Pathogenics in Fresh Water Environments. Journal of Ecology and Environmental Conservation 2: 29-36.

Sharma A. and Khokale D, (2005). Biotyping and Antibiograms Analysis of Aeromonas Isolated from River Narmada. International Journal of Hygiene and Environmental Health 208: 425-433.

Sharma, B.S. (1999). A Study on Water Quality of River Yamuna at Agra. Indian Environ Prot, 19(6): 440-441.

Sharma, S. (2003). Agricultural Use of Sewage Waters in Gwalior: Ionic Quality Assessment. Indian J. Environ. Hlth., 4(40): 343-348.

Sharma, S. (2003). Agricultural Use of Sewage Waters in Gwalior: Ionic Quality Assessment. Indian J. Environ. Hlth., 4(40): 343-348.

Shrivastava, V.S. and Patil, P.R. (2002). Tapti River Water Pollution by Industrial Wastes. A Stastical Approach. Natl. Environ. Pollu. Technol., 1: 285-290.

Shukla. A, Sharma A.R, Gopal K (2009) Impact of Socio Biological Activities on Gomti River Flowing Through Lucknow, Environ Cons. J.10(3): 31-34.

Shyamala, G., Shivananad, K.P. and Babu, S.S. (2008). A Preliminary Report on the Physico Chemical Nature of Water Pollution in and Around Erode Own, Tamil Nadu. Natl. Environ. Pollu. Technol., 7(3): 555-559.

Singh A.K (2002) Quality Assessment of Surface and Sub Surface Water of Damodar River Basin. India. J. Env hlth. 44(1): 41-49.

Singh J.P, Sakun Singh and Khanna D.R (2006) Water Quality Status of River Ganga in Respect to Physiochemical and Microbial Characteristics at Anup Shahar Dist. Bulandshar (U.P), India. Env. Cons. J.7(1-2): 29-34.

Singh M and Gupta K.C (2004) Study of Physiochemical Characteristics of the Yamuna River Water. Indian. J. Env. Port.24(3): 182-186.

Singh, B.N. and Rai, Seema (1999). Physico Chemical Status of Ganga River at Varansi. J. Environ. and Pollu., 6(1): 43-46.

Singh, H.P. (1999). Limnochemistry of River Ganga and Some of its Major Tributaries. J. Inland Fish Soc. India, 31(2): 31-35.

Singh, H.P., Mahaveer, L.R. and Mishra, J. P. (1999). Limnochemical Characteristics of River Ghaghra in U.P. J.Inland Fish Soc. India, 31(1): 28-32.

Singh, K.P. and H.K. Parwana (1999). Groundwater Pollution due to Industrial Wastewater in Punjab State and Strategies for its Control. Indian J Environ Prot, 19(4): 241-244.

Singh, M. and K.C. Gupta (2004). Study on Physico-chemical Characteristics of the Yamuna River Water. Indian J. of Env. Protection, 24(3): 182-186.

Singh, R.K. and Singh, K.N. (2007). Physico-chemical and Biological Analysis of Gomati River Water Affected by Urban Wastes. Mar. Sci. Res. India, 4(2): 233-236.

Singh, S., and V.K. Srivastava. (1988). Variations in Water Quality of Ganga River Between Buxar and Ballia, Poll.Res. 7: 3-4, 85-92.

Sinha, D.K., S. Saxena and R. Saxena (2004) Ram Ganga River Water Pollution at Moradabad –A Physico-chemical Study. Indian J. of Env. Protection, 24(1): 49-52.

Srivastava, C.P.(1992). Pollutants and Nutrient Status in Raw Sewage. Indian J. Envl. Prot., 18(2): pp. 109-111.

Srivastava, R.K. and S. Srivastava (2003). Assessment of Water Quality of River Gaurat Jabalpur. Indian J. of Env. Protection, 23(3): 282-285.

Sustainibility and Water,(2009) Available at World Population Awareness and World Overpopulation Awareness (WAO). htm.

Tamlurkar H.L and Ambore N.E (2006) Correlation Coefficient of Some Physiochemical Characteristics of Alisagar Dam Water, Dist. Nizamabad (A.P) India. J. Aqua. Biol.21(2): 115-118.

Thilaga, A., Subhashini, S., Sobhana, S. and Kumar K. L. (2005). Studies on Nutrient Content of the Ooty Lake with Reference to Pollution. Natl. Env. Poll. Technol., 4(2): 299-302.

Tiwari, R.K., Rajak, G.P. and Mondal, M.R. (2005). Water Quality Assessment of Ganga River in Bihar Region, India. J. Environ. Scei Engng., 47(4): 326-355.

Tiwari, T.N., S.C. Das and P.K. Bose (1986). Water Quality Index for the River Jhelum in Kashmir and its Seasonal Variation. Poll. Res., 5(1): 1-5.

Tripathi, V.M., Tewari, D.D., Tiwari, H.D., Tiwari, S. and Uppadhya. M.P. (2008). Physico-chemical Characteristics of River Rapti Nearby Industrial Area Balrampur, U.P. India.Natl. Envirron. and Pollu. Technol., 7(1): 73-77.

Trivedi R.K and Goel P.K (1989) Chemical and Biological Methods for Water Pollution Studies. Environ. Pub. Karod. Maharastra.

USEPA, (United States Environmental Protection Agency) (1975). Quality Criteria for Water (Ed. R.E. Train) Caste Houe Publication Ltd. Great Britain.

Velge P, Cloeckaert A, Barrow P. (2005) Emergence of Salmonella Epidemics: The Problems Related to Salmonella Enterica Serotype Enteritidis and Multiple Antibiotic Resistance in Other Major Serotypes. Vet Res 36: 267-288.

Verghese Susan P, Singh Monika and Mishra Anjali (2005) An Assessment of Water Quality of River Yamuna during Mansoon at Agra City. Indian. J. Env. Port. 25(10): 893-898.

Verma, S. and Khan, S. A. (2007). Water Quality Criteria and Arpna River Water of Bilaspur City (C.G.). Curr. World Environ., 2(2): 199-204.

Verma, R.G., Kumar.S., Malakar.B.(2012) Evaluation of Water Quality: Physico-chemical Characteristics of Narmada River at Omkareshwar by Using Correlation Study, MP, India Ultra Scientist 24(1)B: 375-379.

Vyas, L.N. (1968). Studies on Phytoplankton Ecology of Pichhola Lake, Udaipur. Proc. Symp. Recent Adv. Trop. Ecol., Int. Soc. Trop. Ecol., Varanasi (ed. R. Mishra and B. Gopal): 334-347.

Wetzel R.G (2000) Fresh Water and the Major Elements. Chem Oceonagraphy. London.1: 365-413.

WHO (2006) Guidelines for Drinking Water, 3rd Ed. World Health Organization, German.

WHO, (1997) Standards for Drinking Water Quality. World Health Organization. Geneva.

Wipple G.C (1954) Microbiology of Drinking Water, John Wiley and Sons London.

Yadav, S.S., & Kumar, R., (2011). Monitoring Water Quality of Kosi River in Rampur District, Uttar Pradesh, India. Advances in Applied Science Research. 2 (2): 197-201.

Yayyantas, O.T., Yilmaz, S., Turkoglu, M., Colakoglu, F.A., Cakir, F., (2007). Seasonal Variation of Some Heavy Metal Pollution with Environmental and Microbiological Parameters in Sub-basin Kocabas Stream (Biga, Canakkale, Turkey) by ICP-AES. Environ. Monit. Assess. (13)4: 321-331.

Zaimoglu, Z., Yavuz Sucu, Davutluoglu, I. O., Hazir, I. and Yuceer, A. (2006) Pollutant Monitoring of a Drainage Canal Receiving Industrial and Agricultural Waste Water Incukurova Plain. J. Biol. Sci., 6(4): 646-650.

Zhang, W.L., Z.X. Tian, N. Zhang and X. Q. Li (1996) Nitrate Pollution of Groundwater in Northern China. Agriculture, Ecosystems & Environment, 59(3): 223-231.

Pages: 105-120

LIMNOLOGY AND AQUATIC SCIENCE
Edited by: Dr. Shailendra Sharma; Dr. Pawan Kumar 'Bharti'
ISBN: 978-93-5056-735-7
Edition: 2015
Published by: Discovery Publishing House Pvt. Ltd., New Delhi (India)

Studies on Some Factors Affecting Aerial and Aquatic Respiration in an Air Breathing Fish, *Channa gachua* (Ham.)

Qaisur Rahman and **D.N. Sadhu**

ABSTRACT

In the present investigation an attempt has been made to study the effects of some factors such as body weight, sex, ambient water temperature, pesticide and hormones on oxygen consumption in an air breathing murrel fish, *Channa gachua* (Ham). The oxygen consumption in *C. gachua* of different body weights in aquatic, aerial and total oxygen uptake was found inversely proportional to body weight. The results indicate that the male fishes consume more oxygen but females take less oxygen due to their activities and life style. In this species the oxygen uptake from water, air as well as total varied considerably with the seasonal variation of ambient water temperature. The oxygen consumption was lowest during the month of December and gradually increased with the rise in temperature reaching at its maximum in June. Thus the nature of oxygen consumption is directly proportional to the ambient water temperature.

Post Graduate, Department of Zoology, Vinoba Bhave University, Hazaribag - 825 301 Jharkhand, India.

A significant positive relationship exists between water temperature and oxygen consumption. The correlation co-efficient (r) for aquatic, aerial and total oxygen consumption was noted as 1.0, 1.0 and 1.04 at lower temperature range (21.6°-28.2° C) and 0.943, 0.9907 and 0.9901 at higher temperature range from (28.2°-31.4° C) respectively. The effect of three different pesticides namely Metacid-50 (Organophosphate), Dithane M-45 (Carbamate) and Kelthane (Organochlorine) were studied on changes in dual mode of oxygen consumption. Exposure of fish to above noted pesticides brought significant decrease in aquatic as well as total oxygen uptake percent while it increased in oxygen consumption through aerial route as compared to control one due to the action of pesticides on respiratory muscles causing paralysis, respiratory failure and death. The treatment of hormones i.e. Hydrocortisone (1mg/100g) and Thyroxine (0.5mg/100g) in *C. gachua* brought significant increase in aquatic, aerial and total oxygen uptake where as Adrenaline (0.000006mg/100g) caused slight decrease in aquatic but abrupt and significant fall in aerial and total oxygen consumption. The treatment of Progesterone (1mg/100g) caused significant increase in aquatic and decrease in aerial and total oxygen uptake whereas Testosterone (2mg/100g) significantly increased in aquatic and total oxygen uptake but slight decrease in aerial oxygen uptake was noticed. Thiouracil (2mg/100g) increased the aquatic oxygen consumption and decreased the aerial and total oxygen consumption respectively. The details have been discussed in this paper.

Key words: oxygen consumption, *Channa gachua*.

INTRODUCTION

The fishes are primarily aquatic vertebrates which exploit every nook and niche of the domain of water. In India the pools, ponds, creeks and also the torrential streams often either dry out during summer or water becomes muddy, highly hypoxic and hyper carbic (Mousa, 1957). Under the above adverse conditions some fishes for their existence develop two modes of respiratory gas exchange mechanisms i.e. in water by gills and in air by highly vascularized air breathing apparatus. Some investigators have studied the rate of oxygen consumption as function of body weight in fishes (Parvatheswara Rao, 1960; HemingSen, 1960; Brett, 1964 and Johansen *et al.*, 1976). Temperature plays an important role in the physiology of fishes.

High temperature tends to increase nearly all the metabolic processes and simultaneously disrupts the structural integrity of the animal. Information on temperature tolerance and resistance is of much value in judging the ecophysiological characteristics of fishes. It has been experimentally shown that one of the causes of thermal death is the osmoregulatory failure at temperature extremes (Fry, 1971). Pesticides affect the respiratory metabolism of fishes (Mount, 1962; Waiwood and Johansen, 1974; Annes, 1975; Gopalakrishna Reddy and Gomathy, 1977; Dalela *et al.*, 1979; Natarajan, 1981;

Sambasiva Rao *et al.* 1984; Ganapathyraman, 1987 and Karuppiah, 1996). Hormones also affect the oxygen consumption in fishes. Some important workers have tried to co-relate the endocrine activity of fishes with metabolic activity including respiratory metabolism (Kaya 1973; Raza *et al.*, 2000). A perusal of literatures also indicates that our information regarding role of body weight, sex, ambient water temperatures, pesticides and hormones on oxygen consumption in Indian air breathing fishes are very scanty. As such the present investigation has been undertaken to advance our information in *C. gachua*.

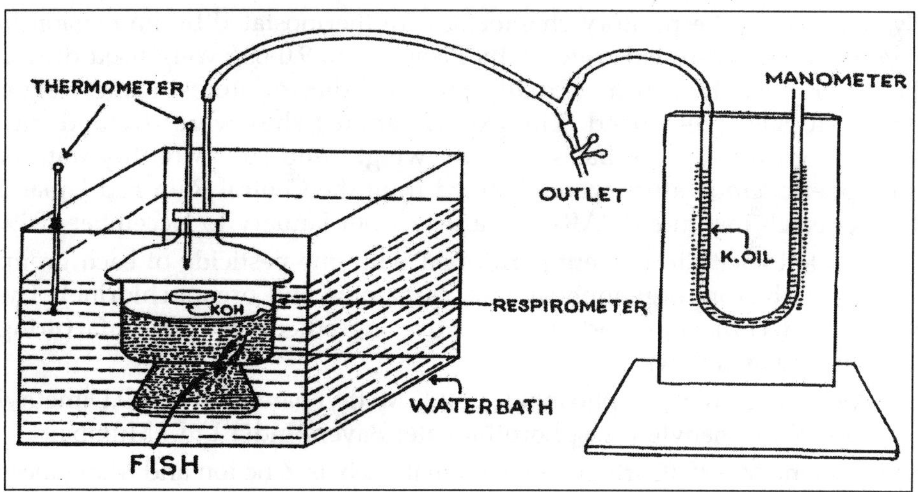

Fig. 7.1: Experimental Set up for the Measurements of Dual Mode of Oxygen Uptake in *Channa gachua*

MATERIALS AND METHODS

Live specimens of *Channa gachua* were procured from local fish dealers at Hazaribag (Latitude 25° 59′N and Longitude 85° 22′E) and maintained in large glass aquaria size (90 x 60 x 60cm) with continuous flow of water. The specimens were fed on chopped goat liver daily during a minimum acclimation period of 15 days in the laboratory. Routine oxygen consumption from air and still water was measured in a closed glass respirometer containing 3 litres of water (initial O2 content = 6.5 mg O2/Iitre; pH = 7.2) and 0.51 ML of air (Fig. 7.1). The fish had free access to air through a small semi circular hole (10 cm diameter) in a disc float. Carbosorb (B.D.H) or KOH in a petridish placed on the float absorbed CO2. Thus the fish could exchange gases with water by way of its gills as well as with the air using the suprabranchial chamber. The air phase of respirometer was connected to a differential manometer. Movement of the manometer fluid follow uptake of oxygen when the CO2 is absorbed by "Carbosorb" (KOH).

The fish were acclimatized to the respirometers for at least 12 hours before the readings were taken. The concentration of dissolved oxygen in the water was estimated by Winklers volumetric method (Welch, 1948). The oxygen uptake through gills was calculated from the difference between the oxygen levels of the ambient water in the respirometer before and after the experiment and the reading of volume of water in the respirometer. Oxygen uptake from air was measured and calculated from the reading of volume change in the manometer and by the use of the combined gas law equations and vapour pressure (Dejours, 1975). Mean values of VO2 of a series of observations, on each fish at standard temperature pressure dry and standard errors were calculated. The experiments were conducted at 29.0 ± 1.5°C. The pH of the ambient water was measured by an electronic pH meter (Systronics). The respiratory chambers were thermostated by immersion in a temperature controlled water bath. Fishes from 9.0-65g were used during the experiment. However, sexually mature fishes of almost same weight group (40-50g) were used. The experimental fishes were divided into different groups on the basis of body weight and sex. Monthly data of atmospheric temperature were obtained from the Central Rain Fed Upland Rice Research Institute (ICAR), Hazaribag from January to December 2009.

Acute toxicity tests were performed with one pesticide of each group (i.e. one each from organophosphate, carbamate and organochlorine). The pesticide's technical or trade name, active ingredients and manufacturing concerns are as follows:

1. Metacid- 50 (Organophosphate): 50%, Methyl parathion= O-O Dimethyl O-P-Nitrophenyle phosphorothionate; Bayers India Ltd., Mumbai.
2. Dithane M - 45 (Carbamate): 75% manozeb as Zinc ion and Manganese Ethylene bis dithio-carbamate. Indofil chemical Ltd., Mumbai.
3. Kelthane E.C. (Organochlorine): 18.15%, 1,1 bi-chlorophenyl. 2, 2, 2 trichloroethanol (DICOFOL): Indofil chemical Ltd., Mumbai.

Metacid and Kelthane were purchased in liquid form but Dithane M-45 was soluble in distilled water. The desired degree of concentrations was prepared by adopting the dilution techniques of APHA *et al.* (1971). The 96 hours bio assay tests were performed employing the technique of static bioassay tests (Doudoroff *et. al.*, 1951). Five fish were used for each set of experiment and mean values of oxygen uptake of all the fish of each set of experiment were taken and compared.

The experimental fishes including controls were divided into six groups each containing ten fishes. To study the effects of hormones on oxygen consumption at different doses of Hydrocortisone, Adrenaline, Testosterone, Progesterone and Thyroxine were injected intra peritoneally on the abdominal side of the fishes slightly anterior to the pelvic fin. The powder form Thiouracil was dissolved in distilled water and were fed orally with the help of catheter rubber pipe. The animals of control group having ten fishes got the treatment of normal saline. The hormones were purchased from local stockists. For every experiment the effective doses of different hormones were standardized and oxygen consumption of animals treated with different hormones was measured in every 24 hours, whereas in case of Adrenaline the O2 consumption was measured after 48 hours. The difference of significance, if any, between the control and experimental groups of fish, was calculated by students 't' test at the level of 5%.

RESULTS AND DISCUSSION

The data showing the effect of different body weights and sex on O2 consumption are summarized in (Tables 7.1 & 7.2). A perusal of Table 7.1 shows that the lowest range of fish body weight (9.0 g) consumed the highest rate of aquatic O2 (68.34 ml/kg/hr) where as the highest range of fish body weight (65.0 gm) consumed the lowest range of aquatic O2 (37.17 ml/kg/hr). The lowest range of body weight (9.0 g) consumed 175.23 (ml/kg/hr) of total O2 where as highest range of body weight (65.0 gm) took 76.32(ml/kg/hr) of total O2. This indicates the percentage of O2 uptake from water was lower and never more than 50%. It ranges from 39.0 to 49.6% of aquatic O2 consumption. Further it was observed that the percentage of aquatic O2 uptake shows an increasing trend with the increasing body weight. The percentage of aerial O2 up take ranges from 61.0 to 50.4% of the aerial O2 consumption. This shows a decreasing trend with the increasing body weight.

A perusal of (Table 7.2) shows that total O2 uptake by male fish was higher in comparison with female fish. Likewise when aquatic and aerial O2 uptake was considered separately it has been observed that the aerial O2 uptake was higher in male than the female and so aquatic O2 consumption was higher in female than male.

The aquatic, aerial and total oxygen consumption due to seasonal variation of ambient water temperature is summarized in (Tables 7.3 & 7.4). It was observed that the oxygen uptake from water and air as well as total (water + air) varied considerably with the seasons (Rahman and Sadhu, 2012). The lowest aquatic, aerial and total oxygen uptake (ml/kg/hr) was observed in December when the temperature was lowest while the aerial and total oxygen uptake gradually increased with the rise in temperature when reached its maximum in June. The aquatic oxygen uptake increased from December onwards reaching at the highest level of 70.53 (ml/kg/hr) in July. Thus it was evident that the O2 consumption was higher in summer than in winter. The percentage of aerial oxygen uptake increased with the rise in temperature and decreased with fall in temperature. The percentage of aerial oxygen consumption was lowest i.e. 51% in December and 58% in June when the temperature reached at its maximum. Again the percentage of aerial oxygen uptake gradually decreased from October to December months. The oxygen consumption has direct bearing on ambient water temperature. The aquatic, aerial and total oxygen consumption in December was 49.8, 52.02 and 102.0 (ml/kg/hr) where as in June it was noted to be 69.3, 95.70 and 165.0 (ml/kg/hr) respectively. Statistically significant positive relationship exists between water temperature and oxygen consumption. The correlation co-efficient (r) for aquatic, aerial and total oxygen uptake was 1.0, 1.0 and 1.04 at lower temperature range (21.6- 28.2°C) whereas 0.943, 0.9907 and 0.9901 at higher temperature range (28.2-31.4°C) respectively. The rate of oxygen consumption increased profoundly at temperature beyond 28.2°C. It was found that at low temperature range (21.6-28.2°C) the aquatic, aerial and total oxygen consumption increased by a power of 3.003, 5.05 and 8.06 respectively with unit increase in ambient water temperature. The effects of sublethal concentrations of different pesticides are recorded in (Table 7.5). This group of fish obtained 46% and 54% oxygen respectively from aquatic and aerial route. Exposure of fish to different sublethal concentrations of all the three pesticides brought significant decrease both in aquatic and total oxygen uptake. The experimental fish obtained 30.0-38% O2 through aquatic route as compared to 46% in control group of fishes while in the experimental group of fishes the O2 uptake through aerial route ranged from 62-70% as compared to 54% in the fishes of control group. Thus a shift in the dependency towards air-breathing was clearly marked out in fishes exposed to different concentration of above three pesticides and Kelthane was found to be more effective as compared to Dithane M-45 and Metacid 50 respectively.

Bimodal oxygen uptake in different doses of hormones and drugs was shown in (Table 7.6). In Hydrocortisone exposed fishes, it was observed that the aquatic O2 consumption increased up to 60.76 (ml/kg/hr) from 52.44 (ml/kg/hr) and the aerial O2 uptake also increased up to 63.24 from 61.56 (ml/kg/hr) and the total O2 consumption increased to 124.00 (ml/kg/hr) from 114.00 (ml/kg/hr) of control ones. When single dose of 0.000006 mg of Adrenaline was injected to the fishes successively for two days, the most remarkable things was observed that aerial O2 uptake decreased up to 6.96 (ml/kg/hr) against 61.56 (ml/kg/hr) to control fishes. The aquatic O2 consumption also slightly decreased to 51.04 (ml/kg/hr) from 52.44 (ml/kg/hr) of control fishes. It showed that the effects of Adrenaline turned the fishes sluggish and compelled to respire under water through gills. The total O2 consumption decreased up to 58.0 (ml/kg/hr) from 114.0 (ml/kg/hr) and when single doses of 2mg of Testosterone was injected to the fish for two days, it was observed that the aquatic O2 consumption increased considerably to 84.68 (ml/kg/hr) from 52.44 (ml/kg/hr).

The aerial O2 uptake remained almost the same which is slightly lower than that the control ones. The aerial O2 consumption was 61.32 (ml/kg/hr) and the total increased up to 146.0 (ml/kg/hr).Thus it was observed that the Testosterone enhanced the aquatic O2 consumption but did not affect aerial O2 consumption. A perusal of (Table 7.6) reveals that the dose of 1 mg of Progesterone to the fish for two days increased the aquatic O2 consumption considerably to 89.25 (ml/kg/hr) as against 52.44 of control ones. The aerial O2 uptake decreased up to 15.75 (ml/kg/hr) and the total O2 was

105.0 (ml/kg/hr). It was observed that the Progesterone enhanced the aquatic O2 consumption but decreased the aerial ones. When single dose of 0.5 mg of Thyroxine was given to the fish for two days the aquatic O2 uptake slightly increased to 53.60 (ml/kg/hr) from 52.44 (ml/kg/hr). The aerial and total O2 consumption increased up to 80.40 (ml/kg/hr) and 134.0 (ml/kg/hr) respectively. It was observed that Thyroxine did not affect aquatic O2 consumption but elevate aerial O2 uptake to a significant level as compared to control ones. Similarly when single dose of 2.0 mg of Thiouracil was fed to the fish for four days, the aquatic oxygen consumption increased up to 61.80 (ml/kg/hr) where as aerial and total decreased to 41.20 (ml/kg/hr) 103.0 (ml/kg/hr) respectively.

Munshi and Dube (1973) reported that O2 consumption per unit body weight in *Anabas testudineus* decreases with increasing body weight similar with the finding in other fishes had been reported by (Hakim *et al.* 1978; Ramaswami and Reddy 1979). Munshi *et al.*, (1978) while studying in *H. fossilis* obtained different values of small and adult fishes when they were provided free access to air the small fishes depend more on aerial breathing for their total metabolic demand where as for growth and maturation they depends on more aquatic respiration. In present investigation in *Channa gachua* respiratory behavior is quite different from that of *Heteropneustes fossilis* the larger fishes depend more on air breathing than gill breathing even in well oxygenated water. The oxygen consumption per unit body weight was higher in smaller fishes but lower in larger ones. This contention is true for almost all the bony fishes Zeuthen (1953 & 1955) and Tamura and Moriyama (1976). Hughes and Singh (1970) reported that *Anabas testudineus* weighing about 29-51grams consume about 53.6% of total O2 requirement through air breathing organs thus it is suggested that larger fishes having a larger respiratory surface will depend on more air than on gills breathing because of the higher diffusing capacity of air breathing organs than on gills (Hughes *et al.* 1970). It was found that total and aerial O2 uptake in male fishes were significantly higher as compared to females, the views consistent with findings of (Raffy and Fountain 1930; Stanley and Tescher 1931; Pandey 1976).

It was observed by Pandey (1975) that during summer when water temperature was highest the fishes *H. fossilis* come to the surface of water frequently to engulf air but the case was just reverse in winter at lower temperature. This behaviour of the fish was similar with the finding of De Roth (1973) in *Lepidosteus occulatus* and Horn and Riggs (1973) in *Amia calva.* The gills are more efficient in winter months with minimum aerial respiration but in summer the aerial respiration increased as the fishes come to the surface of water to engulf air. The increased aerial respiration in summer (June) might be correlated with the fall in dissolved oxygen content of the water at high temperature. Sinha and Pandey (1985) tried to establish direct relationship between ambient water temperature and oxygen consumption through gills in three species of fresh water fishes viz, *A. testudineus M. aculeatum* and *C.punctatus*. It is interesting to note that the rate of aquatic, aerial and total oxygen uptake increased as soon as the temperature level reaches beyond 28° C. This further emphasizes the contention that in *C. gachua* more oxygen is needed during breeding season and also suggests that temperature is not the only factor to cause the rise in aquatic, aerial and total oxygen consumption. The mode and site of action of different pesticides also differ and therefore, it is very difficult to generalize the effect of different pesticides in fishes unless a detailed investigation is carried out Palanichamy *et al.* (1989).

One of the early symptoms of acute pesticide poisoning is the alteration of respiratory metabolism in fishes. However, in *Channa gachua* significant decrease in both aquatic and total oxygen uptake was observed due to different concentration of pesticides Mazairka (1975). This fish relies on aerial gas exchange obtaining 54% of its total oxygen uptake by the air breathing organ where as only 46% was contributed by gill Karuappiah (1996) in *Channa striatus.* The contribution of gas exchange through the aerial route increased between 62-70% similar with the findings of (Konar, 1969; Lunn *et al.* 1976; Verma *et al.* 1979; Pandey *et al.*, 1999). Marinescu (1971) has reported that in *Gobius melanostomus* (Pallar) the treatment of Adrenaline induced a depression of metabolic rate. Pandey *et al.* (1985) in *Macrognathus aculeatum* found that treatment of Adrenaline causes a sharp and substantial decrease in O2 consumption performed for (3-10 hours) and stated that it results from carotid sinus response to the increase in blood pressure. It is also possible that it results from prompt relaxation of the respiratory muscles and slow heart beat rate evoked by epinephrine contrary to Adrenaline the treatment of Hydrocortisone results in a significant rise in O2 consumption in *M. aculeatum*.

The exact reason of increasing O2 consumption due to Hydrocortisone treatment could not be understood, but Chatterjee (1975) has also reported an increase in O2 consumption as a result of Adrenocortical hormone. In some fishes gonadal steroids have shown stimulating while in other depressing effects on cellular metabolism and the effect appears to depend markedly on the concentration of steroids. Hoar (1958) in gold fish and Pandey (1976) in *H. fossilis* have reported an increase in O2 consumption when treated with Testosterone. In *Anabas testudineus* they found a significant correlation in between the cyclic changes in gonadal activity and seasonal variation in O2 consumption in both the sexes. A perusal of literature reveals that male and female sex hormones do not have same effect on oxidative metabolism in fishes. The O2 uptake in male is higher as compared to female because males are metabolically more active than female Chanchal and Pandey (1979). The treatment of Testosterone brought highly significant increase in O2 consumption in *Channa gachua* because male hormones directly or indirectly influence the oxidative metabolism in fishes. The effect of female hormones on the respiratory metabolism was contrary to the effect of Testosterone.

Table 7.1: Showing the Mean Value of Aquatic, Aerial and Total O_2 Consumption, Percentage of Aquatic and Aerial VO_2; Aquatic/Aerial Quotient and E.E.U. in Different Body Weight of *Channa gachua*

Sl.No.	Body Wt. (gm.)	Bimodal Oxygen Consumption									
		Aquatic		Aerial		Total		Aquatic %	Aerial %	Aquatic/ Aerial	E.E.U K. cal/hr
		ml/hr	ml/kg/hr	ml/hr	ml/kg/hr	ml/hr	ml/kg/hr				
1.	9.0	0.615	68.34	0.962	106.89	1.577	175.23	39.0	61.0	0.639	0.0076
2.	18.0	1.097	60.93	1.465	91.39	2.742	152.32	40.0	60.0	0.666	0.0132
3.	29.0	1.488	51.33	1.986	68.49	3.474	119.52	42.8	57.2	0.749	0.0167
4.	37.0	1.870	53.02	2.392	64.65	4.262	115.18	43.8	56.2	0.782	0.0204
5.	41.0	2.174	50.53	2.453	59.83	4.627	112.85	46.9	53.1	0.886	0.0222
6.	51.0	2.334	45.76	2.368	46.43	4.702	92.19	48.7	51.3	0.949	0.0225
7.	65.0	2.416	37.17	2.545	39.15	4.961	76.32	49.6	50.4	0.986	0.0238

Table 7.2: Showing the Mean Value of Aquatic, Aerial and Total O_2 Consumption, in Male and Female *Channa gachua*

Sl. No.	Body Wt. (gm.)	Sex	Bimodal Oxygen Consumption									
			Aquatic		Aerial		Total		Aquatic %	Aerial %	Aquatic/ Aerial	E.E.U K. cal/hr
			Ml/hr	ml/kg/hr	ml/hr	Ml/kg/hr	ml/hr	ml/kg/hr				
1.	35	M	1.84	52.5714	2.280	65.1428	4.120	117.7142	44.7	55.3	0.807	0.019
2.	35	F	1.89	54.0	1.994	56.97	3.884	110.97	48.7	51.3	0.947	0.0186

Table 7.3: Showing Seasonal Variations of Bimodal Oxygen Uptake Percentage of Aerial Oxygen & Aquatic/Aerial Quotient in Relation to Ambient Water Temperature (°C) and Photoperiod in *Channa gachua*

Sl. No.	Month	Ambient	Day		VO2 (ml/kg/hr)		%	% of Aerial Aquatic/Aerial	
		Water Temp. (°C)	Length (Hr)	Aquatic	Aerial	Total	Aquatic VO2	VO2	Quotient
1.	January 2009	22.5	1 0.29	50.88	55.12	106.0	48	52	0.9230
2.	February	25.4	10.59	52.44	61.56	114.0	46	54	0.8518
3.	March	29.3	11.19	56.7	69.30	126.0	45	55	0.8181
4.	April	29.8	12.29	62.03	78.96	141.0	44	56	0.7855
5.	May	31.4	13.14	65.36	86.64	152.0	43	57	0.75.43
6.	June	31.5	13.29	69.3	95.70	165.0	42	58	0.7241
7.	July	30.6	13.14	70.53	84.47	155.0	45.5	54.5	0.8349
8.	August	30.4	12.44	68.4	83.60	152.0	45	55	0.8181
9.	September	29.8	12.14	63.28	74.72	138.0	45.85	54.15	0.8468
10.	October	28.2	11.14	56.4	63.60	120.0	47	53	0.8867
11.	November	26.5	10.29	55.7	60.30	116.0	48.02	51.98	0.9237
12.	December 2009	21.6	10.14	49.98	52.02	102.0	49	51	0.9607

Table 7.4: Correlation Coefficient and Equation Showing the Different VO2 Parameters Under Two Different Temperature Ranges in *Channa gachua*

Sl.No.	Temp. (°C)	Parameters (Temp. VS VO2)	Equation (y = a + bx)	Correlation
	Coefficient (r)			
1.	21.6 -----------------------28.2	a. Through water	y=21.45+3.003x	1.0
2.	21.6 -----------------------28.2	b. Through air	y=66.94+5.05x	1.0
3.	21.6 -----------------------28.2	c. Total	y=88.45+8.06x	1.04
4.	28.2 -------------------- 31.4.	a. Through water	y=70.43+4.49x	0.943
5.	28.2 -------------------- 31.4.	b. Through air	y=281.41+9.95x	0.9907
6.	28.2 -------------------- 31.4.	c. Total	y=289.15+14.45x	0.9901

Y= VO2 (oxygen consumption ml/kg/hr), X=Temp, a = intercept, b = regression coefficient

Table 7.5: Effects of Pesticides on Bimodal Oxygen, Percentage Decreased in Total VO2 and Percentage Increase in Aerial VO2 in *Channa gachua*

Sl. No.	Condition	Dose mg/l	Oxygen uptake (ml/kg/hr)			% O_2 Uptake		Aquatic	% Decrease in O_2 uptake	
			Aquatic	Aerial	Total	Aquatic	Aerial	Aerial Ratio	Aquatic	Total
1.	Control	–	52.44±0.93*	61.56±1.08	114.0±1.93	46.0	54	0.852	–	–
2.	Metacid-50	2.0	24.98±1.64*	46.37±1.24*	71.35±1.08*	35.0	65	0.538	52.36	37.41
3.	-Do-	4.0	26.65±1.04*	43.47±1.33*	70.12±1.04*	38.0	62	0.613	49.17	38.49
4.	Dithane M-45	4.0	26.20±1.23*	56.65±1.28*	82.85±1.12*	31.6	68.4	0.462	50.04	27.32
5.	-Do-	8.0	30.9±1.12*	50.42±1.12*	81.32±1.48*	38.0	62	0.613	40.50	28.67
6.	Kelthane	5.0	25.0±2.68*	58.32±0.61*	83.32±1.93*	30.0	70	0.428	52.33	26.91
7.	-Do-	8.0	29.06±1.36*	52.09±0.28*	80.15±1.04*	35.0	65	0.538	44.58	29.69

N=5: Body wt. = 40.0 ± 1.5gm: water temp.= 29.0 ± 1.5°c ± SEM : *=Significant

Table 7.6: Bimodal Oxygen Uptake in Different Doses of Hormones and Pharmacological Drug in *Channa gachua*. (Body wt. 40.0 ± 2.5 gram)

Sl. No.	Condition	Injection in Days	Total Dose (mg/100g.)	VO_2 (ml/kg/hr)		Total
				Aquatic	Aerial	
1.	Control	–	–	52.44	61.56	114.00
2.	Hydrocortisone	2	1.0	60.76	63.24	124.00
3.	Adrenaline	2	0.000006	51.04	06.96	58.00
4.	Testosterone	2	2.0	84.68	61.32	146.00
5.	Progesterone	2	1.0	89.25	15.75	105.00
6.	Thyroxine	2	0.5	53.60	80.40	134.00
7.	Thiouracil	4	2.0	61.80	41.20	103.00

Almost all the female hormones (progesterone, ovacycline and duogynon forte) lowered the O2 consumption. In the present investigation it had been found that treatment of Testosterone resulted significant increase in aquatic and total O2 consumption while dose of Progesterone decreases the aerial as well as total O2 uptake in *Channa gachua*. It may be concluded that thyroid gland is an important regulator of O2 consumption and functionally the thyroid is known to be more metamorphic than metabolic in its effect in poikilothermic vertebrates (Dehadrai, 1972; Pandey *et al.*, 2002). The treatment of Thiouracil resulted in significant decrease in total and aerial oxygen uptake in this fish.

REFERENCES

Annes, M A 1975, Acute Toxicity of Four Organophosphorous Insectides to Fresh Water Teleost *Channa punctatus* (Bloch). Pak. J. Zool. 7: 135-141.

APHA AWWA and WPCF, 1971, Standard Method for the Examination of Water and Waste Water. 14th Edition American Public Health Association Wasington, INC pp. 1193.

Brett J R 1964 The Respiratory Metabolism and Swimming Perforance of Young *Sockeye salmon*. J. Fish. Res. Bd. Can. 21: 1183-1226.

Chatterjee C C 1975 Human Physiology, Vol. I, Medical Allied Agency Calcutta, pp. 1-764.

Dalela R C Rani Saroj and Verma S R 1979, Acute Toxicity of Phenol and Pentachlorophenol of Few Freshwater Teleosts. Proc. Sym. Environ. Biol. pp. 349-359.

Dehadrai, P V., 1972, Thyroid in Relation to Aerial Respiration in *Notopterus notopterus* (Ham.) teleostei. J. Biol. Sci. 14.

De Roth G C 1973, Effect of Temperature and Light on Aerial Breathing Behaviour of the Spotted gar, *Lepidosteus occulatus*. Ophio. J. Sci. 1: 34-41.

Dejour's P 1975, "Principles of Comparative Respiratory Physiology." Amsterdum. North Holland Publishing company pp. 253.

Doudoroff, P Anderson, B G Burdick G E 1951, Bioassay Methods for the Evaluation of Acute Toxicity of Industrial Wastes to Fish. Sewage Ind. Waste, 23: 1380-1397.

Fry F E J 1971, The Effect of Environmental Factors on the Physiology of Fish. *In:* "Fish Physiology" Edited by S. Hoar and D.J. Randall, Vol. vi, 1-98.

Ganapathyraman S., 1987, Impact of Organophorous Pesticides, Monocrotophos on Dual Mode of Respiration and Protein Metabolism in the Air Breathing Fish, *Channa punctatus* (Bloch) M.Phil. Dissertation Annamalai University, Tamilnadu.

Gopalkrishna Reddy T., and Gomathy S 1977, Toxicity and Respiratory Effects of Pesticide, Thiodon on Catfish *Mystus vittatus*. Indian. J. Environ. Hlth. 19(4): 360-363.

Hakim A Munshi J S D and Hughes G M 1978, Morphometrics of Respiratory Organs of Indian Green Snake Headed Fish, *Channa punctatus*. J. Zool. Lond. 84: 519-543.

Hemingsen, A 1960, Energy Metabolism as Related to Body Size and Respiratory Surfaces and its Evolution. Rept. Steno. Meml. Hosp. Nord. Insulin Lab.9: 1-11.

Hoar W S 1958, Effect of Synthetic Thyroxine and Gonadal Steroids on the Metabolism of Gold Fish Can. J Zool. 36: 113-121.

Horn M H and Riggs C D 1973, Effect of Temperature and Light on the Rate of an Air Breathing of the Fish *Amia calva* Copeia. 4: 653 -657.

Hughes G.M and Singh B N 1970, Respiration in an Air Breathing Fish the Climbing Perch *Anabas testudineus* (Bloch) Oxygen Uptake and Carbon Dioxide Release into Air and Water J. Exp. Biol. 53: 265-280.

Jabde P V and Ansari M 1993, Effect of Acute Exposure of Cypermethrin on the Oxygen Consumption of a Fresh Water Fish, *Naemechillus aureus* (Day). Proc. Acad. Environ. Biol. 2 (1): 95-98.

Johansen K Lomholt J P and Maloy G M 1976, Importance of Air and Water Breathing in Relation to Size of African Lung Fish *Protopterus amphibious* (Peters) J. Exp. Biol. 65(2): 395-399.

Karuppiah D 1996, Toxicity and Effects of a Carbamate Pesticide Sevin, on Some Physiological Aspects of a Freshwater, Edible Air Breathing Fish, *Channa striatus* (Bloch). Ph.D. Thesis, Bharathiar University, Coimbatore, Tamilnadu.

Kaya M K 1973, Effects of Temperature on Response of the Gonads of Green Sunfish *lepomia cynellus* to Treatment with Carp Pituitaries and Testosterone Propionate Fish. Res. Bd. Can. 30: 905-912.

Konar S K 1969, Lethal Effects of the Insectides DDVP on the Eggs and Hatchings of the Snake Headed *Channa punctatus* (Bloch) (Ophiocephaliformes Ophiocephalidae:) Jap. J. Ichthyol. 15: 130-133.

Lunn C R Toews D P and Pree J D 1976, Effects of Three Pesticides on Respiration Coughing and Heart Rates of Rainbow Trout *Salmo gairdneri* (Richadson). Can. J. Zool. 54: 214-219.

Marinescu AG 1971, The Influence of Adrenaline on Oxygen Consumption in the Pertilor *Gobius melanostomus* in High Temperature Condition Stud. Cerlet. Biol. Ser. Zool. 23: 536-546.

Mawdesley Thomas L E 1971, Toxic Chemicals, the Risk of Fish. News. Scientist, 49: 74-75.

Mazairka S 1975, Effects of Organophosphate Pesticide (Malathion, Foschlor, Dichlorophos) on Aquatic Organism. Roczn. Pzh. 26(3): 393-399.

Mousa T A 1957, Physiology of the Accessory Respiratory Organs of Teleost *Clarias lazera* (C&V) J. Exp. Zool. 136: 419-454.

Mount D I 1962, Chronic Effects of Endrin on Bluntnose Minnows and Guppies, U. S. Fish Wild. Ser. Rept. 58: 1-38.

Munshi J S D Pandey P K and Ojha. J 1978, Oxygen Uptake Through Gills and Skins in Relation to Body wt. Air Breathing Siluroid Fish Saccobranchus *H. fossilis* J. Zool. London. 184: 171-180.

Munshi J S D and Dube SC 1973, Oxygen Uptake Capacity of Gills in Relation to Body Size of the Air Breathing Fish *Anabas testudineus* (Bloch). *Acta. Physol. Acad. Sci. Hun.,* 44: 113-123.

Natarajan G M 1981, Changes in the Dual Mode Gas Exchange and Some Blood Parameters in the Air Breathting Fish, *Channa striatus* (Bleeker) Following Lethal (LC50/48hrs) Exposure to Metasystok (Dimeton) Curr. Sci. 50 (I): 40-41.

Pandey B N 1976, Effects of Gonadal Steroids on Oxygen Consumption in *H. fossilis* (Bloch) Pol. Arch. Hydrobiol. 23: 327-332.

Pandey B N and Munshi. J S D, 1976, Role of the Thyroid Gland in the Regulation of Metabolic Rate in an Air Breathing Siluroid Fish *Heteropneustes fossilis* (Bloch) J. Endocrinol. 69: 421-425.

Pandey B N Prasad S and Sinha S P 1985, Cyclic Variations in the Activity of Internal Tissue and Oxygen Consumption in the Fresh Water Mud eel *Macrognathus aculeatum* Ad. Bios.4(II): 87-91.

Pandey, B N Prasad S Singh B K and Umesh P., 2002, Thyroidal Control of Respiratory Metabolism in Fresh Water Mud eel *Macrognathus aculeatum* (Bloch). Proc. Zool. Soc. India (1&2): 53-58

Pandey, B N Arun K Ram S Pyare K Dhananjay Ranja K and Arshi R., Toxic Effect of a Carbamate Pesticide Sevin on Gas Exchange in an Air Breathing Fish, *Clarias batrachus* (Linn) Him J. Env. Zool. 13: 103-10.

Pandey B N 1975, Effect of Salinity and Low pH on the Blood and Oxygen Consumption in an Air Breathing Fish *H. fossilis* (Bloch) J. Indian.Bio.Assoc. 1: 137-140.

Parvateshwara Rao, V 1960 Oxygen Consumption in the Fresh Water Fish *Puntius sophore* (Ham) in Relation to Size and Temperature, Proc. Inst. Sci. India. 268: 64-72.

Palanichamy S Arunachalam S and Bhaskaran P 1989, Impact of Pesticides on Protein Metabolism in the Fresh Water Cat Fish *Mystus vittatus*. J.EcoBiol.1: 90-97.

Prichard, A.W., and A. Gorbman 1960 Thyroid Hormone Treatment and Oxygen Consumption in Embryos of the Spiny Dog Fish Biol. Marine. Biol. Lab. Wood. Hole Mass. 119: 109-119.

Raffy A and Fountain M 1930, Recherches Surla Respiration in *Girardinus guppy* C.R. Soc. Biol., Paris 104: 287-288.

Rahman Qaisur and Sadhu D N 2012, Factors Affecting Aerial and Aquatic Respiration in the Air Breathing Fish *Channa gachua*. J. Ecotoxicol. Environ. Monit. 22 (1): 17-30.

Ramaswamy M and Reddy T G., 1979, Bimodal Oxygen Consumption of an Air Breathing Fish *Colisa lalia*. Indian Zoologist 3 (I & II): 21-25.

Raza Bushra Luxmi Sah and Lakra. G., 2000, Effect of Adrenaline in the Cortical Secretion in Air Breathing Teleost *Clarias batrachus*. Proc. Nat. Conf. on Endocrinology held at Ranchi Abst. No. 35: pp. 35.

Sambasiva Rao K Siva Prasad Rao R S and Raman Rao K V 1984, Impacts of Technical and Commercial Grade Phenothoate on Some Selected Parameters of Oxidative Metabolism in the Fish, *Channa punctatus* (Bloch) Indian. J. Eco. 11 (1): 6-11.

Sinha, D P., and Pandey B N., 1985, Effect of Ambient Water Temperature on Oxygen Uptake in Some Fresh Water Fishes. Intl.J. Acad. Ichthyol (Proc.v) 6: 31-35.

Stanley L L and Tescher G L., 1931, Activity of Gold Fish on Testicular Substance diet. J. Endocrinology, 15 : 55-56.

Tamura O and Moriyama T., 1976, On the Morphological Features of the Gill of Amphibious Air Breathing fishes, Bull. Pac. Fish. Nagasaki, Univ. 41: 1-8.

Verma S R Tyagi, A K Bhatnagar, M C and Dalela R C., 1979, Organophosphate Poisoning to Freshwater Teleost, *Channa gachua* Acetylcholinesterase Inhibition. Bull. Environ. Contam. Toxicol. 21.

Waiwood K G and Johansen, A H., 1974, Oxygen Consumption and Activity of the White Sucker (*Catastomus commersoni*) in Lethal and Non Lethal Levels of Organochlorine Insecticide, Methoxychlor Water Res. 8 (7): 401-406.

Welch P S., 1948, Limnological Methods McGraw Hill Book Co. Inc. New York, London pp. 206-213.

Zeuthen E 1953 Oxygen Uptake as Related to Body Size in Organism. Quart. Rev. Biol. 28: 1-12.

Zeuthen, E., 1955, Comparative Physiology (Respiration) Ann. Rev. Physiol. 17: 459-482.

Pages: 121-131

LIMNOLOGY AND AQUATIC SCIENCE
Edited by: Dr. Shailendra Sharma; Dr. Pawan Kumar 'Bharti'
ISBN: 978-93-5056-735-7
Edition: 2015
Published by: Discovery Publishing House Pvt. Ltd., New Delhi (India)

8

Assessment of Revitalization of Certain Biomolecules of Different Organ Systems of the Nutritionally Important Catfish *Clarias Batrachus* Following Withdrawal of Arsenic Exposure

Randhir Kumar* and **T.K. Banerjee**

ABSTRACT

The present investigation deals with the recovery in arsenic concentration along with repair of the damaged biochemical configuration of five different organ systems (skin, gills, liver, brain and muscle) of the nutritionally important catfish *Clarias batrachus* following return of the 60 day sodium arsenite exposed fish to clean water without arsenic contamination. Although the amount of arsenic deposition in all the five tissues decreased significantly in recovery studies, they failed to reach the untreated control limits indicating incomplete recovery.

Similarly the concentrations of different biomolecules (total proteins, total free amino acids, DNA, RNA, lipids, glycogen, and activity of protease enzyme) in all these tissues improved substantially. However they also failed to reach the levels of untreated controls.

Eco-physiology Unit, Department of Zoology, Banaras Hindu University, Varanasi - 221 005 (UP), India.

This indicates that even after 90 days of withdrawal of the arsenic stress the recovery and regeneration were partial and the fish might not be suitable for consumption.

Key words: Arsenic recovery; *Clarias batrachus*; free amino acids; nucleic acids; lipids; protease activity.

INTRODUCTION

In recent past extensive work have been done to illustrate the toxic impact of different metals (Banerjee 2007, Chatterjee 2008) including arsenic (Roy and Bhattacharya 2006; Singh and Banerjee 2008; Palaniappan and Vijayasundaram 2009; Kumar and Banerjee 2012a, 2012b, 2012c) on various organ systems of fishes. These data mainly deal with the histopathological as well as biochemical alterations inflicted to different organ systems of the fish body that even lead to death of the individual.

Recently Kumar and Banerjee (2012a) reported extensive alteration in the biochemical configuration of certain macromolecules (proteins, nucleic acids, lipids and glycogen) of several organ systems (skin, gills, liver, brain muscles) of the economically important catfish *Clarias batrachus* following exposure to sublethal concentration of sodium arsenite for prolonged period (60 days).

The aim of present study has been to analyse the extent of recovery in the biochemical configuration of the arsenic stressed fish if returned to safer arsenic free media. Data related to such studies illustrating the withdrawal effect on the damaged tissue systems of variously stressed fishes are meager (Singh and Banerjee 2007).

MATERIALS AND METHODS

Live and healthy specimens of catfish *Clarias batrachus* (Linn) (15±1 cm in length and 45±5 g weight) purchased from a single population at Chaukaghat fish market, Varanasi were acclimated for three week in large plastic aquaria of 25 L capacity containing tap water (having dissolved 6.3 O_2 mg/L, pH=7.2, water hardness 23.2 mg/L and room temperature 28±3 °C) for 30 days. The concentrations of most of the toxic metals in the tap water were below the detection level of the instrument.

Regular feeding followed by renewal of all the media were done after every 24 h interval during acclimation as well as entire experimental period. For treated control twenty batches of ten fish each were exposed separately for 60 days to ten litres of sublethal concentration (1 ppm; 5% of LC_{50} value Kumar and Banerjee 2012b) of sodium arsenite (Batch No. G270707 Loba Chemie Pvt. Ltd. Mumbai, minimum assay 98.5-102.0%) prepared in tap water. Half of the surviving fish were sacrificed for analyses (Kumar and Banerjee 2012b).

For untreated controls (also called wild control), similar batches of ten fish were kept in plain tap water under identical laboratory conditions. For withdrawal experimentation, remaining 50% of the 60 days-arsenic ($NaAsO_2$) pre-treated fish were transferred to arsenic free tap water. Eventhough six fish died during arsenic exposure experiment no casualty was noticed during withdrawal of the arsenic stress. The sets of the entire experimental setups were simultaneously run. Nine (3 × 3=9) fish each from untreated control as well as withdrawal experiment were also sacrificed after 90 days by spinal dislocation. The arsenic concentration was measured by Parkin-Elmer atomic absorption spectrophotometer (Kumar and Banerjee 2012b).

Biochemical estimation of nucleic acid contents were performed by Schneider (1957) technique. The protein contents estimated using Lowry's method (Lowry et al. 1951). For analyses of total lipids tissue samples were subjected to extraction in chloroform methanol mixture (2:1) following the method of Folch and Stanley (1957). Glycogen content was analysed following the method of Carroll et al. (1956). Fish are known for main source of proteins to illustrate the damaged inflicted to these macromolecules the activity of the protein degrading enzyme protease and total free amino acids were estimated using the method of Moore and Stein (1954) and Spices (1957) respectively. Results are expressed as mean±SEM (n=9) calculated for each parameter considered in the present study. Pair wise comparison was also done between unexposed, arsenic-exposed and withdrawal groups by employing student'*t*-test to determine the statistical significance between the groups. The value of $p<0.05$, and $p<0.01$ were considered statistically significant.

RESULTS

Kumar and Banerjee (2012b) reported decreased body weight in arsenic stressed *C. batrachus* marked improvement in body mass took place when the arsenic stress was withdrawn for 90 days (Table 8.1). Table 8.1 also suggest improved condition factor (well-being) of the fish following withdrawal of the arsenic stress. All the five tissues showed active bioaccumulation of the arsenic salt after 60 days of exposure. (Kumar and Banerjee 2012b). Following withdrawal of the arsenic stress up to 90 days the amount of arsenic load in all the tissues decreased significantly (Fig. 8.1).

PROTEINS

The protein contents of the tissues of untreated control fish ranged between 35.11±0.889 mg/g (in brain) to 82.78 ±1.42 mg/g (in muscles) (Table 8.2). Following exposure to sodium arsenite the protein contents of all the five tissues decreased and ranged from 28.55±0.77 in gills to 72.55±1.26 mg/g in muscle (Kumar and Banerjee 2012a). Due to withdrawal of arsenic stress the protein contents in all the tissues recovered substantially with highest concentration achieved in the muscles (72.55±1.26 mg/g) and lowest in the gills (28.55±0.76 mg/g) table 8.2.

Table 8.1: Morphological Parameters in Arsenic Exposed and Withdrawal of Stress in Catfish *(Clarias batrachus)* Linn.

Period of Exposure	Morphological Parameters		
	Body Weight (g)	Body Length (cm)	Condition Factor (K)
60 days	33.55±1.13* Ψ	15.05±0.20 Ψ	0.91±0.039
90 days withdrawal	44.01±0.85*[a]	15.26±0.08	1.19±0.034[a]
0 day CTRL	47.00 ±0.66 Ψ	15.44±0.07 Ψ	1.39±0.026

Values are shown as mean ± SEM, the degree of significance was denoted as:

- $p < 0.05$ for comparisons of arsenic exposed to zero day control.
- [a]- significant difference with 60 days exposed.

Ψ - Cited from Kumar & Banerjee (2012 b).

CTRL- Control.

K factor denotes:

1.60 Excellent condition, trophy class fish.

1.40 A good, well proportioned fish.

1.20 A fair fish, acceptable to many anglers.

1.00 A poor fish, long and thin.

0.80 Extremely poor fish, resembling a big head and narrow, thin body.

FREE AMINO ACIDS

The total free amino acid contents of different tissues of untreated control fish ranged from 3.14±0.61 (gills) to 7.65±0.107 (muscles) mg/g wet wt of tissue. Following exposure the total free amino acid contents of all the tissues increased (8.32±0.038 in gills to 28.30±0.312 (in muscles) mg/g wet wt (Kumar and Banerjee 2012c). Following withdrawal of arsenic stress the total free amino acid contents in all the tissues recovered substantially with maximum concentration found in muscles (12.85±0.136 mg/g) and minimum in brain (5.85±0.119 mg/g) (Table 8.3).

DNA

The DNA content of the tissues of untreated control fish ranged between 1.46±0.044 mg/g in brain to 7.13±0.09 mg/g in gills. Following exposure the DNA content of all the tissues decreased (1.33±0.044 in brain to 4.77± 0.44 mg/g in gills) (Kumar and Banerjee 2012a). Following withdrawal of the arsenic stress there was significant increase in the DNA content of the tissues with highest concentration observed in gills (5.37±0.164), and lowest in brain (1.41±0.035 mg/g) (Table 8.2).

RNA

The RNA contents of the tissues of untreated control fish ranged between 0.49± 0.016 mg/g (in brain) to 7.03±0.060 mg/g (in gills). The RNA content of the tissues also decreased following arsenic stress (0.38± 0.001

mg/g in brain to 4.06±0.066 mg/g in gills) (Kumar and Banerjee 2012a). Following withdrawal RNA content of all the five tissues recovered significant with highest concentration noticed in gills (6.14±0.140 mg/g) and lowest in brain (0.44± 0.080 mg/g) Table 8.2.

LIPIDS

The lipid concentration of the tissues of wild control fish ranged between 21.32±0.606 (in skin) to 66.16± 0.871 mg/g (in brain) (Table 8.2). In exposed fish the amount of lipids decreased in four tissues namely skin (14.83±0.673 mg/g), gills (17.91±0.891 mg/g), brain (48.11±1.148 mg/g), and muscles (26.74±1.036 mg/g). In liver however the lipid concentration increased (64.93 ±0.724 mg/g) (Kumar and Banerjee 2012a).

Following exposure to clean water the lipid contents increased in four tissues (skin, gills, brain and muscles). In liver it decreased to 61.74±1.409 mg/g from 64.93±0.724 mg/g in exposed fish) (Table 8.2).

GLYCOGEN

The glycogen content in tissues of the untreated control fish ranged between 3.46±0.078 mg/g (in muscles) to 33.58±0.621 mg/g (in liver) (Table 8.2). In exposed fish its amount decreased in all the tissues ranging from 1.40±0.108 mg/g in muscles to 10.80±0.115 mg/g in brain (Kumar and Banerjee 2012a). Due to withdrawal of arsenic stress the glycogen content in all these tissues recovered substantially with highest concentration found in liver (28.68±0.760 mg/g) and lowest in muscle (2.42±0.081 mg/g) Table 8.2.

PROTEASE ACTIVITY

The protease activity of skin, gills, liver, brain and muscles of untreated control fish ranged from 0.26±0.011 (in skin) to 0.70±0.015 mmoles of tyrosine equivalent /mg protein/hour (in liver). The protease activity increased significantly in all the five tissues after 60 days of arsenic exposure 1.48±0.014 (in liver) to 0.63±0.014 (in gills) mmoles of tyrosine equivalent/mg protein/ hour (Kumar and Banerjee 2012c). The significant decrease in the stress of arsenic on the activity of the enzyme in all the tissues was noticed after 90 days of withdrawal with maximum (0.66±0.025) in liver and minimum (0.46±0.033) in gills (Table 8.3).

DISCUSSION

The severely damage caused to various biomolecules of *C. batrachus* due to toxic impact of trivalent arsenic has recently been illustrated by Kumar and Banerjee (2012a). The degree of amelioration achieved following withdrawal of arsenic stress by returning the stressed fish to clean water has been documented in this paper. The protein contents of all these tissues showed significant recovery with increased concentration following withdrawal of the arsenic stress. However the amount of proteins in these regenerating tissues could not reach the levels of the untreated control fish.

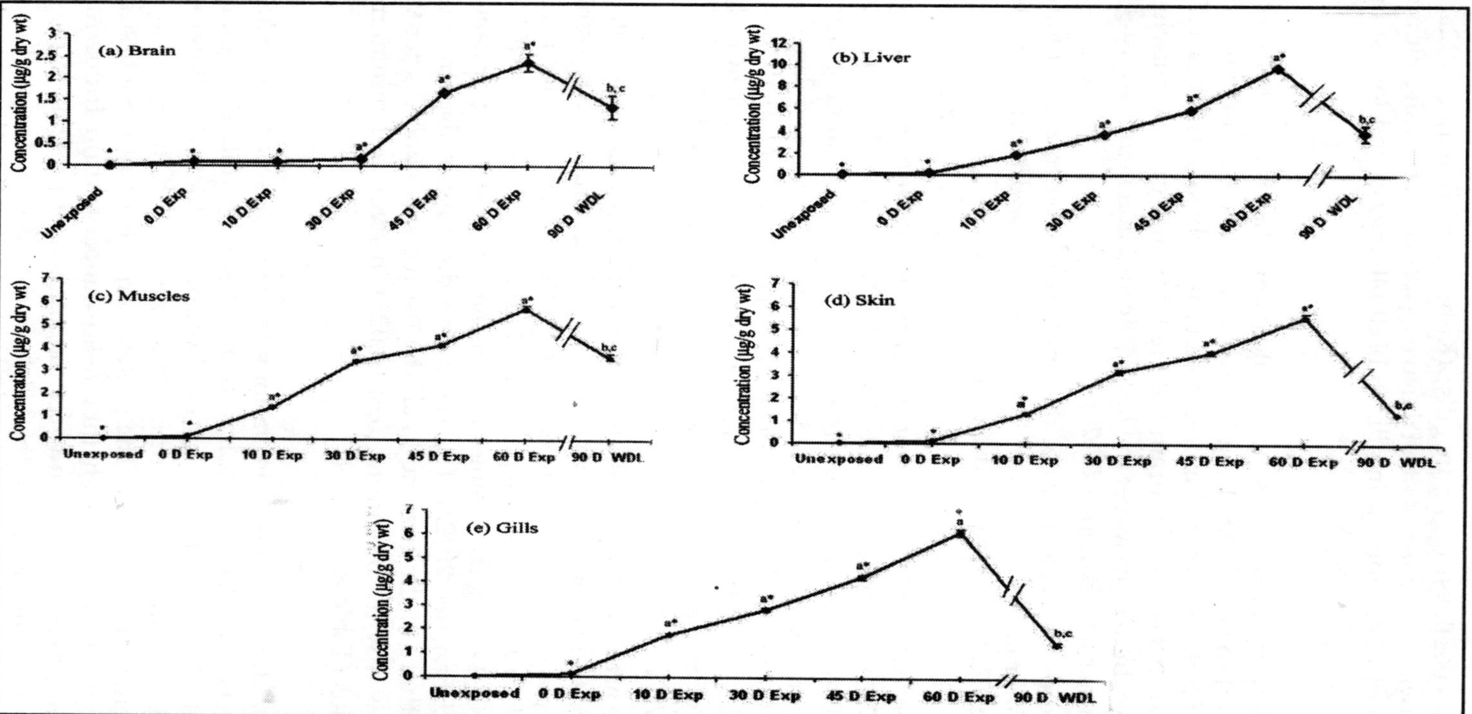

Fig. 8.1 (a-e): Concentration (μg/g dry wt) of Arsenic in Different Tissues **(a)** Brain, **(b)** Liver, **(c)** Muscles **(d)** Skin, **(e)** Gills of *C. batrachus* after 90 days of withdrawal of stress

Symbol:

[a] Significant (p<0.05) difference when exposed groups were compared with 0 day control group.

[b] Significant (p<0.05) difference when withdrawal groups were compared with 60 days exposed group.

[c] Significant (p<0.05) difference when withdrawal groups were compared with 0 day control group.

* Kumar and Banerjee (2012c).

Table 8.2: Fluctuations in Different Biomolecules in Various tissues of *C. batrachus* at Different Periods of Exposure and 90 Days Withdrawal (of mg/L of Sodium Arsenite).Total Protein, DNA, RNA, Lipids, Glycogen were Expressed in mg/gm wet wt of Tissue

Biomolecules	Exposure	Tissues					References
		Brain	Liver	Muscles	Skin	Gills	
Proteins	60 D EXP.	22.55±1.248[a]	40.88±1.206[a]	45.66±1.536[a]	33.22±1.289[a]	15.66±0.799[a]	Kumar & Banerjee (2012a)
	90 D WTD	30.44±1.302[b,c]	66.11±0.824[b,c]	72.55±1.259[b,c]	57.66±1.130[b]	28.55±0.765[b,c]	Present findings
	0 D CTRL	35.11±0.889	80.78±2.21	82.78 ±1.42	69.22 ± 0.996	40.88±1.16	Kumar & Banerjee (2012a)
DNA	60 D EXP.	1.33±0.044[NS]	2.26±0.060[NS]	4.76±0.130[NS]	2.53±0.600[a]	4.77±0.044[a]	Kumar & Banerjee (2012a)
	90 D WTD	1.41±0.035[NS]	2.3±0.052 [NS]	5.23±0.093[b]	2.33±0.033[NS]	5.37±0.164[c]	Present findings
	0 D CTRL	1.46±0.044	2.56±0.044	5.63±0.21	4.74±0.128	7.13±0.088	Kumar & Banerjee (2012a)
RNA	60 D EXP.	0.38 ± 0.001[a]	0.576±0.136[a]	1.23±0.44[a]	2.40±0.76[a]	4.06±0.066[a]	Kumar & Banerjee (2012a)
	90 D WTD	0.44±00.8[b]	0.730± 0.018[c]	3.52±0.0846[b]	3.51±0.078[NS]	6.14±0.140[c]	Present findings
	0 D CTRL	0.49±0.016	0.92±0.007	5.46 ±0.142	3.90±0.180	7.03±0.06	Kumar & Banerjee (2012a)
Lipids	60 D EXP.	48.1±1.148 [a]	64.93±0.724 [a]	26.74±1.036 [a]	14.83±0.673 [a]	17.9±0.891[a]	Kumar & Banerjee (2012a)
	90 D WTD	51.86±1.146[c]	61.74±1.409[c]	31.30±0.690[b,c]	21.63±0.617[NS]	21.11±0.478[b,c]	Present findings
	0 D CTRL	66.16±0.871	55.33±0.915	35.45±0.553	21.32±0.606	24.77±0.314	Kumar & Banerjee (2012a)
Glycogen	60 D EXP.	10.80±0.115[a]	8.90±0.551[a]	1.40±0.108[a]	2.93±0.130[a]	2.48±0.144[a]	Kumar & Banerjee (2012a)
	90 D WTD	3.14±0.110[b,c]	28.68±0.760[b,c]	2.42±0.081[b,c]	4.01±0.113[b]	3.85±0.116[NS]	Present findings
	0 D CTRL	15.00±0.330	33.58±0.621	3.46±0.078	4.83±0.197	4.62±0.166	Kumar & Banerjee (2012a)

Note: Data are shown as mean±SEM (n=9). Two way ANOVA followed by Dunnett's t-test was performed to check the level of significance between the treated with Sodium arsenite and untreated group of the fish. The criterion for significance was set at $p < 0.01$. Each experiment was repeated twice with 9 fish.

Symbol:

[a] Significant, when exposed groups were compared with 0 day controls.

[b] Significant, when withdrawal groups were compared with 60 days exposed group

[c] Significant, when withdrawal groups were compared with 0 days unexposed control group

[NS] Not Significant with 60 days exposed group.

D- day, FAA-Free amino acids, EXP- exposure WTD- Withdrawal, CTRL- Control.

Table 8.3: Fluctuations in Different Biomolecules in Various Tissues of *C. batrachus* at Different Periods of Exposure and 90 Days Withdrawal of Exposure of 1mg/L of Sodium Arsenite.

Biomolecules	Exposure	Tissues					References
		Brain	Liver	Muscles	Skin	Gills	
Free amino acids (mg/g)	60 D EXP.	11.02±0.18 [a]	19.1±1.11[a]	28.29±0.31[a,b]	17.45±0.49[a,b]	8.32±0.04[a,b]	Kumar & Banerjee (2012c)
	90 D WTD	5.85±0.12[b,c]	8.29±0.17 [b,c]	12.85±0.14[b,c]	10.46±0.05[b,c]	6.25±0.12[b,c]	Present findings
	0 D CTRL	4.36±0.89	4.17±0.129	7.65±0.11	3.48± 0.08	3.14±0.06	Kumar & Banerjee (2012c)
Protease activity (m moles of tyrosine equivalent/ mgProtein/hour.)	60 D EXP.	0.72±0.01[a]	1.48±0.01[a]	0.73±0.01[a]	0.94±0.012[a]	0.63±0.015[a]	Kumar & Banerjee (2012c)
	90 D WTD	0.48±0.050[NS]	0.66±0.03[b, NS]	0.50±0.046[c]	0.57±0.062[b,c]	0.46±0.033[NS]	Present findings
	0 D CTRL	0.493±0.023	0.70±0.02	0.29±0.012	0.26±0.012	0.42±0.015	Kumar & Banerjee (2012c)

Note: Data are shown as mean±SEM (n=9). Two way ANOVA followed by Dunnett's t-test was performed to check the level of significance between the treated with Sodium arsenite and untreated group of the fish. The criterion for significance was set at p <0.01. Each experiment was repeated twice with 9 fish.

Symbol:

[a] Significant differ, when exposed groups were compared with 0 day controls.

[b] Significant differ, when withdrawal groups were compared with 60 days exposed group.

[c] Significant differ, when withdrawal groups were compared with 0 days unexposed control group.

NS Not significant differ with 60 days exposed group.

D- day, FAA-Free amino acids, EXP- exposure WTD- Withdrawal, CTRL- Control.

The reason for increased level of proteins could either be due to their increased biosynthesis or termination of degradation of proteins because the additional requirement of energy supply for combating arsenic stress was substantially decreased. This increase in the protein level was substantial in the gills and skin perhaps due to decreased quantity of slime secretion which is mainly made up of glycoproteins. Also due to withdrawal of the ambient arsenic stress the rate of sloughing of damaged cells from the surface of the skin decreased significantly. The increase in the protein contents in the liver was also considerable as it is one of the main site of protein synthesis needed so urgently for regeneration of the damaged tissues. Recovery in the protein level in the brain is not so substantial because of tight blood barrier in the brain causing its difficult transportation. In the muscles also the recovery was not so extensive in comparison to the gills, skin and liver because of poor blood circulation in the muscular tissues.

Following withdrawal the amount of the total free amino acids in all the tissues decreased substantially indicating their use in protein biosynthesis or reduction in protein breakdown due to absence of ambient arsenic stress. However the level of the free amino acids of all these tissues still continued to be above the untreated control levels indicating incomplete recovery and regeneration. Withdrawal of toxicity although restored the enzyme activity in brain, liver and gills greatly that almost reached control levels, in skin and muscle the enzyme activity was still above the untreated control levels. Decreased activity of the enzyme in recovery experiment indicates retarded protein breakdowns which got reflected in increased concentration of proteins (Table 8.2).

Following withdrawal of arsenic stress, four out of five tissues showed substantial increase in the lipids contents indicating repair and substantial recovery of these organ systems. However their concentration remained below the untreated control levels. On the contrary liver, the fifth tissue showed significant decrease which still continued to be above the untreated control limit. The higher level of lipids in the liver in comparison to untreated controls following withdrawal indicates the continuation of damaged (fatty degenerated) condition of this organ system even after 90 days of recovery. Recovery of lipid contents of the skin after 90 days withdrawal to the level of untreated control fish indicates the better regenerating capacity of this vital boundary tissue needed for continuous protection of the fish.

The glycogen contents of all the tissues of arsenic stressed fish increased. However its recovery in different tissues was partial and continued to remain below the untreated control levels indicating disturbed glycogen metabolism. Increased level of glycogen in the liver might have perhaps led to increased concentration of lipids. The increase in the glycogen level of the gills in the recovery experiment was not significant perhaps because of continuous utilization of this carbohydrate for breathing requirement. Garg et al. (2009) also observed recovery of lipid and carbohydrate contents in different tissues of three Indian major carps *Labeo rohita, Cirrhinus mrigala* and *Catla catla* following withdrawal of three different metal stresses. Excepting skin which showed decreased level, the DNA contents of all other tissues showed increased concentration indicating their recovery and regeneration due to absence of ambient arsenic stress.

Decreased concentration of DNA in the skin during recovery might perhaps be a process to discard/reject the damage/arsenic loaded cells. Increase in the DNA level in the gills might indicate regeneration leading to hyperplasia (Banerjee 2007) of the epithelial lining of primary and secondary lamellae. The RNA level of all these tissues increased in clean water returned fish. Increased RNA contents indicate synthesis of proteins (Table 8.2) for repair activities during regeneration. In the skin increase in the RNA level might also be due to synthesis and accumulation of slime especially by the goblet cells. However the level of RNA of clean water returned fish did not reach the levels of the untreated control specimens indicating incomplete recovery.

CONCLUSION

60 days of sodium arsenite exposure inflicted severe damage to different organ systems of the air breathing catfish *Clarias batrachus*. Withdrawal of the arsenic stress led to the significant regeneration and repair of these tissue systems. The recovery was however partial and never reached the levels of untreated control fish because of bioconcentration of metalloid in different fish tissues. Hence the consumption of these recovered fish is still may not be safe.

REFERENCES

Banerjee, T.K. (2007), Histopathology of Respiratory Organs of Certain Air-breathing Fishes of India. *Fish Physiology and Biochemistry* 33, 441-454.

Carroll, N.V., Longley, W.R. & Roe, J.H. (1956). The Determination of Glycogen in Liver and Muscle by Use of Anthrone Reagent. *Journal of Biological Chemistry* 220, 583-593.

Chatterjee, I. (2008). Studies on the Toxicity of Manganese Chloride on the Respiratory Organs of Air-breathing Catfish *Heteropneustes fossilis* (Bloch.) Thesis Submitted to Banaras Hindu University, Varanasi, India for the award of Ph.D., Degree.

Folch, J., Iers, M. & Stanley, G. H. S. (1957). A Simple Method for the Isolation and Purification of Total Lipids from Animal Tissues. *Journal of Biological Chemistry* 226, 497-509.

Garg, S., Gupta, R. & Jain, K.(2009). Sublethal Effects of Heavy Metals on Biochemical Composition and Their Recovery in Indian Major Carps. *Journal of Hazardous Materials* 163, 1369-1384.

Kumar, R. & Banerjee, T.K.(2012a). Study of Sodium Arsenite Induced Biochemical Changes on Certain Biomolecules of the Freshwater Catfish *Clarias batrachus.* Neotropical Ichthyology 10, 451-459.

Kumar, R. & Banerjee, T.K.(2012b). Arsenic Bioaccumulation in the Nutritionally Important Catfish *Clarias batrachus* Exposed to the Trivalent Arsenic Salt, Sodium Arsenite. Bulletin of Environmental Contamination and Toxicology 12, 714-718.

Kumar, R. & Banerjee, T.K. (2012c), Changes in the Level of Certain Biomolecules (Proteins, Free Amino Acids and Protease Activities) of the Catfish *Clarias batrachus* in Response to Sodium Meta-arsenite Intoxication. Clean Soil Air Water, doi 10.1002/clen.201200041.

Lowry, O.H., Rosebrough, N.J., Farr, A.L. & Randall, R.J. (1951), Protein Measurement with Folin-Phenol Reagent. *Journal of Biological Chemistry* 193, 265-275.

Moore, S. & Stein, W.H.(1954), In: Methods in Enzymology. Vol. I (Ed. Colowick and Kaplan). Academic Press, New York.

Palaniappan, P.L.R.M. & Vijayasundaram, V. (2009), Effect of Arsenic Intoxication on Proteins and Lipids of *Labeo rohita* Gill Tissues: An FT-IR Study', *Toxicological and Environmental Chemistry* 91, 1125-1134.

Roy, S. & Bhattacharya, S. (2006), Arsenic-induced Histopathology and Synthesis of Stress Proteins in Liver and Kidney of *Channa punctatus. Ecotoxicology and Environmental Safety* 65, 218-229.

Schneider, W.C. (1957), Determination of Nucleic Acids in Tissues by Pentose Analysis. In: Colowick SP, Kaplan NO (eds) Methods in Enzymology, Vol. 3. Academic Press, New York, 680-684.

Singh, A.K. (2007). Toxicopathological Effect of the Arsenic Salt, Sodium Arsenate on the Respiratory Organs of the Walking Catfish *Clarias batrachus* (L.) Ph.D., Dissertation of Banaras Hindu University, Varanasi, India.

Singh, A.K. & Banerjee, T.K. (2008), Recovery of Damages in the Skin of Arsenic Exposed *Clarias batrachus* (Linn.) Following Withdrawal of the Stress. *Iranian Journal of Environmental Health Science and Engineering* 4, 217-224.

Spices, J.R. (1957). Colorimetric Procedures for Amino Acids. In: Methods of Enzymology (S.P. Calowick and N.O. Kaplon. Eds.). Academic press, New York. 468.

Pages: 132-137

LIMNOLOGY AND AQUATIC SCIENCE
Edited by: Dr. Shailendra Sharma; Dr. Pawan Kumar 'Bharti'
ISBN: 978-93-5056-735-7
Edition: 2015
Published by: Discovery Publishing House Pvt. Ltd., New Delhi (India)

9

Effects of Seasonal Variations of Ambient Water Temperature on Oxygen Consumption in an Air Breathing Murrel Fish, *Channa gachua*

D.N. Sadhu* and Qaisur Rahman

ABSTRACT

In the present investigation an attempt has been made to study the effects of seasonal variations of ambient water temperature on dual modes of oxygen consumption in an air breathing murrel fish, *Channa gachua* as a mark of metabolic activities. In this species the oxygen uptake from water, air as well as total varied considerably with the seasonal variation of ambient water temperature. The aquatic, aerial and total oxygen consumption was 49.98, 52.02 and 102.0 ml/kg/hr respectively lowest during the month of December. The oxygen uptake gradually increased with the rise in temperature reaching at its maximum in June i.e. 69.30, 95.70 and 165.0 ml/kg/hr.

The aquatic oxygen consumption also showed rising trends from December on wards reaching its peak 70.53ml/kg/hr in Ju1y. The percentage of aerial oxygen uptake was lowest i.e.51% in December and 58% in June when the temperature reached almost maximum 31.4 °C. Thus the nature of oxygen consumption is

Department of Zoology, Vinoba Bhave University, Hazaribag - 825 301 Jharkhand, India.

directly proportional to the ambient water temperature. A significant positive relationship exists between water temperature and oxygen consumption. The correlation co-efficient(r) for aquatic, aerial and total oxygen consumption was noted to be 1.0, 1.0 and 1. 04 at lower temperature range (21.6° - 28.2° C) and 0.943, 0.9907 and 0.9901 at higher temperature range from (21.6° - 31.4° C) respectively.

Key words: Ambient water temperature, Oxygen consumption, *Channa gachua*.

INTRODUCTION

Organisms live in a particular environment which is subject to marked seasonal fluctuations (Wolfson, 1964). Seasonal changes in the environmental conditions (viz-temperature, pH, rainfall etc) have pronounced effect on the life of poikilothermic animals. Successful living demands a continual adjustment or regulation of the internal media with the changing environmental conditions. For ecological adaptations, it is not the animal which as a whole changes but they gradually acclimatize their physiological machinary to the changing external environmental conditions. According to Welch (1948) no other single factor has so many profound direct influences than temperature in aquatic organisms.

Fishes are also poikilothermic vertebrates, always in danger of various sorts of stress, either living in a home of vast pond or small ditch, which are rnainly influenced by temperature changes in the environment. Temperature is one of the most important physical factor in the environment of an animal particularly the fishes. High temperature tends to increase nearly all the metabolic processes and simultaneously disrupts the structural integrity of the animal. Information on temperature tolerance and resistance is of much value in judging the ecophysiological characteristics of fishes. It has been experimentally shown that one of the causes of thermal death is the osmoregulatory failure at temperature extremes (Fry, 1971). In a changed environmental condition organism tries to adapt and adjust to sustain its life is called acclimatization or it must try to prevent or minimise changes in its body temperature is called thermoregulation. Changes in the environment and its composition compel the organism to alter its body physiology and biochemistry in order to cope up with this novel threat. A perusal of literature (Sinha, 1988, Perween, 1988 and Kaur, 1996) indicates that our information regarding the effect of seasonal changes of ambient water temperature in *Channa gachua* is very limited as such the present work has been undertaken as an endeavour to fill up the gap of our knowledge in this regard in a fresh water teleost.

MATER1ALS AND METHODS

Live *Channa gachua* were procured from the local fish market at Hazaribag (Latitude 25°59′ N and Longitude 85°22′E) and maintained in glass aquaria of size (90x60x60 cm). The fishes were fed on chopped goat liver daily and acclimatized for 15days in laboratory. The concentration of dissolved oxygen in the water was estimated by Winkler's volumetric method (Welch, 1948). Routine oxygen consumption was measured with the help of respirometer after Munshi and Dube (1973). Aquatic oxygen consumption was calculated from the difference between the oxygen level of the ambient water in the respirometer before and after the experiment and the volume of water inside the respirorneter. Oxygen consumption from air was calculated from the range of imbalance by the level of the fluid in the manometer and by the use of combined gas law equation of vapour presure (Dejours, 1975). The experimental animals including control ones were divided into different groups each containing ten fishes. To study the effects of seasonal variation of ambient water temperature the experiments were conducted at 29.0 ± 1.5°C. Monthly data of atmospheric temperature were obtained from the Central Rain Fed Upland Rice Research Institute (ICAR), Hazaribag from January to December 2008. Sexually mature fishes of same weight group (40-50gm) were used in the present study.

RESULTS

The aquatic, aerial and total oxygen consumption due to seasonal variation of ambient water temperature are summarized in table 1. It was observed that the oxygen uptake from water and air as well as total (water +air) varied considerably with the season. The lowest aquatic, aerial and total oxygen uptake (ml/kg/hr) was observed in December when the temperature was lowest and found to be 49.8, 52.02 and 102.0 (ml/kg/hr) respectively. The aerial and total oxygen uptake gradually increased with the rise in temperature when reached its maximum in June and was calculated to be 95.75 and 165.0 (ml/kg/hr) respectively. The aquatic oxygen uptake increased from December onwards reaching at the highest level of 70.53 (rnl/kg/hr) in July. Thus it was evident that the O consumption was higher in summer than in winter.

A perusal of table1 showed that the percentage of aerial oxygen uptake increased with the rise in temperature and decreased with fall in temperature. The percentage of aerial oxygen consumption was lowest i.e. 51% in December and 58% in June when the temperature reached at its maximum. Again the percentage of aerial oxygen uptake gradually decreased from October to December months. The aquatic and aerial oxygen consumption Quotient also showed decreasing trend with the rising in temperature reaching at its lowest at the highest temperature in June and afterwards gradually increased and reached the highest in December. The oxygen consumption increased with the increased in ambient water temperature and decreased with fall in ambient water temperature. The aquatic, aerial and total oxygen consumption in December was 49.8, 52.02 and 102.0 (ml/kg/hr) where as in June it was noted to be 69.3, 95.70 and 165.0 (ml/kg/hr) respectively.

Statistically significant positive relationship exists between water temperature and oxygen consumption. The correlation co-efficient(r) for aquatic, aerial and total oxygen uptake was 1.0, 1.0 and 1.04 at lower temperature range (21.6-28.2°C) whereas 0.943, 0.9907 and 0.9901 at higher temperature range (28.2-31.4°C) respectively. The rate of oxygen consumption increased profoundly at temperature beyond 28.2°C. It was found that at low temperature range (21 .6-28.2°C) the aquatic, aerial and total oxygen consumption increased by a power of 3.003, 5.05 and 8.06 respectively with unit increase in ambient water temperature.

DISCUSSION

In majority of fishes the metabolic rate increases with the increasing water temperature. Schaperclaus (1933) found that the rate of metabolic activities in fishes gets doubled with 10° C rise of water temperature. Fry and Hart (1948) reported that a change from 10°-20°C increased the standard oxygen uptake in gold fish by 25%. In *Salmo gairdneri* the maximum active oxygen uptake occurs at 15-20°C Dickson (1968) and in *Salmo clarki* the maximum point has reached at 15°C (Dwyer, 1969). The oxygen consumption of *Pomato schistus* species at resting and during forced swimming increased exponentially with rise in water temperature from 5°-20°C Fond and Veldhuis (1973).

Rajgopal and Kramer(1974) also reported that the active metabolic rate of *Gila atria* (Giard) were 3.25, 3.60, 3.07, 4.83 and 3.85 times the standard metabolic rate at 6°, 9°, 12°, 18° and 22° C respectively. In *H. fossilis* the increase in oxygen consumption has been found to be closely associated with an increasing water temperature. It was observed by Pandey (1975) that during summer when water temperature was high the fishes *(H.fossilis)* come to the surface of water frequently to engulf air but the case was just reverse in winter at lower temperature. This behaviour of the fish was similar with the finding of De Roth (1973) in *Lepidosteus occulatus* and Horn and Riggs (1973) in *Amia calva*. Such behaviour in *H.fossilis* Pandey (1975) reveals that gills are more efficient in winter months with minimum aerial respiration but in summer the aerial respiration increased as the fishes come to the surface of water to engulf air. The increased aerial respiration in summer (June) might be correlated with the fall in dissolved oxygen content of the water at high temperature. In June the oxygen content was low (5.2ppm) which increased to a value of (8.2ppm) in winter.

De Roth (1973) studied the effect of temperature and light on aerial breathing behaviour of the spotted gar, *Lepidosteus occulatus*. He reported that number of aerial breathes per hour increased as temperature increased from 15°- 28°C. Rate of breathing were consistently higher during hours of darkness than during light hours. Pandey (1978) in *H. fossilis* observed a clear trend of increase in oxygen consumption with increasing water temperature. The correlation coefficients between the water temperature and oxygen consumption under both the experimental conditional (viz. surfacing prevented and surfacing allowed) were high. Sinha and Pandey (1985) tried to established direct relationship between ambient water temperature and oxygen consumption through gills in three species of fresh water fishes viz, *A. testudineus M. aculeatus and C.punctatus*. They found the best fit between temperature and oxygen consumption by showing the relationship by two separate regression lines in all the three species of fishes. The temperature ranges for *A. testudineus* were 21.5°-29°C and 29°-31°C for *M.aculeatum* it was 20°-29°C and 29°-31°C and for *C.punctatus* this range was 21.7°-29.1°C and 29.1-31.7°C. They reported that at lower temperature range with unit increased in temperature the oxygen consumption increased by a power of 2.347, 2.493 and 2.211 respectively in *Anabas testudineus, M. aculeatum* and *C.punctatus*. Sinha and Pandey (1985) have also calculated mean Q10 values of oxygen uptake at low and high temperature ranges.

In the present investigation in *Channa gachua* the relationship between the ambient water temperature and oxygen uptake were established by showing the relationship by two separate regression lines i.e. between 21.6°-28.2°C and 28.2°-31.4°C. It was found that at lower temperature range (21.6°-28.2°C) the oxygen consumption through water, air and total increased a power of 3.003, 5.05 and 8.06 respectively with unit increase in water temperature. It is interesting to note that the rate of aquatic, aerial and total oxygen uptake increased as soon as the temperature level reaches beyond 28° C. It may be noted that 28.2°-31.4°C which is available in March to July. This period is of preparation for reproductive activity, gonadal maturation and breeding which requires more energy and consequently greater oxygen demand. Another point of interest that 30°C temperature is available to the fish after breeding season (August to October), but oxygen consumption is lower than that of breeding season.This further emphasizes the contention that more oxygen is needed during breeding season and also suggests that temperature is not the only factor to cause the rise in aquatic, aerial and total oxygen consumption. Thus it is evident from the above discussion that ambient water temperature imparts considerable effects on the bimodal gas exchange mechanism in *Channa gachua* and also has direct bearing on breeding of fishes.

REFERENCES

Dejours, I975. "Principles of Comparative Respiratory Physiology." Amsterdam. North Holland Publishing Company, 253.

De Roth. G.C. 1973, Effect of Temperature and Light on Aerial Breathing Behaviour of the Spottedgar, *Lepidosteus occulatus.* Ophio. J.Sci. 1: 34-41.

Dickson. I. 1968. Factors Influencing Respiratory Metabolism in Rainbow Trout. *Salmo gairdneri.* Ph.D. Thesis Utah State University. 104

Dwyer. W.P. 1969. The Influence of Temperature on Scope for Activity of Cut Throat Trout. *Salmo clarki*. Ph.D. Thesis Utah State University. 33

Fry, F.E.J. 1971. The Effect of Environmental Factors on the Physiology of Fish. In "Fish Physiology" Edited by W.S.Hoar and D.J. Randall. Vol. VI, 1-98.

Fry, F.E.J. and Hart, J.S. 1948. The Relation of Temperature to Oxygen Consumption in the Gold Fish. Bio. Bull 94: 66-77.

Fond, M and Veidhuis, C. 1973. The Oxygen Consumption of Four *Pomatoschistus* Species (Pisces, Gobidae) in Relation to Water Temperature. Nether. J. Sca. Res. 7: 376-386.

Horn, M.H. and Riggs, C.D. 1973. Effect of Temperature and Light on the Rate of an Air Breathing of the Bow Fish *Amia calva* copeia. 4: 653-657.

Kaur, Manjeet. 1996. Haernatological Studies in a Fresh Water Fish, *Rita rita* (Ham.) Ph.D. Thesis. Magadh Univ, Bodh Gaya.

Munshi. J.S.D. and Dube, S.C. 1973. Oxygen Uptake Capacity of Gills in Relation to Body Size of the Air Breathing Fish. *Anabas testudineus* (Bloch.) Acta.Physol. Acad. Sci. Hung. 44: 113 - 123.

Pandey, B.N. 1975. Effect of Salinity and Low pH on the Blood and Oxygen Consumption in an Air Breathing Fish, *H. fossilis* (Bloch) J.Indian Bio. Assoc. 1: 137-140.

Pandey, B.N. 1985. Seasonal Variation in Oxygen Consumption of *H. fosslis* (B1och) Z.Tier Physiol. Tierer Hating U.F.U. herrnittelkde. 40: 165-170.

Perween, R.1988. Studies on Some Aspects of Dietary Requirements and Other Factors Affecting Growth in *Catla catla* (Ham) Ph.D. Thesis. Magadh Univ, Bodh Gaya.

Rajgopal, P.K. and Kramer, R.H. 1974. Respiratory Metabolism of Utah Chub. *Gila atria* (Giard) and Speckled dace, *Rhinichthys oscenlus* (Giard). J.Fish. Biol.6: 215-222.

Schaeperclaus, W. 1933. Text Book of Pond Culture U.S. Fish, Wild Life Serv. Fishery Leaflet. 311: 1-240.

Sinha, Archana 1988. Studies on the Effect of Heat Stress on the Air Breathing Teleost *Heteropneustes fossilis* Ph.D. Thesis L.N.M. Univ. Dharbhanga.

Sinha, D.P. and Pandey, B.N. 1985. Effect of Ambient Water Temperature on Oxygen Uptake in Some Fresh Water Fishes. Intl.J.Acad. Ichthyol (Proc.v) 6: 31-35.

Welch, P.S. 1948. Limnological Methods. Mc Graw Hill Book co. Inc. N.Y. London, 206-213.

Wolfson, A. 1964. Animal Photoperiodism "In Photo Physiology". Edited by A.G. Giese. A.P.N.Y:47-58.

Pages: 138-156

LIMNOLOGY AND AQUATIC SCIENCE
Edited by: **Dr. Shailendra Sharma; Dr. Pawan Kumar 'Bharti'**
ISBN: 978-93-5056-735-7
Edition: **2015**
Published by: **Discovery Publishing House Pvt. Ltd., New Delhi (India)**

Limnology of Sahastradhara River at Dehradun (Uttarakhand), India

Kehar Singh[1] and **Pawan K. Bharti**[1, 2, 3]

ABSTRACT

Sahastradhara stream is a major tributary of river Saung, 15 Km. far away from Dehradun city in Uttarakhand. It has a great importance as a picnic tourist spot of the region, whereas there is not much industrial and agricultural pollution. Hill streams of the area are the cradle of nutrients especially calcium and magnesium in the form of ions. Anthropogenic factors mainly tourists activities and catchments runoff may influence the index of nutrients in stream water. Nutrients play a vital role into niche restoration maintenance, self-regulation and water quality. Location variation in ions concentration of the stream was studied with special reference to correlation with physico-chemical parameters of the stream water. Calcium and Magnesium were observed in

1 Department of Zoology and Environmental Sciences, Gurukula Kangri University, Haridwar (Uttarakhand) - 249 404, India.

2 Society for Environment, Health, Awareness of Nutrition & Toxicology (SEHAT-India), 1775, Sohanganj, Near Clock Tower, Delhi-7, India.

3 Antarctica Laboratory, R&D Division, Shriram Institute for Industrial Research, Delhi-7, India.

higher range in Sahastradhara stream as comparison to other hill-streams. Calcium and Magnesium were found maximum 104.21 mg/l and 68 mg/l respectively in summer season. Planktonic diversity and primary productivity was also measured at different selected sites.

Key words: Sahastradhara, Water quality monitoring, Aquatic pollution, physico-chemical parameters

INTRODUCTION

Himalayas are the cradle of a large number of streams and mighty rivers. Lesser Himalayas consists of a main part of Uttarakhand i.e. Kumaon and Garhwal Himalaya. Dehradun, Hardwar & Rishikesh are the main religious and beautiful cities, situated in the foothills of Garhwal Himalaya. A hill-stream Sahastradhara, a major tributary of river Song flows downward through Dehradun valley.

Dehradun valley rests in the arms of the Himalaya in the North and Shiwalik in the South and transversely bordered by Ganga in the South-East. Yamuna in the North-West forms an intermontane valley ecosystem extending from 29° 55′ to 30° 30′ N latitude and 77° 35′ to 78° 20′ E longitude with the area of about 2000 square kilometer ranging from 330 meter to 1800 m above msl (Valdiya, 1975).

The main sources of water in Himalayas are glaciers. The glaciers are an important resource of fresh water stored in the solid state and regulated by climate. Glacier melts and the water pass through heavy & porous sediment materials in the form of river. Water is the basic requirement of all living organisms. Lotic habitats are those exiting in relatively fast running streams, springs, river and brooks. The lentic habitats represent lakes, marshes, swamps, ponds and wetlands. A hill-stream consists of two major zones, Rhithron and Potamon. Aquatic biodiversity is mainly occurring in potamon zone due to the slow velocity of running water.

Ecological study of hill stream describes the distribution & abundance of aquatic living organisms and also their contribution into environment. Biological diversity mainly influenced by the physicochemical characteristics of the aquatic ecosystem through the food chain. The biotic community in the stream exhibited the quantitative and qualitative fluctuations due to varied nutrient dynamics and ultimately changed the different trophic status of species community and limnological status of aquatic ecosystem.

Physico-chemical and biological parameters play an important role in population dynamics of phytoplankton, zooplankton, benthos and fishes. Various parameters that affect the population dynamics of phytoplankton may be broadly classified as light intensity, photoperiod, chlorophyll content, nutrient availability, transparency, turbidity, temperature, velocity, water column depth. Light intensity, duration and water column depth are the basic parameters and others are the derived ones (Khanna *et al.*, 2005)

The present chapter deals with biological diversity, primary productivity and physico-chemical characteristics of Sahastradhara stream, which gives a baseline data about the biological status of stream. The purpose of this work is to provide preliminary observations of the ecology of natural water from Sahastradhara at Dehradun and to make geo-chemical comparison between 'Sahastradhara' water and water from other regions of the country. The present work is aimed towards developing baseline data for river water quality of *'Sahastradhara'* stream, a major tributary of Song River and to understanding the ecological processes active in Himalayan river basins.

MATERIAL AND METHODS

The sampling site is situated in Sahastradhara valley, 15 km far from Dehradoon, selected five sampling station along with stream for limnological study. The water samples were collected monthly from different sampling site s_1, s_2, s_3, s_4 and s_5 during 2003 to 2004 in morning period (from 9.00 am to 11.00 pm). First upstream S_1 (Karligarh village), second upstream S_2 (Parking bridge), main tourist spot S_3 (Sulphur Spring), first down steam S_4 (Crossing bridge) and second downstream S_5 (Bus stand) were the sampling stations with a distance of about 1 km for each.

The samples were taken in BOD bottles and plastic Jeri cane for physical, chemical and biological parameters. The samples for different parameter were analyzed with the help of the procedure described by Mark (1977), APHA (1995), Mathur (1982), Trivadi and Goel (1984), Santhanam *et al.* (1989), Admondson (1992) and Khanna (1993).

RESULTS AND DISCUSSION

The impact on water quality of anthropogenic pollution from industrial, agricultural, sources, quarrying and tourists activity has concerned environmentalists and scientists for the past two decades. Plankton is the primary producer of any aquatic ecosystem, which can be as an indicator of water quality. Dissolved oxygen is decreases or increases in an aquatic ecosystem due to the plankton. Plankton takes sunlight directly and makes food for the total ecosystem through the photosynthesis process. Plankton may vary at place-to-place and season-to-season.

Temperature plays a vital role in all physico-biochemical reactions and self-purification power of aquatic system. Organic matter, which is oxidized, is highly influenced by the temperature. Temperature fluctuation measurement is useful to determine the trends of bio-chemical and biological activities. The Sahastradhara stream has a difference in the fluctuation of water temperature was recorded maximum (17.7°C ± 0.4) in the month of May and minimum (13.1°C±0.66) in January. The temperature of water decreases form September and increases from January onward. Badola and

Singh (1981) observed similar trend in the river Alaknanda in the Garhwal region. The maximum value of velocity of Sahastradhara stream was recorded in the month of May (0.64m/s ± 0.257) and minimum (0.58m/s ± 0.1315) in December. During the study period it has been observed that form January onward the velocity starts increasing up to April. Similar observation has been recorded by Joshi *et al.* (1995) in western Ganga canal at Hardwar.

The seasonal fluctuation of pH depends chiefly on amount of free carbon-dioxide, which is ultimately related to the rate of photosynthesis and also the decomposition of organic matter. The pH of natural water was controlled in a greater extent by the interaction of hydroxyl ions, resulting form the dissociation of carbonic acid and form hydroxyl ion arising from the hydrolysis of bicarbonate. In this study, it was recorded that the pH was always slightly alkaline. The pH of stream water was recorded highest (8.02 ± 0.1166) in December and lowest (7.4 ± 0.1414) in the month of April. Various workers in their studies have shown similar results in other rivers of Garhwal region. Sharma (1986) has also indicated the same trend of pH values on seasonal basis in the Bhagirathi River, Garhwal Himalayas.

The dissolved oxygen showed an inverse relationship with temperature as reposted by Das and Srivastava (1956) and Dobriyal (1985). The dissolved oxygen in water is often attributed to the fact that the oxygen is dissolved more during the period of active photosynthesis. Hutchinson (1957) reported that when the water has low temperature has greater capacity for holding dissolved gases. The highest value of dissolved oxygen was recorded (9.85 mg/l ± 0.776) in the month of January and the lowest value of dissolved oxygen was observed (6.68 mg/l ± 0.387) in the month of May. This trend was also stated by Khanna *et al.* (1992) in Ganga river at Hardwar. The higher value of dissolved oxygen during winter months can be attributed to increased solubility of oxygen at lower water temperature and high photosynthetic rate.

Free carbon dioxide released during the decomposition of certain substances and respiration of living organism since higher temperature accelerate the decomposition of organic substances as well as the respiratory activity of the biota and shown direct relationship between the water temperature and free carbon dioxide (Hynes, 1970). The maximum value of free carbon dioxide was observed (2.2 mg/l ±0.155) in May and minimum value in January (1.70 mg/l ± .066). Free carbon dioxide and dissolved oxygen showed a negative relationship to each other. The similar observations have also been reported by Quadri and Shah (1989) in some fresh water ecosystem. The highest rate of photosynthesis decreases free carbon-dioxide content and higher rate of decomposition increases free carbon dioxide. An inverse relationship between dissolved oxygen and free carbon- dioxide has been reported by Khan and Siddiqui (1971).

Chloride was found in form of chloride ion, and one of the major inorganic anions present in natural water. The maximum chloride concentration was recorded (17.14mg/l ± 1.33) in the month of May and minimum in the month of January (11.36 mg/l±2.008), chloride and hardness showed a positive relationship to one another. Chopra and Patrick (1994) also stated similar trend in aquatic ecosystem in the river Ganga at Rishikesh. The maximum calcium concentration was observed (15.99mg/l ± 5.53) in the month of May while the minimum value of calcium was observed (80.336mg/ l ± 2.64) in the month of January. Similar type of relationship of calcium was observed by Ahemad and Hasnain (2001) in fresh water bodies. Khanna & Singh (2000) also reported similar trend of calcium distribution in river Suswa, Raiwala, Dehradun. Sahastradhara stream may be regarded as rich in calcium and other geochemical nutrients. Calcium is one of the essential nutrients, which plays an important role in biological system. In fact, Calcium content in water is responsible for bone growth of children.

Magnesium is also an essential and beneficial element, but it is toxic at higher concentration. The recommended acceptable limit of magnesium for domestic purpose is 30mg/l in the river. The amount of magnesium in the river Sahastradhara was found maximum (57.2mg/l ± 7.24) in the month of May while the minimum value of magnesium was recorded (52.2mg/l ±6.55) in the month of January. Castante *et al.* (1985) in river Parana and Meybeck (1984) in river Zaire also reported similar trend of magnesium availability in natural water.

Sodium at lower concentration has no adverse effect on human health. The maximum sodium concentration was recorded (9.44 mg/l ± 1.016) in the month of May and minimum value of sodium was observed (7.1mg/l ± 0.663) in the month of January. Pande and Mishra (2000) observed similar results on Sahastradhara stream. Sodium is one of the most common cation present in the water bodies. Potassium is naturally occurring elements, like the sodium, however its concentration remains lower than sodium. The potassium is released by the clay mineral, weathering and leaching form the growing vegetation and decomposition of organic matter. Potassium concentration was observed highest in the month of May (17.2 mg/l±0.67) and lowest in the month of January (15.2 mg/l±0.812). Similar results were obtained by Sarin *et al.* (1989) and Subramanian (1989) observed the similar trend on the river Brahmaputra.

The quantitative fluctuation of the planktonic diversity has shown a significant effect on the ecology of river. All natural water contains a variety of plankton as the natural flora and fauna. The phytoplankton community is a heterogeneous group of tiny plants adapted to suspension in the fresh water. The present study showed that the maximum number of total plankton were recorded (1523.6±26.56) in the month of January and minimum (718.6 ± 19.33) in the month of May.

Phytoplankton was recorded maximum (1371 ± 25.77) in the month of January and minimum (633 ± 9.32) in the month of May. Eddy (1993) pointed out that plankton production is mainly influenced by temperature. Badola & Singh (1981) reported high values of plankton during January to March in freshwater of Kumaon Lake. According to Das & Pathani (1978) increment in turbidity will reduces the plankton production in a water body due to low light penetration and low rate of photosynthesis. According to Khanna (1993) the plankton were maximum in the month of winter probably due to low temperature, high content of dissolved oxygen low velocity and transparency of water and other suitable conditions. Allen (1920) stated that water currant is the chief factor influencing the plankton of stream San Joaquin River and its tributaries near Stockton in California.

Zooplankton were recorded maximum (152.6 ± 13.00) in the month of December and minimum (82 ± 13.02) in the month of May. Total diatoms were recorded maximum (1048.8 ± 34.02) in the month of January and minimum (495 ± 9.25) in the month of April. Green algae were recorded maximum (241.2 ± 29.77) in the month of January and minimum (106.4 ± 6.28) in the month of May. Blue Green algae was recorded maximum (81 ± 4.05) in the month of January and minimum (27.6 ± 3.98) in the month of May. Juttner *et al.* (1995) also reported the similar trend of diatom communities in Himalayan Hill Streams. Similar observations have been reported by Khanna *et al.* (1998) in relation to phytoplanktonic communities of Ganga canal at Haridwar. Khanna and Singh (2000) also reported the similar trend of planktonic diversity in Suswa River, Raiwala, Dehradun. Similar observations were also reported by Nautiyal (1982) in Alaknanda River and Khanna (1993) in river Ganga at Hardwar.

It is well established that the primary productivity is controlled by several physico-chemical and biotic interactions. The rate of production of organic mater per unit time is termed as productivity. There are two levels of production, primary and secondary. The amount of new organic matter resulting from photosynthesis is termed as primary productivity. The animal and plant communities inhabiting water bodies are considered as the direct manifestation of the productivity. The maximum net primary productivity was observed (0.335 ± .093) in the month of December and minimum (0.170 ± .04) in the month of May. The maximum gross primary productivity was observed (.796 ± .123) in the month of January and minimum (.569 ± .0379) in the month of May. The maximum net community respiration was observed (.479 ± .0575) in the month of January and minimum (.399 ± .0102) in the month of April. The higher productivity in the present studied was concomitant with temperature range from 14°C to 18°C. Singh and Swaroop (1980) observed positive correlation with productivity and water temperature. A positive correlation existed between gross primary productively and calcium in Cavery (Lakshminarayan, 2001). Vashney *et al.* (1983) present study a positive correlation was recorded between gross primary productivity and dissolved oxygen while the negative correlation between gross primary productivity and temperature and free carbon dioxide.

Net production efficiency shows the positive correlation with dissolved oxygen, while the negative correlation between net production efficiency and carbon dioxide. The maximum mean value of net production efficiency was observed (43.79%) in the month of January and minimum (29.88%) in the month of April. Similar trend was observed by Yeragi and Shaikh (2003) on the primary productivity of Tansa River. Singh *et al.*(1980) and Kar *et al.* (1978) however, recorded low and high productivity in summer and winter respectively.

Table 10.1: Physical Parameters of Sahastradhara River Water

Parameters	Site - I	Site - II	Site - III	Site - IV	Site - V
Temperature (°C) (Range)	15.75±1.14 (14 - 18)	15.37±1.63 (13 - 17.5)	15.0±1.41 (13 - 17)	15.75±1.6 (13.5 - 18)	5.75±2.277 (12 - 18)
Velocity (m/s) (Range)	0.3±0.14 (0.3 - 0.4)	0.9±0.1 (0.28 - 0.32)	0.35±0.05 (0.8 - 1.0)	0.8±0.02 (0.78 - 0.82)	0.65±0.05 (0.6 -0.7)
Turbidity (JTU) (Range)	2.75±1.47 (1.0 - 5.0)	3.25±1.30 (2.0 - 5.0)	4.5±1.15 (3.0 - 6.0)	3.75±1.48 (2.0 - 6.0)	4.75±1.48 (3.0 - 7.0)
Total solids (mg/l) (Range)	1218±183.2 (955 - 1427)	1234.2±89.8 (1090 - 1332)	1277.25±122.6 (1115 - 1443)	1305.7±166.1 (1135 - 1520)	1290.75±146.1 (1148 - 1535)
TDS (mg/l) (Range)	1093.25±175 (840 - 1278)	1094.25±120.5 (895 - 1217)	1140.5±134.6 (1010 - 1322)	1189±158.01 (1039 - 1380)	1134.25±176.1 (965 - 1420)
TSS (mg/l) (Range)	124.75±14.39 (113 - 149)	140.0±28.16 (119 - 195)	136.75±40.95 (105 - 207)	116.75±13.8 (105 - 140)	156.5±41.69 (115 - 211)

Table 10.2: Chemical Parameters of Sahastradhara River Water

Parameters	Site - I	Site - II	Site - III	Site - IV	Site - V
pH (Range)	7.625±0.43 (7.2 - 8.1)	7.6±0.28 (7.3 - 8.1)	7.75±0.15 (7.5 - 7.9)	7.75±1.66 (7.6 - 8.0)	7.6±0.339 (7.2 - 8.1)
Free CO2 (mg/l) (Range)	1.6525±0.39 (1.40 - 1.69)	1.75±0.017 (1.62 - 1.92)	1.825±0.25 (1.62 - 2.20)	1.74±0.09 (1.65 - 1.85)	1.87±0.21 (1.62 - 2.20)
D O (mg/l) (Range)	8.41±1.62 (7.04 - 11.08)	8.46±1.18 (6.84 - 10.07)	8.65±0.95 (7.04 - 9.47)	7.55±0.87 (6.04 - 9.06)	7.49±1.36 (6.04 - 9.47)
BOD (mg/l) (Range)	1.875±0.162 (1.60 - 2.0)	1.98±0.23 (1.7 - 2.2)	2.25±0.18 (2.0 - 2.5)	2.0±0.14 (1.8 - 2.2)	2.05±0.15 (1.9 - 2.3)
COD (mg/l) (Range)	2.55±0.32 (2.1 - 3.0)	2.6±0.25 (2.2 - 2.9)	2.9±0.22 (2.6 - 3.2)	2.68±0.22 (2.4 - 3.0)	2.7±0.18 (2.4 - 2.9)
Hardness (mg/l) (Range)	196.25±8.2 (190 - 210)	200.0±15.41 (185 - 220)	222.5±19.2 (200 - 250)	200.0±18.71 (180 - 230)	198.75±21.02 (185 - 235)
Alkalinity (mg/l) (Range)	250.0±134.7 (150 - 480)	262.5±140.8 (140 - 500)	305±172.1 (170 - 600)	292.5±168.8 (130 - 570)	317.5±175.2 (120 - 540)

Table 10.3: Nutrients Parameters (Major Elements) of Sahastradhara River Water

Parameters	Site - I	Site - II	Site - III	Site - IV	Site - V
Chloride *(mg/l)* (Range)	12.78±1.73 (11.36 - 15.62)	13.73±1.93 (11.36 - 16.58)	15.26±2.1 (12.78 - 18.46)	13.49±3.25 (9.94 - 18.46)	11.6±3.06 (8.52 - 16.58)
Calcium *(mg/l)* (Range)	84.67±3.58 (80.160 - 88.176)	85.67±4.28 (80.160 - 92.184)	91.68±10.13 (77.154-104.208)	89.18±8.26 (79.158-99.198)	88.43±6.19 (80.16-96.192)
Magnesium *(mg/l)* (Range)	48.66±3.09 (45 - 53)	57.33±3.29 (55 - 62)	64.66±2.36 (63.0 - 68.0)	55.33±2.49 (52.0 - 28.0)	51.0±5.29 (45.0 - 55.0)
Sodium *(mg/l)* (Range)	7.375±0.96 (6 - 8.5)	7.725±0.506 (7.0 - 8.2)	8.75±0.75 (8.0 - 9.5)	8.87±1.14 (7.0 - 10.0)	9.25±1.35 (7.5 - 11.0)
Potassium *(mg/l)* (Range)	15.13±0.74 (14 - 16)	15.75±0.901 (14.5 - 17.0)	16.62±0.65 (16.0 - 17.5)	16.5±0.79 (15.5 - 17.5)	17.0±1.35 (16.0 - 18.0)

Table 10.4: Planktonic Diversity of Sahastradhara River Water

Parameters	Site - I	Site - II	Site - III	Site - IV	Site - V
Total plankton (n/l) (Range)	1130.25±316.8 (700 - 1540)	1133±316 (725 - 1525)	1101.5±323.9 (693 - 1480)	1063.75±346.9 (700 - 1490)	1163.25±339.4 (730 - 1583)
Phytoplankton (n/l) (Range)	1018.25±286.1 (625 - 1380)	1023.75±291.5 (635 - 1380)	992.5±296.3 (615 - 1345)	951.25±318.2 (635 - 1340)	1037.5±259.5 (640 - 1410)
Zooplankton (n/l) (Range)	112±31.61 (75 - 160)	109.25±27.09 (77 - 145)	109±28.6 (78 - 140)	112.5±31.72 (65 - 150)	125.75±36.66 (90 - 173)
Total diatoms (n/l) (Range)	764.75±206.6 (492 - 1022)	784.5±218.5 (645 - 1015)	772.25±247.3 (480 - 1064)	732.5±236.5 (495 - 1035)	807±250.5 (495 - 1108)
Green algae (n/l) (Range)	190.5±59.86 (105 - 275)	179.5±64.96 (98 - 278)	161±40.72 (102 - 205)	164.5±57.21 (105 - 228)	157.5±50.13 (102 - 220)
Blue green algae (n/l) (Range)	63±24.53 (21 - 83)	57.25±21.57 (27 - 87)	59.25±17.72 (33 - 76)	54.25±25.86 (27 - 83)	58±32.04 (23 - 97)

Table 10.5: Primary Productivity of Sahastradhara River Water

Parameters	Site - I	Site - II	Site - III	Site - IV	Site - V
Net primary productivity (mg/l) (Range)	0.271±.069 (0.200 - 0.355)	0.220±.0215 (0.200 - 0.255)	0.336±.108 (0.140 - 0.500)	0.231±.086 (0.105 - 0.320)	0.265±.0522 (0.200 - 0.330)
Gross primary productivity (mg/l) (Range)	0.6925±.074 (0.605 - 0.805)	0.640±.0776 (0.600 - 0.705)	0.716±.1344 (0.550 - 1.01)	0.729±.0975 (0.505 - 0.900)	0.676±.0826 (0.580 - 0.810)
Community respiration (mg/l) (Range)	0.420±.0184 (0.405 - 0.450)	0.420±.0635 (0.400 - 0.450)	0.421±.0394 (0.390 - 0.480)	0.498±.156 (0.400 - 0.580)	0.411±.0375 (0.380 - 0.480)
Net production efficiency (%) (Range)	38.77±4.7 (33.05 - 44.09)	34.29±1.101 (33.33 - 36.17)	44.15±15.56 (25.45 - 66.66)	30.485±6.445 (20.79 - 37.03)	38.87±3.069 (34.48 - 42.55)

Table 10.6: Correlation Between Major Element Ions and Physico-chemical Parameters of Sahastradhara River Water

Parameters	Chloride	Calcium	Magnesium	Sodium	Potassium
Temperature *(°C)*	-0.86097	-0.51833	-0.92056	-0.01186	-0.14275
Velocity *(m/s)*	-0.17595	-0.12077	0.007842	0.179873	0.225839
Turbidity *(JTU)*	0.012697	0.818834	0.400371	0.92284	0.959357
Total solids *(mg/l)*	-0.00448	0.788427	0.273292	0.949891	0.906666
T.D.S. *(mg/l)*	0.133154	0.71132	0.25802	0.764443	0.682478
T.S.S. *(mg/l)*	-0.35586	0.096981	0.004271	0.35689	0.46296
pH *(pH unit)*	0.681329	0.761113	0.623067	0.395679	0.345766
Free CO_2 *(mg/l)*	-0.03224	0.686443	0.396104	0.833271	0.90927
D.O. *(mg/l)*	0.679888	-0.12231	0.471533	-0.65112	-0.55633
B.O.D. *(mg/l)*	0.607899	0.912138	0.845587	0.615583	0.694262
C.O.D. *(mg/l)*	0.595229	0.954861	0.801927	0.654354	0.704159
Hardness *(mg/l)*	0.814816	0.795954	0.897315	0.312648	0.386789
Alkalinity *(mg/l)*	-0.04111	0.829565	0.331085	0.97707	0.985243

Table 10.7: Correlation Between Plankton and Physico-chemical Parameters of Sahastradhara River Water

Parameters	Total plankton	Phytoplankton	Zooplankton	Total diatom	Green algae	Blue green algae
Temperature °C	0.140144	0.040568	0.561048	-0.12814	0.203944	-0.06004
Velocity (m/s)	-0.09075	-0.11978	0.096464	-0.00984	-0.18658	-0.81972
Turbidity (JTU)	0.103772	0.005161	0.537763	0.394692	-0.95776	-0.35417
Total solids (mg/l)	-0.40534	-0.52983	0.405479	-0.18218	-0.91516	-0.73149
TDS (mg/l)	-0.70298	-0.80425	0.139674	-0.54607	-0.71164	-0.72652
TSS (mg/l)	0.823334	0.77943	0.635537	0.966082	-0.40829	0.080955
PH	-0.88664	-0.89145	-0.42828	-0.71618	-0.42595	-0.36483
Free CO_2 (mg/l)	0.27888	0.196314	0.548124	0.578174	-0.89315	-0.36232
D O (mg/l)	0.028383	0.184226	-0.75181	0.04589	0.505435	0.574037
BOD (mg/l)	-0.18081	-0.18513	-0.07095	0.161374	-0.74373	-0.20002
COD (mg/l)	-0.27454	-0.29116	-0.05821	0.047125	-0.75928	-0.19054
Hardness (mg/l)	-0.2978	-0.25029	-0.38539	-0.01229	-0.45865	0.023773
Alkalinity (mg/l)	-0.00781	-0.12433	0.568959	0.262619	-0.98348	-0.44697

Table 10.8: Correlation Between Primary Productivity and Physico-chemical Parameters) of Sahastradhara River Water

Parameters	Net Primary Productivity	Gross Primary Productivity	Community Respiration	Net Production Efficiency
Temperature °C	-0.59945	0.006189	0.311429	-0.57232
Velocity (m/s)	-0.82147	-0.40554	0.387568	-0.78591
Turbidity (JTU)	0.459379	0.237629	-0.09751	0.389256
Total solids (mg/l)	0.086601	0.565255	0.544701	-0.16675
TDS (mg/l)	0.01787	0.761621	0.801179	-0.33031
TSS (mg/l)	0.165469	-0.58282	-0.73453	0.444083
PH	0.409892	0.87509	0.647625	0.023325
Free CO_2 (mg/l)	0.335796	-0.03623	-0.24934	0.360837
D O (mg/l)	0.43596	-0.20694	-0.47748	0.522691
BOD (mg/l)	0.715985	0.330189	-0.11921	0.583037
COD (mg/l)	0.757185	0.484589	-0.01968	0.572202
Hardness (mg/l)	0.811178	0.38677	-0.13668	0.659382
Alkalinity (mg/l)	0.380434	0.349649	0.067672	0.259953

Sahastradhara stream has a wide biodiversity of small invertebrates, including some benthos, nekton, phytoplankton, zooplankton, which maintain the water quality of aquatic ecosystem. Planktonic genus and other fauna available in the water of Sahastradhara hill stream at Dehradun depicted in table 10.9.

Table 10.9: Preliminary Study of Biotic Communities in Sahastradhara River at Dehradun

Family/Phylum	Genus/Species
Flora:	
(A) Chorophyceae-	*Ulothrix, Volvox, Cladophora, Chlorella, Vaucheria, Zygnema, Pediasterum*
(B) Bacillariophyceae-	*Diatoms*
(C) Rhodophyceae-	*Batrachospermun*
(D) Cyanophyceae-	*Rivularia, Nostoc*
Fauna:	
(A) Protozoans-	*Vorticalla, Amoeba, Paramoecium, Chrysamocha, Volvox*
(B) Coelentrata-	*Hydra, Ceratella*
(C) Annelida-	*Pheretima*
(D) Arthropods-	*Mayfly nymph*
(E) Macroinvertibrate-	*Snails, Leeches, Flatworms, Beetles*

The endemic fish species about 18 in number occurs in the natural aquatic system of Sahastradhara (Table 10.10). Among these, four to six species may be undertake as sport fishery to enhance or attract the fish anglers on the tourist sites. The limnological and biological status of Sahastradhara stream have shown optimum suitable environment to accelerate the growth and population of endemic fish diversity. There has taken place to increasing use of aquatic resources to cater the needs of tourism. As the present conditions are in sites development of these water bodies has to be taken up for the protection of natural habitats and rehabilitate as fish sanctuaries. The transplantation of healthy stocks of desirable sport fishes have to be done on scientific lines on the basis of optimum biological productivity of the stream. The conservation and management of aquatic ecosystem of hill streams should involve the management of aquatic life including fishes and multiplicity of uses of a whole ecosystem as amenity, ecotourism etc.

Table 10.10: Fish diversity in Sahastradhara river at Dehradun

Scientific Name (Genus/species)	Local Name
Schizothorax richardsonii (Gray)	Asella
Schizothorax plagiostomus	Dhibrua
Schizothorax sinatus	Maseen
Puntius chola (Ham.)	–
Puntius hexasticus	Khront
Barilius barila (Ham.)	
Barilius bendelisis (Ham.)	Chal
Barilius vagra (Ham.)	Chal
Noemacheilus savona (Ham.)	–
Glyptothorax pectinopterus (McClell.)	–
Mastacembelus armatus (Lac.)	–
Garra lamta (Ham.)	–
Garra gotyla gotyla (gray)	Gunthala
Danio devario (Ham.)	Patukari
Chagunia chagunio (Ham.)	Gelhari
Botia durlo (Ham.)	Baghaua
Chipisoma garua (Ham.)	Raikari
Colisa fasciatus (Block & Schn.)	Khosti

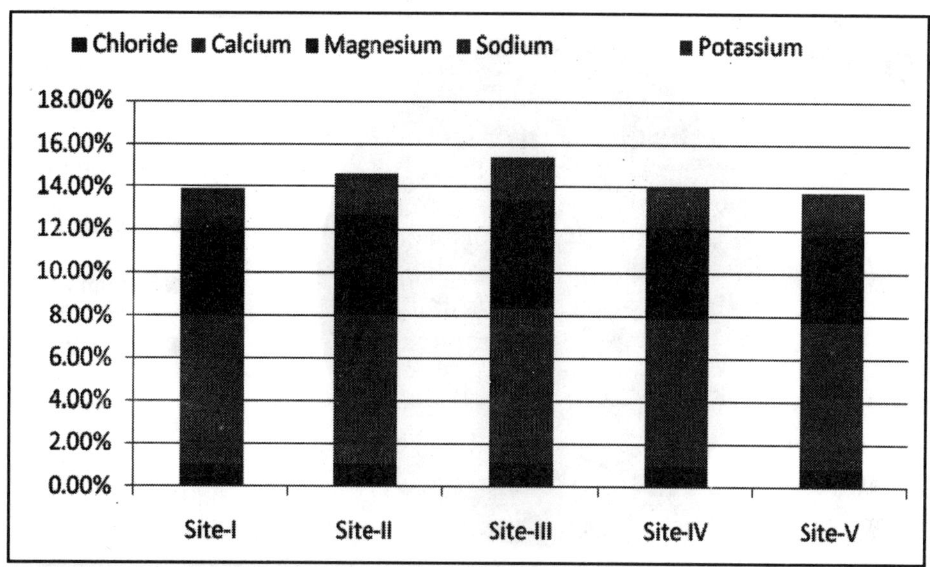

Fig. 10.1: Per cent Composition of Major Elements Among Total Dissolved Solids in Sahastradhara Water

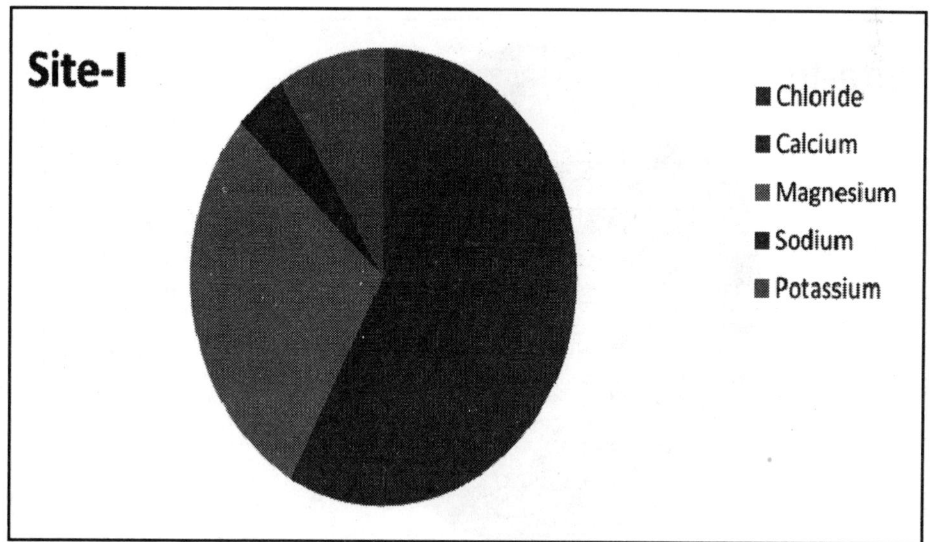

Fig. 10.2: Per cent Composition of Major Elements Among Total Dissolved Solids at Sahastradhara site-I

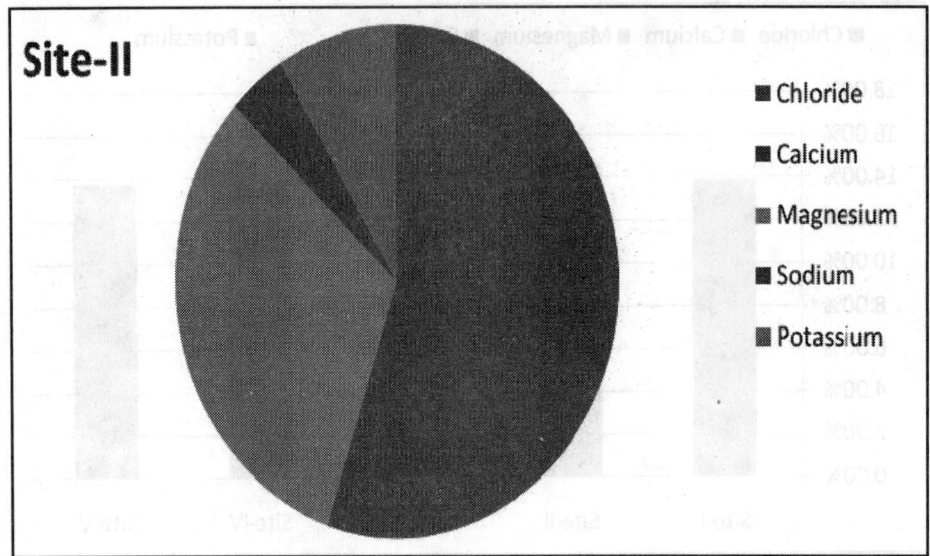

Fig. 10.3: Per cent Composition of Major Elements Among Total Dissolved Solids at Sahastradhara site-II

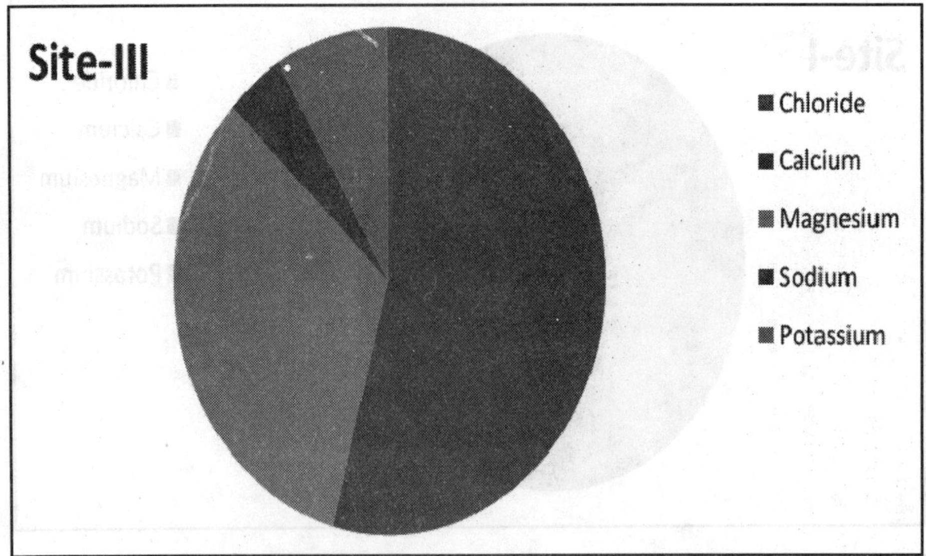

Fig. 10.4: Per cent Composition of Major Elements Among Total Dissolved Solids at Sahastradhara site-III

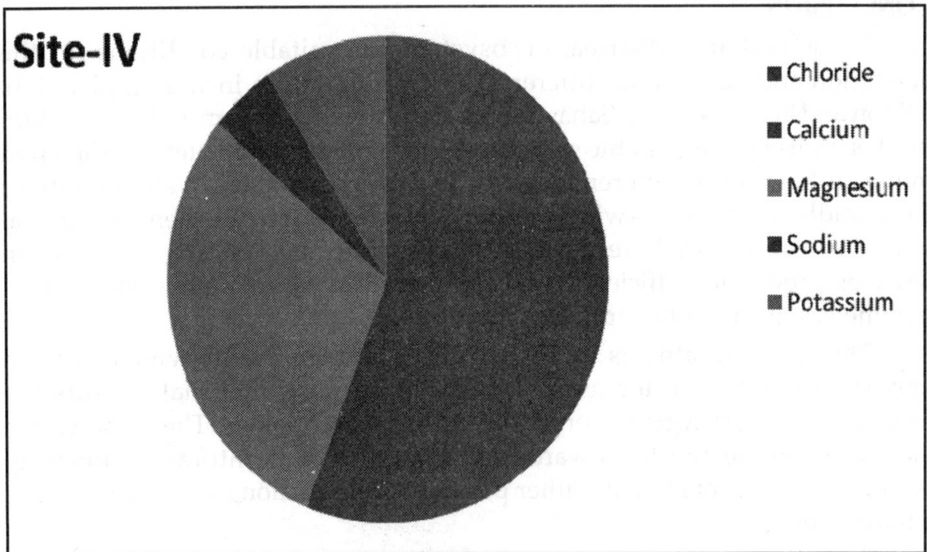

Fig. 10.5: Per cent Composition of Major Elements Among Total Dissolved Solids at Sahastradhara site-IV

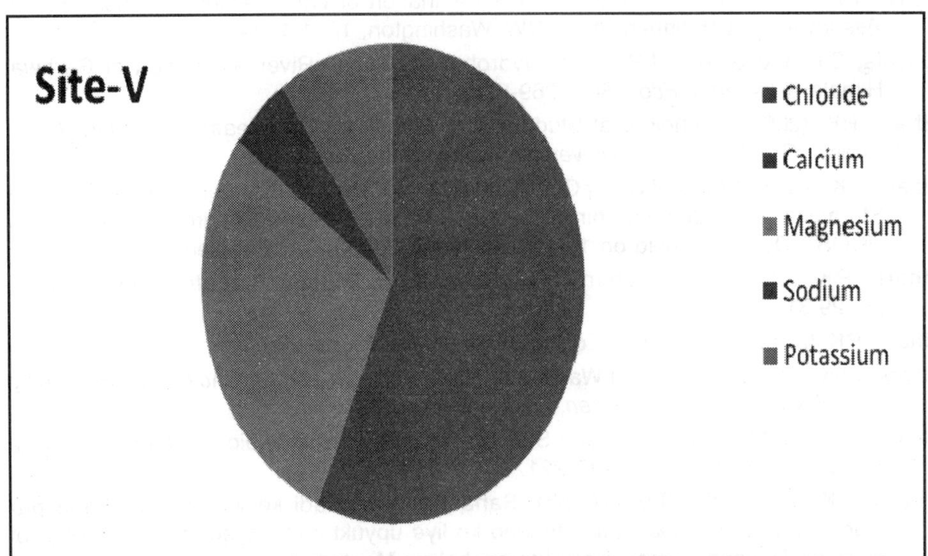

Fig. 10.6: Per cent Composition of Major Elements Among Total Dissolved Solids at Sahastradhara site-V

CONCLUSION

Sahastradhara hill-stream ecosystem has suitable conditions for the habitation and survival of different biotic communities including plankton, nekton and benthos. In the Sahastradhara hill-stream Calcium and Magnesium level is high especially in the summer season. All the parameters studied had minor differences at different sites during the observation. Water quality of Sahastradhara stream has widely affected by tourists activities hence industrial pollution is no more here. Primary productivity is high in winter season whereas production efficiency was influenced by various physico-chemical parameters at different sampling sites.

The water quality is quite rich in natural nutrients which play an important implication for use the drinking purpose after making sure the bacterial and other hygienic condition after clean technology. The conservation measures must be directed towards understanding of the intricate relationship between all biotic organisms either plants or animals along with surrounding environment.

REFERENCES

Ahamed, S. and Hasnain, S.I. 2001. Snow and Stream Water Chemistry of the Ganga Headwater Basin, Garhwal Himalaya, India, *Hydrological Sciences Journal* 46(1): 103-111.

Allen, W.E. 1920. A Quantitative and Statistical Study of the Plankton of the San Joaquin River and its Tributaries in a Near Stockton California in 1913. *Univ. Calif. Publ. Zool.* 22(1): 1-24.

APHA 1995. Ecological Methods for the Examination of Water. *American Public Health Association*, 1015 fifteen Street NW, Washington, 19: 1-1134.

Badola, S.P. and Singh, H.R. 1981. Hydrobiology of the River Alaknanda of Garhwal Himalaya *Indian J. Ecol.*, 8(2): 269-276.

Bharti, P.K. (2004): Limnological Study of Sahastradhara Hill-stream, Dehradun, *M.Sc. Thesis, Gurukula Kangri University, Hardwar, India,* pp: 102.

Bharti, P.K. (2008): Status of Water Quality and Ecotourism Enhancement in Sahastradhara Stream at Dehradun. In: Third Uttarakhand State Science Congress Organised by UCOST, Dehradun held on 10-11 November, 2008 at IIT, Roorkee.

Bharti, P.K. (2010): Sandushan- (Eutrophication), *Vigyan Pragati,* January 2010, pp. 29-31.

Bharti, P.K. (2012a): Hill-stream Ecology, *Biotech Books*, pp. 246.

Bharti, Pawan K. (2012b): Solid Waste and River Ecology, *Lambert Academic Publishing GmbH & Co. KG, Saarbrucken*, Germany, pp. 65.

Bharti, P.K. and Malik, D.S. (2005a): Significance of Rivers in Vedic Literature, *Gurukula Shodha Bharti,* Vol. 4, pp: 217-221.

Bharti, P.K. and Malik, D.S. (2005b): Sahastradhara Nadi ke vibhinna sthhano par machhliyon ke anukool vaas sthhano ke liye upyukt dashaayen, in proceedings of (in Hindi) National Symposium: Uttaranchal me Maatyasyki ki bhaavi sambhaavnaye' organized by department of zoology, H.N.B. Garhwal University, Srinagar on 28-29 October 2005, pp. 84-87.

Bharti, P.K.; Malik, D.S. and Yadav, R. (2008): Influence of Heavy Metals on Abundance of Cyanophyceae Members in Three Spring-fed Lake in Kempty, Dehradun, *Journal of Ecology and Fisheries*, 1(1): 35-38.

Bharti, Pawan K. (2007a): 'Where is Environmental Science Going in India?' *Current Science,* 92 (4): 414.

Bharti, Pawan Kr. (2007b): 'Why are Indian Standards not so Strict?', *Current Science,* 93(9): 1202.

Bharti, Pawan K.; Tyagi, P.K. and Singh, V. (2014): Assessment of Heavy Metals in the Water of Sahastradhara Hill Stream at Dehradun, India. *International Journal of Environment.* 3(3): 164-172.

Chopra, A.K., Patrick, Nirmal, J. 1994. Effect of Domestic Sewage on Self-purification of Ganga Water at Rishikesh. *A. Bio.science,* 13(11): 75-82.

Das, S.M. & Pathani, S.S. 1978. A Study on the Effect of Lake Ecology on Production of Mahaseer (*Tor tor & T. putitora*) in Kumaon Lake. *Indian Matsya.* 4: 25-31.

Das, S.M. and Srivastava, V.K. 1956. Studies of Fresh Water Plankton II Correlation Between Plankton and Hydro-biological Factors *Proc. Nat. Acad. Sci. India*, (13) 26: 243-253.

Dobriyal, A.K. 1985. Ecology of Limnofauna in the Small Streams and Their Importance to the Village Life in Garhwal Himalya. *Uttar Pradesh J. Zool.* 5 (2): 139-144.

Eddy, S. 1934. A Study of Freshwater Plankton Communities. *Illinois Biol. Monogr.* 12 (4): 1-93.

Hutchinson, G.C. 1957. A Treatise on Limnology, Geography, Physical and Chemical, Vol. I, New York: *John Wiley and Sons, Inc.*, pp: 1-1015.

Hynes, H.B.N. 1970. The Ecology of Running Waters. *Liverpool University Press, Liverpool, 4th Impression*: 1-555.

Juttner I., Heike Rothfritz and Steve J. Ormerod 1995. *University of Wales, Cardiff, CFI 3TL UK*- 'Diatom Communities in Himalayan hill streams, pp. 589-597.

Joshi, B.D., Bisht, R.C.S. and Semval, V.P. 1995. Primary Productivity in Western Ganga Canal at Hardwar. *Indian J.Ecol.* 22(2): 123-126.

Kar, O.K., P.C. Mishra, M.C. Das and R.C. Das 1978. Pollution Studies in River Ib. III Plankton, Pollution and Primary Productivity, 175.

Khan, A.A. and Siddiqui, A. 1971. *Hydrobiologia,* 37: 447.

Khanna, D.R., Badola, S.P., Sing, H.R. and Dobriyal, K., Anoop 1992. Observations on Seasonal Trends in Diatomic Diversity in the River Ganga at Sapt-sarover, Hardwar. In: Recent Research in Cold Water: Fisheries, Ed. by K.L. Sehgal, Today and Tomarrow Printers and Publishers, New Delhi: 99-107.

Khanna, D.R. 1993. Ecology and Pollution of Ganga River, *Ashish Publishing House*, New Delhi. pp. 1-241.

Khanna, D.R., Malik, D.S. and Rana, D.S. 1998. Phytoplanktonic Communities in Relation to Certain Physico-chemical Parameters of Ganga Canal at Hardwar. *Him. J. Env. Zool.*, Vol. 12: 193-197.

Khanna, D.R and Singh. R.K. 2000. Seasonal Fluctuations in the Plankton of Suswa River at Raiwala Dehradun. *Env. Conservations J.* 1(2 & 3): 89-92.

Khanna, D.R., Bhutiani, R. and Chandra, K. S. 2005. Modeling to Assess Effect of Light on Phytoplanktonic Growth Dynamics: A Review, *Env. Conservations J.,* 6(3): 103-107.

Lakshminarayana and R.K. Someshekar. 2001. Ecology of Polluted Water by Arvind Kumar Vol. 1, chapter II, pp. 51-60, *APH Pub. Corp.* New Delhi - 110002.

Malik, D.S. and Bharti, P.K. (2005a): Nutrient Dynamics in Rhithron Zone of Shivalik Himalayan Stream Sahastradhara, Dehradun (Uttaranchal), *Env. Cons. J.* 6 (2): 63-68.

Malik, D.S. and Bharti, P.K. (2005b): Fluctuation in Planktonic Population of Sahastradhara Hill-stream at Dehradun (Uttaranchal), *Aquacult.* 6 (2): 191-198.

Malik, D.S. and Bharti, P.K. (2005c): Primary Production Efficiency of Sahstradhara Hill-stream, Dehradun, *Env. Cons. J.* 6 (3): 117-121.

Malik, D.S. and Bharti, P.K. (2007a): Water Resources Conservation in Vedas, *Gurukula Shodha Bharati,* Vol. 7, pp. 231-235.

Malik, D.S. and Bharti, P.K. (2007b): Ecology of Sahastradhara Hill-stream at Dehradun (Uttaranchal), In: 'Advances in Aquatic Ecology, Vol. I' ed. by V.B. Sakhare, Daya Publishing House, New Delhi, (ISBN 81-7035-483-8) pp. 1-11.

Malik, D.S.; Bharti, P. K.; Negi, K.S. and Yadav, R. (2009): Distribution of Metals in Water of an Artificial Lake at Mussoorie, Uttarakhand, In: 'Aquatic Biology and Aquaculture' edited by V.B. Sakhare, Ambajoagi, MS, Manglam Publication, New Delhi, pp: 77-95.

Malik, D.S. and Bharti, P.K. (2006): Sahastradhara me Matasya vinod evam paryatan, in Proceeding of National Seminar on 'Meethajal matsyiki' organized by Rashtriya matsya anuvanshik sansadhan bureau, Lucknow.

Nautiyal, P. 1982. Some Aspects of Bio Ecology of Tarputitora in Relation to Hydrobiology of some Garhwal Hill Stream. *D.Phill. Thesis;* Garhwal University.

Pande, R.K. and Asha Mishra 2000. Water Quality Study of Freshwaters of Dehradun (Sahastradhara Stream and Mussoorie Lake). *Aquacult.* Vol- (1): 57-62.

Quadri, M.Y. and Shah, G.M. 1984. Hydro-biological feature of Hoassar. A Typical Wetland of Kashmir-I, Biotope. *Indian J. Ecol.,* 2(2): 203-206.

Santhanam, R.; Velayntham, P. and Jegatheesan, G. 1989. A Manual of Freshwater Ecology. Daya Publishing House Delhi - 110 006: 3-17, 53-92.

Sarin, M.M., Krishnaswamy, S.K., Trivedi, J.R. and Sharma, K.K. 1992. Major ion Chemistry of the Ganga Source Waters: Weathering in High Altitude Himalaya. In: *Proc, Indian acad. Sci. (Earth Planet Sci.)* 1, 89-98.

Schwoerbel, J. 1991. Handbook of Limnology, *Ellis Horwood Limited, Chichester, England:* pp. 95-114.

Shrama, R.C. 1986. Effect of Physico-chemical Factors on Benthic Fauna of Bhargirathi River Garhwal Himalaya. *Indian. J. Ecol.* 13(1): 133-137.

Singh, S.N.; Gupta, M.L.; and Prakash, P. 1980. Hydro-biological Studies of Some Eutrophic Ponds of Rohtash, Bihar. *Environment and Ecology.* 16 (2): 457-462.

Singh, Kehar 2004. A Study on Water Quality of Sahastradhara Hill-stream, Dehradun, *M.Sc. Thesis, Gurukula Kangri University, Hardwar, India,* pp. 91.

Subramanian, V. 1989. Chemical and Suspended Sediment Characteristics of River of India. *J. Hydrol,* 44: 37-55.

Trivedi, R.K. and Goel, P.K. 1984. Chemical and Biological Methods for Water Pollution Studies Karad: *Environmental Publication,* pp. 1-251.

Valdiya, K.S. 1975. Emergence of the Himalayas, Science Today, 9: 14-18.

Vashney, P.K.; R. Vijayalakshmi, Nair and S.H.H. Abidi .1983. Primary Productivity in Near Shore Water of Thai Maharashtra Coast, India. *J.Mar. Sci.* 12:27-30.

Yeragi, S.G. and Nisar Shaikh. 2003. Studies on Primary Productivity of Tansa River. *J. Natcon* 15 (1): 125-130.

Pages: 157-177

LIMNOLOGY AND AQUATIC SCIENCE
Edited by: **Dr. Shailendra Sharma; Dr. Pawan Kumar 'Bharti'**
ISBN: 978-93-5056-735-7
Edition: **2015**
Published by: **Discovery Publishing House Pvt. Ltd., New Delhi (India)**

Biological Indices of Aquatic Ecosystem

***Shailendra Sharma; Shitika Barkale; Bhagwan Singh Patel**

ABSTRACT

Natural ecosystems are complex, multivariate system and are being simultaneously exposed to a multitude of Stresses, the mechanisms and cumulative effects of which are poorly understood. Understanding assemblages of organisms and how they change in species number and abundance has been a question that has always interested ecologists.

The indices of particular use in aquatic ecosystems for the study of pollution and its effects on the aquatic community. Indices that summarized a large amount of information have appeared to scientist for a long time. However, the wide scale use of indices in biology and particularly ecology is quite recent. Ecosystems change with pollution is stress is apparent, and this has led to the search for manes of quantifying such changes. Two main approaches to study of pollution effects have been used, being the use of measures based on community structure and on measure based on indicator organisms. There are

Adarsh Institute of Management & Science, Devi Ahilya Vishwavidyalaya, Indore, Dhamnod, India.

two different types of indices. Diversity attempt to combine the data on abundance within species in a community into a single number. The state of the community can then be understood from the number. In similarly indicate two samples are compares one of which often a control. The term similarity indices have also come to include its complement, dissimilarity or "distance "indices. When diversity & similarity indices are used, they normally are calculated for a given taxonomic groupings e.g.birds,mammals plants or a given size or structural grouping such as trees, shrubs, herbs etc.When used in aquatic situation such grouping may be macro invertebrates.

INTRODUCTION

In recent years our environment has been put to serious threat as a result of discharge of disastrous chemicals of various kinds which are primarily the byproducts of developmental activities like industrialization, urbanization, use of chemical fertilizers as well as pesticides and burning of fossil fuel emitting green house gases. Huge oil spills in the oceans and radioactive fallout are contaminating air, water and soil. In the event of large scale eco-degradation it is necessary to monitor the nature and degree of change in environment so that due words of caution may be given to the consumers and proper preventive and specific corrective measures may, be adopted.

The approaches where indices based on "indicator organisms" are group are called "Biotic Indices". Biotic indices are highly specialized for a particular type a water pollution, usually organic pollution.Structure and function are both important in aquatic ecosystems such as river, streams etc.and biomonitering should emphasize a combined structure/function testing strategy. Many attempts have been made to condense data obtained from biomonetring into a useful index of community or ecosystems response. Ideally there indices would be applicable to a wide geographic are sensitive and reproducible, suitable for tong term surveillance and able to distinguish seasonal and other natural changes from the stress effects. There are community response indices any be devised into three types:

1. Those based on functional information;
2. Those based on structural information; and
3. Those based on a combination of structural and functional information.

Functional indices include the popular P/R, as well as other less well known indices based on rate. Rodgers (1977) describes several potential functional indices, such as the Autotrophic production index, a ratio between net primary productivity (mg/l m^{-2} $h^{-2)}$ and net microbial productivity (calculated using assimilative sulfate reduction, mg so m^{-2} h^{-2}). Dickson et al.

(1978) suggest three other "functional "indices: The trophic index (chl:a organic carbon estimate/ATP organic carbon estimate) and the viability index (ATP organic carbon estimate/ash free ndry weight organic carbon estimate). Structural indices include such as those based on information theory (Pinkham and pearson, 1976) as well as the viability, trophic, and trophic functional indices. When structural indices make use of the structural/functional pair relationship (eg.chl.'a' and ATP) they may be useful in describing community functional response as well as structural changes. Another structural index that benefits from use of structure/function pairs is the Autotrophic index (AI) (APHA 1976, weber 1973). This index divides ash free dry weight from plankton or preiphyton samples by chlorophyll 'a'levels,with increasing AIS corresponding to increasing heterotrophy in the system. The AI usually works well in lentic systems. however; in streams here a consideration portion of the ash free dry wt.may come from allochthonous, nonviable sources, and gravimetric measurement may not reflect an accurate response (Clark et al.1979).

The use of existing biological indices in aquatic systems:

The exiting biological (Diversity, comparative or similarity and pollution or biotic) indices are used considering their ecological application, both theoretical and practical. Eighteen diversity indices in eight groups, twenty biotic (pollution) indices in ten groups and seven comparative (similarity) indices are examined for their applicability to biological systems (Washington, 1984), particularly aquatic ecosystems. A summary of the properties of indices method of data analysis are presented in table 11.1.

(a) Diversity indices

What is diversity?

The oxford dictionary defines diversity as the condition of being diverse where diverse means "different is character or quality, not of the same kind" elsewhere "diversity" is equated with variety; diversity has also been equated with "complicity".

The diversity indices are based upon the concept that the structure of normal communities may be change by perturbation in the environment and the degree of change in community structure may be used to assess the intensity of the environmental stress. Various definition have been put forwarded as a diversity index. Margal (1951) states that a diversity index should be a relation between the number of species and the number of individuals, and should include the distribution of the species by their abundance range. Goodman (1975) says that a measure which takes account both of the number of species and their relative abundance seems necessary.hurlbert (1971) notes that species diversity is a function of the number of species, and the evenness. Thus diversity can increase as evenness increase while specie number actually decreases slightly. He also notes that the problem with diversity has been to determine the appropriate relative weight to be give to species richness (species number) and species evenness (abundance in species) in the index. Cairns (1977) describes a diversity index as a numerical expression that can be used to make comparisons between communities. He status that the diversity index in probably the best single means of assessing biological integrity in fresh water streams.

According to eight category by which people have approached the problem of formulating a diversity index is:

1. Simpson (1949) wishes to define and examine a measure of contration in terms of population contants.
2. Relatives of species number (kothes 1962) Odum 1960; gleasion 1922; and Margalef's 1958; Menhinick's 1962.
3. Curve fitting approach by motomure's 1932; fisher's 1943; Yule 1944; Prestons, 1948.
4. Information Theory is given by Brillouins 1951,shannon's 1949, Lloyd & Ghelardi 1964; Margalef's 1962.
5. Interspecific encounters by Herlberts (1971).
6. Based on "ecological distance" relative by Mc Intosh's (1967).
7. Theory of runs (SCI) by cairns (1971) and Keef's & Bergerson's (1976, 1977) theory of runs (unbiased) by T.U.

(b) Biotic (or pollution) indices:

"Biotic indices are approach to water pollution making use of the indicator organisms' concept; as such they do not represent community structure.

The Concept of indicator species:

According to Johnson et al. (1993). The concept of indicator species is of central important in the use of benthic macroinvenabrates in biological monitoring "indicator species" is defined here as a species (or species assemblage) that has particular requirement with regard to a known set of physical or chemical variables such change in to present/absent, number, morphology, physiology, or behavior are outside its prefered lomits.The factor or factors that regulate pollution abundance or present/absents may act at any stage of the life cycle, and may be of abiotic (e.g. chemical variables O_2 H^+,or trace metal concentration. physical variables : sedimentation) or abiotic (e.g. competition, predation, parasitism)origin. The "ideal" indicator should have following characteristics (Rosenberg and Wiens 1976, Hellawell 1986):

1. Taxonomic soundness and easy recognition by the nonspecialist. Taxonomic uncertainties will complicate long-term monitoring and between-site interpretation.

2. Cosmopolitan distribution (or distribution involving an ecological analog). Choice of a cosmopolitan species would allow for comparative studies on regional, nation and international scales.
3. Numerical abundance. Numerical predominance. Of an indicator species allows for ease of sampling and for conclusions regarding quantities patterns.
4. Low genetic and ecological variability. Again, indicators should have relatively narrow ecological demands.
5. Large body size. This would facilitate sampling and sorting.
6. Limited mobility and relatively long life history. These would allow for ease of integration on spatial and temporal scales.
7. Ecological characteristic are well known. Background physiological and autecological information should be available widely.
8. Suitable for use in laboratory studies. These may allow for determination of causality.

The saprobiensystem and modifications:

The saprobiensystem of kolkwitz and marsson (1909) is one of the oldest classification system using benthic macro invertebrates in pollution analysis. Kolkwitz and marsson (1909) recognized four zones: (1) polysaprobic (a zone of grossly polluted by organic matter); (2) Alpha and beta mesosaprobic (zone where dissolved oxygen content and diverse fauna and flora). Animals associated with the above are classified depending on the animals' presents in the system, the stream is put on the one of the classes. These animals are in fact bacteria and protozoa which are classified according to their preferred habitats.Chandeler's (1970) states that kolkwitz and Marsson's "saprobiensystem" rapidly gained acceptance in Erope and America and that it was later modified by many workers. Hynes (1960) belives that the saprobiensystem is unwieldy in use and takes no account of local factors in assessment of pollution. Chutters (1972) finds the saprobiensystem to be of limited usefulness (i.e. for sewerage only). The USEPA (1972) notes that the system needs precise identification of organisms to work.Wurtz (1955) creates pollution zone modifies from the saprobiensystem to apply to all types of pollution, erroneously implying that organisms are consistently tolrent to different types of pollution.saprobity indices have also been calculated by Pantle and Buck (1955), Zelinka and Marvab (1961) (with 5 saprobic zones) and Dittmar (1959) (with six saprobic zones). However, most of these criticisms also apply to many of the more recently derived biotic index or score classification schemes. Moreover, many of these criticisms do not apply to the conditions under which the saprobiensystem was intended for use. The saprobiensystem still is used widely in the original or a modified from; and example, Germany recently accepted a substantially improved and simplified version of the saprobiem system as a standredlized method for the Biological – Ecological examination of lotic systems (Friendrich 1990).The Saprobity index of a site is calculated as:

Where S= Saprobity index of the site;

Si= Saprobicvalue of the I th taxon;

Ai= Abundance index of the I th taxon;and

Gi= Indication weight of the I th taxon.

The terns are scroed according to the explations given in Friedrich (1990).

Almost all pollution indices have been derived from the observation that there is a progressive loss of component of the clean water biota with increasing pollution load. From this phenomena Kothe (1962) developed a simple index, the 'Attenfehlbetrag' or species deficit, which measure the percentage difference between the number of species occurring above and below the point of discharge of a pollutant, but the index takes no cognizance of charges in the relative abundance of individual species. Another index, proposed by Back (1954),measures the different between the number of 'tolerance' and 'intolerance' species, the distribution being made on subjective assessments of their limits of tolerance to organic pollution, but again no allowance is made for relative abundance.

Other indices utilizes the ratio between groups of organisms. King and bell (1964) have suggested the use of the ratio of wet weights of insects and tubificid worms but this seems both crude and haive, as does the proposal of Goodnight and whitely (1960) in which the proportion of tubificid worms to other macro invertebrates is used.Brinkhurst (1966) considered that a useful index of organic enrichment was provide by nothing the number of tubificid worms and the proportion of limnodrillus hoffnesatri in abundance with organic pollution but this may vary with seasonal abundance. Indices based on the ratio of readily recognized taxa may prove useful in detecting subtle changes in water quality when one species increasingly replaces another where their environmental tolerances overlap.raffacelli & Mason's nematode/ copepod ratio (1981) propose a ratio of nematodes to copepods as a means of assessing marine pollution. This resembles Goodnight & whitleys (1966) index. The nematode/copepod ratio has been severely criticized by coull et al. (1981) however, and currently the question of its usefulness is unclear. Hellawell (1977) belives that the worm of Hawkes & Davies (1971) suggest that the ratio of two other invertebrates, gammarus and assellus may prove a useful indication of organic pollution.

In addition to the very simple indices describe above, there are several, more complex, method for calculating pollution indicies which tend to incorporate common factor. Patricks "Biological measure of stream condition "was proposed in 1949 and 1950. It is intresting that this index has component of both a diversity index approach and a biotic index. It has the classification to actually call this "Biological measure" a biotic index histograms are use for the comparison, and not numbers as in other indices. Patricks organizes histograms for streams in five classes: (1) healthy; (2) semi healthy; (3) polluted; (4) very polluted; & (5) atypical. Palmers Biotic index (1969) differs from most other spcial in that it employ a large taxa not macroinvertebrates. Sander's rarefaction method (1968) claims to present a new diversity measurements for marine system. This method is based only on the polychate/bivalve fraction of the aquatic community. Beaks river index (1965) studies the macro invertebrates living in and on the silty bottom of a large Canadian river. This index based on the feeding habits, sensitivity to pollution and density of macroinvertebrates.Beak's (1965) also states that the index is based on a study of the ecological changes taking place in a river system exposed to a combination of toxicity and reduced dissolved oxygen. The index ranges from) for severe pollution (usually toxic) to 6 for an unpolluted area. The trent biotic index (1960) (The woodiwiss index) was first proposed by woodiviss who was working in the Trent river Authorty. Woodiwiss used benthic macroinvertebrates inhabiting riffle reaches of midland rivers in England. Woodiwiss (1960), devised a scheme in which the number of group (of defined taxa) of benthic macroinvertebrates was related to the presence or absence of six key organisms: (1) plecoptera nymph's; (2) Ephemeroptera nymph's; (3) Trichoptera larvae; (4) Gammarus ; (5) Asellus; and (6) Tubificids and/or red worms (chironomid larvae). The rankings presumably reflect the relative oxygen requirements of these indicator organisms: The Trent Biotic Index ranging from 0 (= polluted site where none of the above animal groups are present) to 10 (= clean water site where none then one species of plecoptera and several other taxanomic groups are presents). Woodwiss based the index on the order in which he observed benthic macroinvertebrates species to disappear with deterioration in the water quality (Balloch et al.1976). Modifications of the TBI have been used extensively in continental Europe (e.g. France: Tuffery and Verneaux 1968, Verneaux and Tuffery 1976, Varneaux et al. 1982, Belgium: De Pauw & Vanhooren 1983, Denmark :anderesen et al. 1984, Norvay: Borgstrom and saltviet 1978). The trent biotic index was adopted by Graham (1965) for the lothians River purification Board. Graham used a six point scale in which a clean stream scored a value of 1.0,higher values correlating with increasing deterioration in water quality with an upper index valve of 6 indication that no benthic macroinvertebrates were present. Chandler's Biotic score (CBS), a frequently used variation of the TBI that was developed in Scotland (Chandler's 1970), also divides the fauna into key indicators groups, but it requires quantities data and a higher degree of taxonomic expertise. Each taxon in a sample is scored according to its sensitivity to pollution and its relative abundance, the sum of individual scores yields the site score. CBS's generally range from 0 (= polluted site where notexa are present) to >3,000 (=Unpolluted site). Because chandler's score tended towards lower score values at the upper unpolluted stations of a river ballot et al. 1976 divided the total score obtained for a station to give an average score. They reduced the scale to a range of 0-100. The use of CBS or (average) CBS Depend really on whether one is interested in seeing the stress in the stream or merely the stress caused by pollution. Chutter's (1972) Claims that his Biotic index is a measure of the pollution of flowing water by allochthnous (i.e. *ex situ*) readily oxidisable organic matter and its breakdown products. It is based on three hypotheses concerning the fauna. These are: (1) that the faunal communities of clean stream and rivers are definable; (2) that they change in a predictable way as organic matter is added to the water; and (3) that the greater the amount of ox disable organic matter added, the greater will be the change in the fauna. He arranged the index value to be between 0-1 (clean) and 1.0 (polluted).chutter drew up a list of riffle taxa and then used the literature to allocated each taxon to the quality values between (1-10). Clean water species were valued at and polluted water species at 10. This index is shown in appendix IT. hilsenhoff (1977), working for the U.S. Dept.of Natural resources, proposed an index based on chutter's however, his quality values ranged from 0 to 5 instead of chutter's 0 to 10 and also drew up his own extension list of taxa and their corresponding quality value, depending on the animals sensitivity or tolerance, suitable for North American condition.

Lotic Ecologist in the England have began using the Biological Monitering working party (BMWP) score (ISO 1979, Armitage et al. 1983) to standardize the assessment of water quality. The system uses binary data and relies on taxonomic resolution to the family label only. Pollution intolerant families gain high scores (e.g. siphlonuride =10), where as pollution tolerance families are given low scores (e.g. Chironomide = 2). The sum of score of individual families present in a sample yields the site score. Armitage et al. (1963) recognized that using site score for comparative purpose could be influenced disproportionately by the presence/absence of particular taxa as artifacts of sampling efforts.To suppress this effect, each site score was divided by the number of scoring taxa in the sample to give an "Average score per Taxon" (ASPT). Armitage et al. (1983) evaluates the sensitivity of BMWP and ASPT and showed that ASPT was less sensitive to sampling effect and seasonal change than BMWP.Both indices presently being evaluated and use in predictive modeling by British Research groups (e.g. wright et al. 1988) More recently, wright et al. (1989) and wright et al (in press) presented River Invertebrates prediction and classification system (RIVPACS) programme. RIVPACS, which uses the probability of capture of taxa as described by moss et al. (1987), predicts the occurrence of macroinvertabreates fauna at a given site from a small number of environmental variables and is a promising method for environmental monitoring and assessment studies. The BMWP index (National water council 1981) requires only qualitative data but quantitative data or semi-quantitative data (relative abundance) data are necessary for the indices of Knopp's (1954) pantle and buck (1955), Dittmer (1959), Zelinka & Marvan (1961) and Chandler's (1970).

The biotic (or pollution) indices that have been used can be enumerated (possibly barring some obscure once used by local water authorities) in temporal sequence:

1. Kolkwitz and Marsson's Saprobensystem (1908, 1909).
2. Wright nad tidds "Oligochaete indicators" (1933).
3. Patrick's histograms (1950).
4. Knopp's (1954, 1955) relative putity index.
5. Beck's index (1955).
6. Pantle & Buck saprobity index (1955).
7. The Trent Biotic index (woodiwiss index) (1960).
8. Goodnight and Whitleys "Oligochaetes"index (1960).
9. Zelinka and Marvan Saprobic Index (1961).
10. Kothe 's Species Deficit index (1962).
11. King & Ball's index (1964).
12. Fjerdinstad saprobic index (1964).
13. Grahm's index (1965)
14. Beak's River index (1965)
15. Brinkhurst's index (1966).
16. Sander's Rarefaction index (1968).
17. Palmer's index (1969).
18. Chandler's biotic index (1970).
19. Chutter's index (1972).
20. Heister's modification to Beak's index (1972).
21. The Average Chandeler's Biotic score (CBS) (Balloch,1976).
22. Hilsenhoff's index (1977).
23. Rafaelli and Mason's index (1981).

However some of the above indices are related. In five cause the indices metniond developed out of earlier indices so they will be considered in the following order:

1. The Saprobiensystem:
   (a) Kilkwitz & Marsson's (1908).
   (b) Pantle and Buck (1954).
   (c) Knopp index (1954,1955).
   (d) Zelinka and Marvan (1961).
   (e) Kothe's index (1962)
   (f) Fjerdinstad saprobic index (1964).

2.
   (a) Wright and Tidds index (1933).
   (b) Goodnight and Whitley's index (1960).
   (c) King and Ball's index (1964).
   (d) Brinkhurst's index (1966).
   (e) Rafaelli and Mason's index (1981).
3. Patrick's Histograms (1950).
4. Palmer's index (1969).
5. Sander's Rarefaction method (1968).
6.
   (a) Beck's index (1955).
   (b) Hester's modification (1972).
7. Beak's River index (1965).
8.
   (a) The Trent Biotic index (1960).
   (b) Graham's index (1965).
9.
   (a) The Chandler's Biotic score (1970) or CBS
   (b) The Average Chandler's Biotic score (1976) or CBS.
10.
   (a) The Chutter's index (1972).
   (b) Hilsenhoff's index (1977).
11.
   (a) BMWP index (1981 NWC,England wright et al. 1988)
   (b) ASPT.score (Armitage 1983).
   (c) Belgian Biotic index (Depauw vanhooren, 1983)
   (d) RIVPACS (moss et al. 1987).

(c) Comparative or Similarity (or dismilarity) indices:

Comparative or similarity indices are often used for ordination i.e. ordering samples relative to the overall similarities and then examining the major gradients for correlation with environmental factors. A similarity index is basically a measure of the similarity of the structure of two communities, different indices may actually compare abundance in particular species (i.e. similarity of areas in terms of shared species) or, merely abundance in any species (i.e. similarity of areas by species number). Comparative or similarity indices may be used in river quality surveillance studies to identify spatial discontinuities between communities which may be attributable to environmental change or to detect and measure temporal changes between successive samples. at the simplest level one may compare the species composition of the communities. Several indices are available but only those which compare joint presences (e.g. Jaccord 1912,) are preferred since joint absences may arise circumstantially and the close affinity indicated between samples or stations which has similar lists "missing" species would be spurious. Better comparisions are made with comparative indices in which the relative or absolute abundances of species are utilized, for example those of czekanowski (1913) and Raabe (1952).another useful method for comparing communities is the "distance measure" (Sokal 1961, Sokal and Sneath 1963) in which the abundances of a species within the two communities are represented in an dimensional hyperspace and the spatial separation or "distance "between three communities provides a measure of their affinity.

Finally, communities may be compared by name of ranking method in which the relative importance of species in each community are ranked and then compared (Spearman 1913, Kendall 1962). This approach has the advantage that only the relative importance of species need be measured and sampling difficulties are thereby reduced. It is, however, possible to have identical ranking in communities with very dissimilar structure.

The indices which discussed here briefly are as follows:

1. Jaccard's index (1908).
2. Percent similarity (1952).
3. Bray-Curtis dissimilarity (1957).
4. Pinkham and Pearson's index (1976).
5. Euclidean or Ecological distance (1961).

The summary and properties of each indices (above mentioned). Jaccord (1908) index is included because it the oldest and simplest similarity indesx.Williams (1964) states that Jaccord's index is independent of the number of individuals and the number of species in the communities to be compared. The US EPA (1972) calls Jaccord's coefficient is the most common diversity index used to express species overlap and does not call it a similarity index. Cairns (1977) also lists Jaccord's index as a diversity species "overlap".

Brock (1977) states that percentage similarity coefficient (PSC) was the "original index" used for community similarity and was discussed by Whittaker (1952) and used by Whittaker and Fairbanks (1958) to compare copepod communities of small lakes and ponds. Bray and Curtis (1957) reports the index $c = 2w/(a+b)$; where a= the sum of the quantitative measure of the plants in one stand, b=the similar some for a second stand and w= the sum of the lesser value for only those species which are in comman between the two stand. Bray and Curtis use a score system based on normalized data from different measurement. Beal's (1960) did not use the score system of Bray and Curtis but developed a system of "Prominence values" calculating the density of a taxa multiplied by the square root of its frequency. Burlington

(1962) uses the Bray-Curtis index to discover variations in populations of bottom macroinvertebrates at various river stations. Dean and Burlington (1963) state that it is possible to express a quantitative relationship between biotic population in variable ecology habitats and thus assess pollution.dean and Burlington believe that the use of a similarity index can yield quantitative data which can be meaningful to both the engineer and the biologist.

Pinkham and Pearson's index (1976) discuss various situations in which similarity indices or biotic indices (i.e. Chutter's) fail to depict changes in community. They state that indices that examine species abundance or species occurrence are inadequate for pollution surveys. They also feels that when the sample consists of organisms from the same trophic level, the desirability of assigning the sum weight to each taxon may be lessened. Under these condition the dominant taxa may be considered to play amore significant role in that trophic level. They concluded that agood weighting factor that reflects this dominance is the relative abundance of each taxon.

Sokal (1960), Williams (1971), Goodall (1973),Sneath and Sokal (1973), Clifford and Williams (1976), Clifford and Stephenson (1975), discussed Euclidean distance which is a dissimilarity measure.This index formed the basis for Mcintosh's M (Mcintosh, 1967), a diversity index which Hurlbert (1971) has criticized. Orloci (1968) suggest replacing "absolute" Euclidean or Ecological distance by a "relative" distance, each observation being standardized by dividing by the length of the standard vector. Clifford and Williams (1976) state that Euclidean distance is the simplest and oldest similarity coefficient. Clifford and Stephenson (1975) note that in an ecological context Euclidean distance givs considerable, or possibly undue weighting, to abundance species.Finally Euclidean distance are all acceptable indices but need extensive field testing and comparison to evaluate the most reliable index.

CONCLUSION

1. This attempt has considered three types of biological index, those called diversity indices, biotic indices and similarity indices. The first and last are basically indices of community structure, the middle one being specifically a toxicological. "Indicator organism" index. All three have been used for aquatic ecosystems and water pollution, the biotic index being generally specific for organic pollution.
2. Under the category of diversity indices, threre is a need to find an index that meaningful biological explanation and includes both species number and abundance of the individuals in species. The eight category discussed for diversity indices "relative of species number", is unsatisfactory because it has no abundance data and none of these categories have any attempts biological explanation. Simpson's index, information theory, Hurlbert's index, Mcintosh's index and the Theory

of runs, all have abundance data included. The biological relevance of Simpson's index, Hurlberts PIE and the Theory of Runs, is more apparent than the others.

3. (a) Under the Biotic indices,The "saprobiensystem" is difficult to use,the "Oligochaete group" lacks sensitivity and can give erroneous reading in certain areas. Patricks Histograms was an advanced measure at the time of its inception and can still be of graphic use visually but require a lot of work. Sander's rarefaction method requires a lot of data collection to be used properly and even then is basically a marine index. Beck's index group, appears somewhat arbitrary.

   (b) Beak's River index is comprehensive as to probably be impractical, barring a major study. Beak's river index requires not only all the toxicological work of other indices but extensive ecological data as well.

   (c) The Trent index group is unsatisfactory because of its very poor sensitivity Chandler's and Chutter's approach appears to be the most favored in the literature for biotic indices. Average Chandler's Biotic score (CBS) seems to be the most favored biotic index at the present time. More evaluation is needed of Beck's index, chutters index and Chandler's Score in field conditions.

   (d) The BMWP and ASPT score system (ISO, 1979, Armiteag, 1983) sensitivity showed that ASPT was less sensitivity to sampling effort and seasonal change than BMWP. RIVPACS (Wright et al. 1989), which uses the probability of capture taxa predicts the occurrence of macroinvertebrates fauna at a given site from a small number of environmental variables and is a promising method for environmental monitoring and assessment studies.

   (e) Belgian Biotic index (BBI) method (De pauw and Vanhooren 1983) combines the scoring procedure of the indies biotique from france (Tuffeny and verneaux 1968) and the sampling procedure of the Trent Biotic index from Great Britian (Woodiwiss 1964). This index reflect richness of the benthic macroinvertebrates community and gives weighted scores reflecting richness in various indicators group.

4. Similarity indices are many in number but few have been used on aquatic ecosystems. The simplest and oldest index is that of Jaccord, however it measure only species numbers hence cannot compare abundance in number, only species. PSC, an index which includes abundance in not sensitive to rare species changes, but has been considers worthwhile in the literature.

The Bary nad Curtis index, originally one of similarity, has been converted to dissimilarity. Pinkham and Pearson's index is a recent similarity index, but is sensitive to rare species. All of these indices are currently in use. PSC, the Bray-Curtis Pinkham and Pearson's index and Euclidean distance all include abundance of individual in species and all have q reasonable theoretical basis. PSC, Bray-Curtis and Eucildean distance are all acceptable indices but need extensive field testing and compression to evaluate the most reliable index.

FUTURE RECOMMENDATIONS

1. Pollution or biotic indies have been used extensively to evaluate pollution stress. They were devised originally to measure the effects of organic pollution, so their application to other forms of pollution or even to complex sewage effluents mat pose problems. Emphasis on improving the efficiency, accuracy, precision and predictive ability of biotic indices and scoring systems is needed. A need also exists to combine laboratory – derived tolerance data and field observation in the development of Biotic indices.
2. Pollution or Environmental monitoring studies should consist not only of qualitative and quantitative analyses of benthic macro invertebrates communities, but also of hypothesis generation through classification, ordination and model construction, the accuracy of model prediction also must be tested.
3. International standardization of macro invertebrates identification codes would enhance data transfer and allow for the creation of an international data bank for lentic and lotic macroinver tebrates.This would a major step toward the establishment of tolerance levels of macro invertebrates and their ordination along environmental gradients.
4. The old and new biotic indices and score systems work reasonably well along univariate environmental gradients (e.g. changes in O_2 or H^+ conc.) However, the confounding factors often associated with pollution indicate that a multivariate approach may enhance our understanding of the effects of pollution stress.
5. In pollution assessment, behavioral endpoints are likely to be of physiological origin, they may provide a sensitive, early warning measure of sub lethal toxicity. Laboratory studies have shown that ecologically relevant results can be obtained in short term behavioral experiments. The shorts time is necessary to complete an assay, combined with the ability to obtain sub lethal, ecologically relevant results, makes this approach attractive and cost effective.
6. The use of morphology deformities in freshwater benthic macroinvertebrates to detect the presence of contaminants in an ecosystem is currently a taxonomically restricted, quantitative measure.

Therefore a greater variety of macroinvertebrates needs to be examined, and morphological deformities need to be used in a more quantitative fashion. The experimental production of morphology deformities, and the establishment of dose response relationship between stressors and deformities are high priorities for future research on this subject.

7. Although the need for applied freshwater ecology is obvious, it is impossible to apply knowledge that one does not have. A sound understanding of macroinvertebrates ecology is a prerequisite to the implementation of a biological approach to ecosystem management.
8. During the design phase of biomonitoring study both accuracy and precision must be considered.
9. Scientist need to communities better to legislators that attempt to standardize biomonitoring procedures and analyses (such as basing impact on changes in value of the Shannon Diversity index).
10. Scientist working in biomoniterning and environmental assessment need to continue to employ imaginative thinking in both the design of studies as well as specific method used. biologists need to take advantage of technological advancements in developing new sampling devices, laboratory procedures and method of analysis.

Table 11.1

(1) Diversity indices simpson's index

(a) Simpson's d: (1949)

Where d=

(2) Relatives of species number

(b) Kothe's species deficit (1962)

$$\frac{A_1 - A_x \times 100}{A_1}$$

(c) Odum's species per thousands individuals (1960)

(3) Guesses by data fitting

(d) Gleason's index $D = \dfrac{S}{\text{in N}}$ (1922)

(e) Margalef's index $D = \dfrac{S-1}{\text{in N}}$ (1958)

(f) Menhinick's index $D = \dfrac{S}{\sqrt{N}}$ (1964)

(4) Curve fitting approach

(g) Motomura's geometric series, $Y=A_c^{(x-1)}$ (1932)

(h) Fisher's a Where $S_1 = \alpha \ln\left(1+\frac{N}{\alpha}\right)$ (1943)

(i) The modified Yules "characteristic"

$$=\frac{\left(M^2{}_1\right)}{M_2-M_1}=\frac{\eta^2}{\Sigma\eta\left(\eta-1\right)}$$

(1944) (1964)

(j) Preston's log-normal "a" where

$Y= Y_0 \exp(-aR)^2$ (1948)

(5) Information theory

(k) Brillouins $H=\frac{1}{n}\ln\frac{N!}{\prod_{S} N1!}$ (1951)

(l) Shannon's H′ =

(m) Evenness $E=\frac{H'}{H'_{max}}$ (1966)

(n) Redundancy R= $E=\frac{H'_{max}-H'}{H'_{max}-H'_{min}}$ (1962)

The Present use of some biological (structural and functional index in the river Yamuna:

During last 8 year several indices were tride on the river Yamuna Data.It was found that BMWP index (or score), SCI,SDI and Production/Respiration index were the best suited index for evaluation of Indian river water quality which are mostly polluted by untreated sewage. These effect indices such as the Benthic saprobity index (BSI) will b evaluated accorfing to the modified method prescribed by the Biological Monitoring working party (BMWP). The Biological diversity index (BDI) will be quantified according to the sequential comparision index (SCI) and an estimate of a species Defeat score (SDS), comparing the local number of species with the number of species at a reference or upstream area. The evaluation of the benthic fauna diversity and defeat level can easily be combined with the field work for estimating the saprobity index,which is also ensuring an evaluation with sufficient elaboration. Both SCT and SDS have values in the range of 0 to 1 and canbe transformed into quality function on a scale of 0-100 present acceptability by multiplying with a factor of 100.to combine the reading of SCI and SDS,formula ann be applied given below:

$$\text{BID} = e1\sum^{n} wn.L_{n(PQI)_n}$$

Where BDI= the Benthic diversity index.

$(PQI)_n$ = ... n= .... Wn = ...

The production Respiration index (PRI) is evaluated according to the method first prought forward by odum (1956). This method has recently been adopted has a standard method by the American public Health Association (1985). Primary and community respiration are estimated by a 24 h... measurement of the changes in the dissolved oxygen concentration. The following formula is applied:

ΔDo = Production- respiration + Diffusion.

Summary of the Properties of Indices and Methods of Data Analysis (After Hellawell, 1977b)

Pollution (Biotic) indices:

1. Species deficit (Kothe,1962)

$$I = \frac{S_u - S_d}{S_u} \times 100$$ S_u = no. of species upstream

S_d = no. downstream of outfall

2. Relative purity (knopp, 1954)

$$I = \frac{\Sigma(o+b)}{\Sigma(o+b+a+p)}$$ No. of species in each class

o = Oligosaprobic

b = beta-mesosaprobic

a = alpha-mesosaprobic

p = polysaprobic

3. Saprobity index (Pantle and Buck, 1955)

$$I = I = \frac{\Sigma sh}{\Sigma h}$$ s = degree of saprobic (liebmann

1951) oligo = 1, poly = 4

h = abundance (rare=1, 3 = frequent,

5 = abundance)

4. Saprobic index (Zelinka and Marvan,1961)

$I = \frac{\Sigma ahg}{\Sigma hg}$ a = saprobic valency in each of 5

Saprobic classes (sum = 10)

h = abundance

g = indicator value (1-5; 5 = high)

5. Trent biotic index (Woodiwiss,1964)
Derived from table provided. Highest score (10 upwards) is equivalent to lowest population. Uses qualitative data.

6. Biotic score (Chandler, 1970)
Sum of scores derived from table provided.Score of clean water rarely exceeds 2500. Uses quantitative data.

7. Pollution index (Beck,1954)

$I = 2S_1 - S_t$ S_1 = no of species, intolerant

S_t = Tolrent to pollution rarely exceeds 10

Table 11.2

1. Hurlbert's "encounter" index

(o) Hulbert's PIE = $\left(\frac{N}{N-1}\right)\left(1 - \Sigma_{1-1}^{s} P^2{}_1\right)$ (1971)

2. McIntosh's "Ecological distance" relative

(p) McIntosh's M = $\frac{n - \sqrt{\Sigma_{1-1}^{s} N_1^2}}{n - \sqrt{n}}$ (1967)

3. Theory of run:

(q) Cairns SCI = DI_1 x No. taxa

$$DI_1 = \frac{\Sigma \frac{\text{No. runs}}{\text{No. specimens}}}{\text{No.times done to be statistically significant}}$$ (1971)

(R) Keef's TU $= 1 - \left(\frac{n}{n-1}\right)\left(\Sigma KP^2{}_1 - \frac{1}{n}\right)$ (1976)

{ }

(1-1)

(Table Contd...)

List of terms:

S = the number of species in either a "sample" or a "population"
K = number of taxa in either "sample" or a "population'
N = the number of individual in a population or community
N_1 = the number of individual in species i of a population or community
n = the number of individual in a sample form a population
n_1 = the number of individual in a species i of a sample from a population
$p_1 = n_1/n$ = the fraction of a sample of individual belonging to species i.
$n_1 = N_1/N$ = the fraction of a population of individual belonging to species i.

Symbols of indices from the literature have been changed to conform to the above.

Table 11.3: Comparative indices

1. Coefficient of similarity (Jaccard, 1912)

$$I = \frac{c}{a + b - c}$$

a = no.of spp. In community A
b = no.in B
c = no.common to both

2. Coefficient of similarity (Kulezynski, 1948)

$$I - \frac{c}{2}\left(\frac{1}{a} + \frac{1}{b}\right)$$

symbol as above

3. Quotient of similarity (Sorensen, 1948)

$$I = \frac{2c}{(a + b)}$$

symbol as above

4. Index of similarity (Mountford, 1962)

$$I = \frac{2c}{2ab - (a + b)c}$$

symbol as above

5. Comparative measure (Raabe, 1952)
I = Σmin (d, e, f … …) d, e, f, etc. are minimum % values of each Species common to both communities.

6. Comparative measure (Czekanowski, 1913)

$$I = \frac{2\Sigma \min(g, h, \ldots z)}{A + B}$$

g, h, etc. = lesser measure of abundance of Species common to both communities; A and B Are sums of measure of abundance in each Community.

(Table Contd…)

7. Distance measure (Sokal, 1961)

$$\sum_{\sqrt{i}=1}^{S}\left(P^1{}_j - P^1_h\right)^2$$

D_{jh} = distance between communities
P^1_j = proportion of spp.i in community j
P^1_j = proportion of spp.i in community h

REFERENCES

Aanes, K.J., Baekken, T., (1995), Use of Macro Invertebrates to Classify Water Quality. Norwegian Institute for Water Research (NIVA), Report No. 2A, Acidification.

Andersen, M.M.; Riget, F.F. And Sparholt, H. (1984), A Modification of the Trent Biotic Index for Use in Denmark. Water Res., 18 (2), 145-151.

Armitage, P.D.; Moss, D.; Wright, J.F. And Furse, M.T. (1983): The Performance of a New Biological Water Quality Score System Based on Macroinvertebrates Over a Wide Range of Unpolluted Running-water Sites. Water Res., 17 (3), 333-347.

Barbour M.T., Gerritsen, J., Snyder, B.D., Stribling, J.B., (1999), Rapid Bioassessment Protocols for Use in Streams and Wade-able Rivers: Periphyton, Benthic Macroinvertebrates and Fish, Second Edition. EPA 841-B-99-002. U.S. Environmental Protection Agency; Office of Water; Washington, D.C.

Chandler, J.R. 1970, A Biological Approach to Water Quality Management. Wat. Pollut. Control., 69: 415-422.

Hilsenhoff, W.L. (1988), Rapid Field Assessment of Organic Pollution with a Family-level Biotic Index. J.N. Am. Benthol So., 7, 65-68.

Moog, O. (1991), Biologische Parameter zum Bewerten der Gewassergute von FlieBgewassern. Landschaftswasserbau 11, 235-266, TU Wien.

Moog, O. and Sharma, S. (1996), Biological Assessment of Water Quality in the River Bagmati and its Tributaries, Kathmandu Valley, Nepal. Proceedings of the International Conference on Ecohydrology of High Mountain Areas, 24-28 March, 1996, Kathmandu, Nepal.

Persoone, G. And De Pauw, N. (1979), Systems of Biological Indicators for Water Quality Assessment. In: (Ed.) O. Ravera, Biological Aspects of Freshwater Pollution Oxford, Pergamon Press, 39-75.

Plafkin, J.L., Barbour, M.T., Porter, K.D., Gross, S.K., Hughes, R.M., 1989, Rapid Bioassessment Protocols for Use in Streams and Rivers: Benthic Macroinvertebrates and Fish. EPA/444/4-89-001. United States Environmental Protection Agency, Assessment and Watershed Protection Division, Washington, DC.

Pittwell, L.R. (1976), Biological Monitoring of Rivers in the Community, pp. 225-261. In: Amavis, R. and Smeets, J. (Eds), Principles and Methods for Determining Ecological Criteria on Hydrobiocenoses. Pergamon Press, Oxford, 531 pp.

Riza (1995), Biological Assessment Methods for Watercourses. UN/ECE Task Force on Monitoring and Assessment, Draft Report III. Institute for Inland Water Management and Waste Water Treatment (RIZA), Lelystad, the Netherlands.

Resh, V.H., Rosenberg, D.M., (Eds.) 1984, The Ecology of Aquatic Insects. Praegers Publishers, New York, USA.

Rosenberg, D.M., Resh, V.H. (Eds.), (1993), Freshwater Biomoni-wring and Benthic Macroinvertebrates. Chapman and Hall, Inc., New York.

Schwoerbel, J. (1970), Methods of Hydrobiology-Freshwater Biology. Pergamon Press, London, 200 pp.

Sharma, S. and Moog, O. (1996), Use of Biotic Indices and Score Methods in Biological Water Quality Assessment of the Nepalese Rivers. Proceedings of the International Conference on Ecohydrology of High Mountain Areas, 24-28 March, 1996, Kathmandu, Nepal.

Sharma, S., (1996). Biological Assessment of Water Quality in the Rivers of Nepal. Ph.D. Dissertation, University of Agricultural Sciences, Vienna, Austria.

Sharma, S. (2000), Capacity Building in Community: Water Quality Assessment in the Ihikhu Khola Watershed Kavrepalanchok District, Nepal. Introducing NEPBIOS Method in Surface Water Quality Monitoring. International Centre for Integrated Mountain Development (ICIMOD), Nepal.

Sladecek, V. (1973b), The Reality of Three British Biotic Indices. Water Res.7, 995-1002.

Stark, J.D. (1985), A Macroinvertebrate Community Index of Water Quality for Stony Streams. Water and Soil Miscellaneous Publication No. 87.

Vongprasert, R. (1990), Application of Biotic Index for Water Quality Assessment of Rivers in Tropical Countries: Case Studies in Thailand and Indonesia. A Master's Thesis at the State University of Ghent, Centre for Environmental Sanitation, 78 pp.

Wright, J.F.; Armitage, P.D. and Fruse, M.T. (1988), A New Approach to the Biological Surveillance or River Quality Using Macroinvertebrates. Verh. Internat. Verein. Limnol. 23, 1548-1552.

Wright, J.F.; Furse, M.T. and Armitage, P.D. (1993): A Technique for Evaluating the Biological Quality of Rivers in the UK. European Water Poll. Control, 3 (4), 15-25.

Pages: 178-189

LIMNOLOGY AND AQUATIC SCIENCE
Edited by: Dr. Shailendra Sharma; Dr. Pawan Kumar 'Bharti'
ISBN: 978-93-5056-735-7
Edition: 2015
Published by: Discovery Publishing House Pvt. Ltd., New Delhi (India)

12

Techniques for Monitoring Water Quality

[1]Chitralekha Bagul, [2]Harshada Kulkarni,
[3]G.D. Mhaske*, and [4]Resham Bhalla

ABSTRACT

It is needless to emphasize the importance of water in our life. Without water, there is no life on our planet. We need water for different purposes. We need water for drinking, for industries, for irrigation, for swimming, fishing, etc.

Water for different purposes has its own requirements as to composition and purity. Each body of water needs to be analyzed on a regular basis to confirm to suitability. The types of analysis could vary from simple field testing for a single analyte to laboratory based multi-component instrumental analysis. The measurement of water quality is a very exacting and time consuming process, and a large number of quantitative analytical methods are used for this purpose.

Key words: Physico-chemical analysis, water quality monitoring.

1, 2 & 3 Department of Biotechnology, HPT Arts and RYK Science College Nashik - 422 005, M.S., India.

4 Department of Zoology, LVH Arts, Science and Commerce College, Panchavati, Nashik - 3, M.S., India.

THE IMPORTANCE OF WATER MONITORING

Every living thing on earth needs water to survive. Human bodies are made up of more than 60 percent water! We use clean water to drink, grow crops for food, operate factories, and for swimming, surfing, fishing and sailing. Water is vitally important to every aspect of our lives. Monitoring the quality of surface water will help protect our waterways from pollution. Farmers can use the information to help better manage their land and crops. Our local, state and national governments use monitoring information to help control pollution levels. We can use this information to understand exactly how we impact our water supply and to help us understand the important role we all play in water conservation.

Water quality can be difficult to measure. Water is a vast network of branching rivers, springs, creeks, swamps, estuaries, wetlands, lakes, bays, etc. Each water body can contain dramatically different levels of pollution. Water quality issues influence human and environmental health, so the more we monitor our water the better we will be able to recognize and prevent contamination problems.

Why monitoring?

Monitoring can be conducted for many purposes. Five major purposes are:

- Characterize waters and identify changes or trends in water quality over time;
- Identify specific existing or emerging water quality problems;
- Gather information to design specific pollution prevention or remediation programmes;
- Determine whether programme goals – such as compliance with pollution regulations or implementation of effective pollution control actions – are being met; and
- Respond to emergencies, such as spills and floods.

ABOUT WATER QUALITY

Each water body has its own standards. For example, water used for drinking has to be much cleaner than water used for crop irrigation or to cool machinery in a factory. Scientists use information from water monitoring to determine how a water body rates based on its intended use. If scientists rate water quality as GOOD, then the water can fully support its intended uses. If, however, scientists rate the water quality as IMPAIRED, the water cannot support one or more of its intended uses. Shown at left are three pie charts comparing the quality of various water bodies. On average, about 45 percent of tested water bodies are rated as impaired.

MEASURING WATER QUALITY

Analyses of physical, chemical and biological parameters.

The parameters used to assess the water quality are broadly divided into:

- **Physical parameters**: Colour, Temperature, Transparency, Turbidity , Odour, Total Solids (TS), etc.
- **Chemical parameters**: pH, Electrical Conductivity (E.C), Total Hardness, acidity, alkalinity, Nitrates, Phosphates, Sulphates, Chlorides, Dissolved Oxygen (D.O), Biological Oxygen Demand (BOD), Chemical Oxygen Demand (COD), Fluorides, Potassium and Sodium.
- **Heavy metals**: Lead, Copper, Nickel, Iron, Chromium, Cadmium and Zinc.
- **Biological parameters**: The biological parameters involved the qualitative analyses of planktons (zooplankton and phytoplankton) and microbial load.

PHYSICAL PARAMETERS

Colour

In natural water, colour is due to the presence of humic acids, fulvic acids, metallic ions, suspended matter, plankton, weeds and industrial effluents. Colour is removed to make water suitable for general and industrial applications and is determined by visual comparison of the sample with distilled water.

Temperature: (By Thermometer- 0.1 °C Division)

The temperature of water can affect it in many different ways. Some organisms prefer cool water, while some like it warm. Most aquatic organisms are cold-blooded. This means that the temperature of their bodies match the temperature of their surroundings. Reactions that take place in their bodies, like photosynthesis and digestion, can be affected by temperature. It is also important to know that when the temperature goes up, water will hold more dissolved solids (like salt or sugar) but fewer dissolved gases (like oxygen). The opposite is true for colder water. Plants and algae that use photosynthesis prefer to live in warm water, where there is less dissolved oxygen. Generally, bacteria tend to grow more rapidly in warm waters. Colder water contains more oxygen, which is better for animals like fish and insect larvae.

Transparency (Light Penetration) (by Secchi disc Method)

Solar radiation is the major source of light energy in an aquatic system, governing the primary productivity. Transparency is a characteristic of water that varies with the combined effect of colour and turbidity. It measures the light penetrating through the water body and is determined using Secchi disc.

Secchi Disc

A metallic disc of 20 cm diameter painted alternately black and white color in a radial fashion on the upper surface. The disc with centrally placed weight at the lower surface, is suspended with a graduated cord at the center.

Procedure: Transparency is measured by gradually lowering the Secchi disc at respective sampling points. The depth at which it disappears in the water (X1) and reappears (X2) is noted.

The transparency of the water body is computed as follows:

Transparency (Secchi Disc Transparency) = (X1 + X2)/2

Where, X1 = Depth at which Secchi disc disappears

X2 = Depth at which Secchi disc reappears

Turbidity: (By Using Nephelometer)

Turbidity refers to the clarity of water, or how clear it is. This determines how much light gets into the water and how deep it goes. Excess soil erosion, dissolved solids or excess growth of microorganisms can cause turbidity. All of these can block light. Without light, plants die. Fewer plants mean less dissolved oxygen. Dead plants also increase the organic debris, which microorganisms feed on. This will further reduce the dissolved oxygen. No dissolved oxygen means other aquatic life forms cannot live in the water.

Material that causes water to be turbid includes:

- Clay.
- Silt.
- Finely divided organic and inorganic matter.
- Soluble coloured organic compounds.
- Plankton.
- Microscopic organisms.

It is usually measured in nephelometric turbidity units (NTU) or Jackson turbidity units (JTU).

TOTAL SOLIDS

Total solids is the term applied to the material residue left in the vessel after evaporation of the sample and its subsequent drying in an oven at a temperature of 103-105°C. Total solids include Total Suspended Solids (TSS) and Total Dissolved Solids (TDS).

Apparatus: Evaporating dishes-100ml porcelain dish, steam bath, drying oven, desiccator, Monopan balance and measuring jars.

Procedure: A known volume of the well-mixed sample (50ml) is measured into a pre-weighed dish and evaporated to dryness at 103° C on a steam bath. The evaporated sample is dried in an oven for about an hour at 103-105° C and cooled in a desiccator and recorded for constant weight.

Calculation:

$$\text{Total solids (mg/L)} = \frac{(W1-W2)\ (1000)}{\text{Sample volume (ml)}}$$

W1 = Weight of dried residue + dish

W2 = Weight of empty dish

CHEMICAL PARAMETERS

pH: (by pH meter)

The potential of Hydrogen, also known as pH, is a measure of acidity and ranges from 0 (extremely acidic) to 14 (extremely basic) with 7 being neutral. Most water is in the range of 6.5-8.5. Let's see some examples to compare pH values.

Lemon juice has a pH of 3 – this makes it an acid. We all know how it feels to accidentally get lemon juice on a cut finger. Stronger acids have the ability to eat through solid objects if spilled. Liquid bleach has a pH of 11 – this makes it a base. Strong bases, just like acids, can burn your skin. Let's think about why. Our bodies are made mostly of water. Water has a pH of 7. Things that are close to pH 7 work well with our bodies. The same holds true for aquatic organisms. If the water becomes too acidic or basic, it can kill them. Not all acids and bases are bad. Aspirin and tomatoes are acidic, while milk of magnesia and baking soda are both bases.

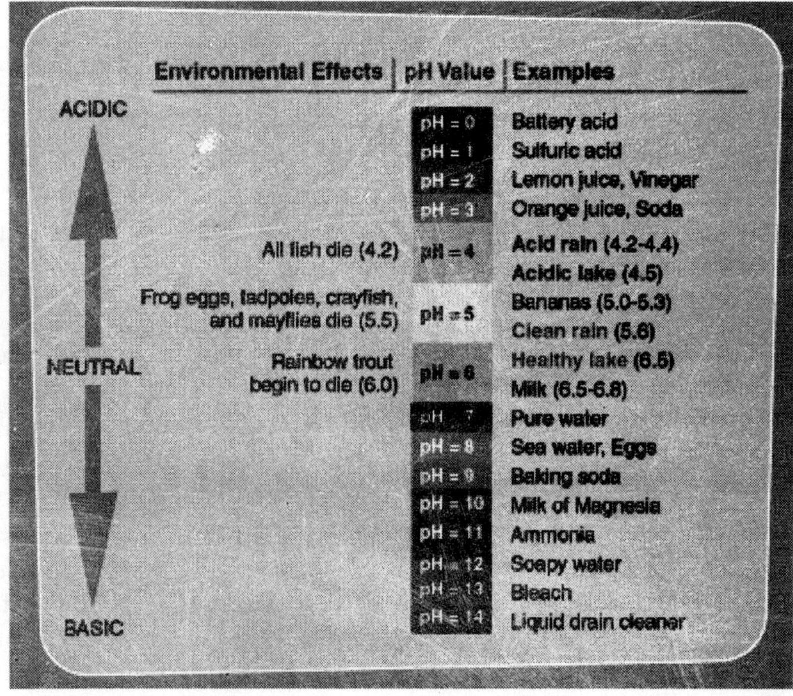

Electrical Conductivity (By Conductivity meter)

Conductivity (specific conductance) is the numerical expression of the water's ability to conduct an electric current. It is measured in micro Siemens per cm and depends on the total concentration, mobility, valence and the temperature of the solution of ions. Electrolytes in a solution disassociate into positive (cations) and negative (anions) ions and impart conductivity. Most dissolved inorganic substances are in the ionised form in water and contribute to conductance. The conductance of the samples gives rapid and practical estimate of the variation in dissolved mineral content of the water supply. Conductance is defined as the reciprocal of the resistance involved and expressed as mho or Siemen (s).

G = ———

R

G – Conductance (mho or Siemens) and R – Resistance

Total Hardness (By EDTA Titrimetric Mehod)

Hardness is predominantly caused by divalent cations such as calcium, magnesium, alkaline earth metal such as iron, manganese, strontium, etc. The total hardness is defined as the sum of calcium and magnesium concentrations, both expressed as CaCO3 in mg/L. Carbonates and bicarbonates of calcium and magnesium cause temporary hardness. Sulphates and chlorides cause permanent hardness.

Hardness Chart *(for drinking water)*:

Soft = 0-60 mg/L

Medium = 60-120 mg/L

Hard = 120-180 mg/L

Very Hard = > 180 mg/L

Total Acidity and Total Alkalinity: (Acid Base Titration)

The total *alkalinity* of water is a measure of its acid-neutralising capacity to a designated pH. It is the sum of all titratable bases, including carbonates, bicarbonates, and hydroxides, and also borates, phosphates, silicates and other bases if they are present.

Total *acidity* is a quantitative measure of the capacity of water to react with a strong base to a designated pH.

Nitrates (By Phenoldisulphonic Method)

Nitrates are the most oxidized forms of nitrogen and the end product of the aerobic decomposition of organic nitrogenous matter. The significant sources of nitrates are chemical fertilizers from cultivated lands, drainage from livestock feeds, as well as domestic and industrial sources. Natural waters in their unpolluted state contain only minute quantities of nitrates. The stimulation of plant growth by nitrates may result in eutrophication, especially due to algae. The subsequent death and decay of plants produces secondary pollution. Nitrates are most important for biological oxidation of nitrogenous organic matter. Certain nitrogen fixing bacteria and algae have the capacity to fix molecular nitrogen in nitrates. The main source of polluting nitrates is domestic sewage. Nitrates may find their way into ground water through leaching from soil and at times by contamination.

Phosphates (Stannous Chloride Metho

Phosphates occur in natural or wastewaters as orthophosphates, condensed phosphates and naturally found phosphates. Their presence in water is due to detergents, used boiler waters, fertilizers and biological processes. They occur in solution in particles or as detritus. They are essential for the growth of organisms and a nutrient that limits the primary productivity of the water body. Inorganic phosphorus plays a dynamic role in aquatic ecosystems; when present in low concentration is one of the most important nutrients, but in excess along with nitrates and potassium, causes algal blooms.

Sulphates (Turbidometric Method)

Sulphates are found appreciably in all natural waters, particularly those with high salt content. Besides industrial pollution and domestic sewage, biological oxidation of reduced sulphur species also add to sulphate content. Soluble in water, it imparts hardness with other cations. Sulphate causes scaling in industrial water supplies, and odour and corrosion problems due to its reduction to hydrogen sulphide. It can be calculated by turbidometric method.

Chlorides (Mohrs Method)

The presence of chlorides in natural waters can mainly be attributed to dissolution of salt deposits in the form of ions (Cl-). Otherwise, high concentrations may indicate pollution by sewage, industrial wastes, intrusion of seawater or other saline water. It is the major form of inorganic anions in water for aquatic life. High chloride content has a deleterious effect on metallic pipes and structures, as well as agricultural plants

Dissolved Oxygen (Azide Modification of Winkler Method)

Oxygen is necessary for many aquatic species to survive. This test tells you how much oxygen is dissolved in water for fish and other organisms to breathe. Most healthy water bodies have high levels of DO. Certain water bodies, like swamps, naturally have low levels of DO in the water. Lots of organic debris (fallen leaves, sewage leak) can cause a decrease in DO concentration. Microorganisms, in the process of decomposing the organic material, use all the oxygen in water. How does oxygen get in water in the first place? Much of the oxygen in water comes from plants during photosynthesis and also from air as wind blows across the water's surface.

Biological Oxygen Demand (BOD. 5-Day Test)

Biological Oxygen Demand (BOD) is the amount of oxygen required by microorganisms for stabilizing biologically decomposable organic matter (carbonaceous) in water under aerobic conditions. The test is used to determine the pollution load of wastewater, the degree of pollution and the efficiency of wastewater treatment methods. 5-Day BOD test being a bioassay procedure (involving measurement of oxygen consumed by bacteria for degrading the organic matter under aerobic conditions) requires the addition of nutrients and maintaining the standard conditions of pH and temperature and absence of microbial growth inhibiting substances.

Chemical Oxygen Demand (Open Reflux Method)

Chemical oxygen demand (COD) is the measure of oxygen equivalent to the organic content of the sample that is susceptible to oxidation by a strong chemical oxidant. The intrinsic limitation of the test lies in its ability to differentiate between the biologically oxidisable and inert material.

Fluoride (SPADNS Method)

Fluorides have dual significance in water supplies. High concentration causes dental fluorosis and lower concentration (<0.8 mg/L) causes dental caries. A fluoride concentration of approximately 1mg/L in drinking water is recommended. They are frequently found in certain industrial processes resulting in fluoride rich wastewaters. Significant sources of fluoride are found in coke, glass and ceramic, electronics, pesticide and fertiliser manufacturing, steel and aluminium processing and electroplating industries.

Potassium (By Flame Photometer)

Potassium ranks seventh among the elements in order of abundance, behaves similar to sodium and remains low. Though found in small quantities (<20mg/L) it plays a vital role in themetabolism.

Method: Trace amount of potassium can be determined by direct reading of flame photometer at a specific wavelength of 766.5nm by spraying the sample into the flame.

Sodium (Flame Photometric Method)

Sodium is one of the most abundant elements and is a common constituent of natural waters. The sodium concentration of water is of concern primarily when considering their solubility for agricultural uses or boiler feed water. The concentration ranges from very low in the surface waters and relatively high in deep ground waters and highest in the marine waters. It is calculated by flame photometric method.

HEAVY METALS

Heavy metals are elements (properties of metals satisfied) of high atomic numbers. They have high utilities in industrial applications from papers to automobiles, by their very characteristic properties. They are found in the deep bowels of the earth as ores (complexes of mixtures). The metals are segregated from these ores, leaving behind the tailings that find their way into the environment as toxic pollutants. They get into the water bodies directly from point sources as sewage, and non-point sources as runoff and more insidiously as atmospheric deposition that are transported from long distances. Heavy metals affect every level of the food web, from producers in the trophic levels to the highest order carnivore by residing in the system and magnifying at every trophic status.

Lead (Atomic Absorption Apectrophotometer (AAS) Method)

Lead is relatively a minor element in the earth's crust but is widely distributed in low concentrations in uncontaminated soils and rocks. Lead concentration in freshwater is generally much higher. High concentration of lead results from atmospheric input of lead originating from its use in the leaded gasoline or from smelting processes. Industrial processes such as printing and dyeing, paint manufacturing, explosives, photography and mine or smelter operations may contain relatively high values in lead. Lead is toxic to aquatic organisms.

Copper (Atomic Absorption Spectrophotometer (AAS) Method)

Copper is a widely distributed trace element because most copper minerals are relatively insoluble and is sorbed to solid phases, hence only low concentrations are normally present in natural waters. Because of the presence of sulphide, copper would be expected to be even less soluble in anoxic systems. The presence of higher concentrations of copper can usually be attributed to corrosion of copper pipes, industrial wastes or particularly in reservoirs, which uses copper as algaecides. Copper is an essential trace element in the nutrition of plants and animals including man. It is required for the function of several enzymes and is necessary in the biosynthesis of chlorophyll. High levels are toxic to organisms but the response varies greatly with species.

Iron (Atomic Absorption Spectrophotometer (AAS) Method)

Iron is an abundant element in the earth's crust, but exists generally in minor concentrations in natural water systems. Iron is found in the +2 *(ferrous)* and +3 *(ferric)* states depending on the oxidation-reduction potentials of the water. The ferric state of iron imparts orange strain to any settling surfaces, including laundry articles, cooking and eating utensils, and plumbing fixtures.

Chromium (Atomic Absorption Spectrophotometer (AAS) Method)

The concentration of chromium in natural waters is usually very low. Elevated concentrations of chromium can result from mining and industrial processes. Chromate compounds are routinely used in cooling waters to control erosion. Chromium in water supplies is generally found in the hexavalent form.

Cadmium (Atomic Absorption Spectrophotometer (AAS) Method)

Cadmium is largely found in nature in the form of sulphide, and as an impurity of zinc – lead ores. The abundance of cadmium is much less than that of zinc. Cadmium may enter the surface waters as a consequence of mining, electroplating plants, pigment works, textile and chemical industries, and is toxic to man. There is evidence that cadmium affects reproductive organs in humans and is also a potential carcinogen. A specific disease called "itai-itai" has been absorbed in Japan due to excess cadmium. In addition, due to bioaccumulation, certain edible organisms may become hazardous to the ultimate consumer.

Zinc (Atomic Absorption Spectrophotometer (AAS) Method)

Zinc is an abundant element in rocks and ores and is present in natural waters only as a minor constituent. The main industrial use of zinc is in galvanizing and may enter the drinking waters from galvanized pipes. Another important use is in the preparation of alloys, including brass and bronze. It is an essential element in human nutrition. Food provides the main source of zinc to the body. Zinc may be toxic to aquatic organisms but the degree of toxicity varies greatly depending on water quality characteristics as well as the species being considered.

BIOLOGICAL PARAMETERS

Plankton Analysis

The physical and chemical characteristics of water affect the abundance, species composition, stability and productivity of the indigenous populations of aquatic organisms. The biological methods used for assessing water quality includes collection, counting and identification of aquatic organisms; biomass measurements; measurements of metabolic activity rates; toxicity tests; bioaccumulation; biomagnification of pollutants; and processing and interpretation of biological data. The work involving plankton analysis would help in:

1. Explaining the cause of colour and turbidity and the presence of objectionable odour, tastes.
2. and visible particles in waters.
3. The interpretation of chemical analyses.
4. Identifying the nature, extent and biological effects of pollution.
5. Providing data on the status of an aquatic system on a regular basis.

Classification of Inland Surface Waters (CPCB Standards)

Sl. No.	Characteristics	A	B	C	D	E
1.	Dissolved Oxygen, mg/L, Min	6	5	4	4	–
2.	Biochemical Oxygen Demand, mg/ L Max	2	3	3	–	–
3.	Total Coli form Organisms* MPN/100 ml, Max	50	500	5000	–	–
4.	Total Dissolved Solids mg/L Max	500	–	1500	–	2100
5.	Chlorides (as CL), mg/L, Max	250	–	600	–	600
6.	Colour, Hazen Units, Max	10	300	300	-	-
7.	Sodium Absorption Ratio, Max	–	–	–	–	26
8.	Boron (as B), mg/L Max	–	–	–	–	2
9.	Sulphates (as SO4), mg/L Max	400	–	400	–	1000
10.	Nitrates (as NO3), mg/L Max	20	–	50	–	–
11.	Free Ammonia (as N), mg/L Max	–	–	–	1.2	–
12.	Conductivity at 25?C, micromhos/cm, Max	–	–	–	1000	2250
13.	pH value	6.5-8.5	6.5-8.5	6.5-8.5	6.5-8.5	6.5-8.5
14.	Arsenic (as As), mg/L Max	0.05	0.2	0.2	–	–
15.	Iron (as Fe), mg/l, Max	0.3	–	50	–	–
16.	Fluorides (as F), mg/L, Max	1.5	1.5	1.5	–	–
17.	Lead (as Pb), mg/L Max	0.1	–	0.1	–	–
18.	Copper (as Cu), mg/L, Max	1.5	–	1.5	–	–
19.	Zinc (as Zn), mg/L, Max	15	–	15	–	–

If the coliform is found to be more than the prescribed tolerance limits, the criteria for coliform shall be satisfied if not more than 20 percent of samples show more than the tolerance limit specified, and not more than 5 percent of samples show values more than 4 times the tolerance limits. Further, the faecal coliform should not be more than 20 percent of the coliform.

Source: Indian Standard (IS : 2296 – 1982).

A - Drinking water surface without conventional treatment but after disinfection

B- Outdoor bathing (organized)

C - Drinking water source with conventional treatment followed by disinfection

D - Propagation of wild life, fisheries

E - Irrigation, industrial, cooling, controlled waste disposal.

REFERENCES

APHA. AWWW and WPCF (1975): Standard Methods for the Examination of and Waste Water 14th Edition. Washington D.C American Public Health.

Asthana D.K., Meera Asthana (1999): Environment, Problems and Solutions, S. Chand and Company, New Delhi, 24: 365-369.

De A.K (1994): Environmental Chemistry, New Age International (p) Limited Publisher, New Delhi (India). 7: 235-278.

G.S. Birdie & J.S. Birdie, (1994): Water Supply & Sanitary Engg, Dhanpat Rai & Sons. 9: 127-142.

J.C.Akan, F.I.Abdulrahman, G.A.Dimari, V.O. Ogugbuaja (2008:) Physicochemical Determination of Pollutants in Wastewater and Vegetable Samples Along the Jakara Wastewater Channelin Kano Metropolis, Kano State, Nigeria.

R.K. Trivedi & P.K. Goel (1994): Chemical and Biological Methods for Water Pollution Studies, Environmental Public. Karad.

R.S. Boyd & S.N. Martens. Chemo Ecology .(1998): The Significance of Metal Hyper Accumulation for Biotic Interactions.

Santra S.C. (2001): Environmental Science, New Central Book Agency, Calcutta (India), 11: 183.

Shittu, O.B., Olaitan, J.O. and Amusa, T.S. (2008): Physico-Chemical and Bacteriological Analyses of Water Used for Drinking and Swimming Purposes in Abeokuta, Nigeria.

Index